Xeriscape
for
Central Texas

A Water-Wise Approach to Home Landscaping

Published by The Xeriscape Garden Club of the Austin Area, Inc.

The information in this book first appeared in *Xeriscape Landscaping in the Austin Area* published in 1993 by the Xeriscape Garden Club of the Austin Area, Inc. The concept and ideas behind Xeriscape have grown and changed significantly since that time, which prompted several XGC members to update the information for the Central Texas area. The result is this book, *Xeriscape for Central Texas*. The information in this book has been carefully researched, and all efforts have been made to ensure accuracy.

August 1998

Authors

Chapter 1   Julia Marsh, *XGC Vice President of Communications*, with the help of Dick Peterson, *City of Austin Xeriscape Program Coordinator and Master Gardener*

Chapter 2   Brenda Barger, *Landscape Architect and XGC Vice President of Programs*

Chapter 3   Chuck Simms, *Founding Member of XGC of the Austin Area, Inc.*

Chapter 4   Janie Bolger, *Landscape Designer, Botanist, and XGC President*

Chapter 5   Lyle Boardman, *XGC Treasurer and experienced Xeriscape gardener*

Chapter 6   Janie Bolger, *Landscape Designer, Botanist, and XGC President*

Chapter 7   John Gleason, *Landscape Architect, Licensed Irrigator, and XGC Past President*

Chapter 8   Julia Marsh edited the wildscaping information provided by Texas Parks & Wildlife Nongame and Urban Program. The section on *Co-Existing With Deer* is based on XGC Fact Sheet #13, which was originally authored by Will Walker and Susan DuBar (with credit to the Lady Bird Johnson Wildflower Research Center publication *Deer Resistant Plants* for the information and wording about deer characteristics). Brenda Barger compiled the extensive list on deer resistant plants.

Editors   Gerre Boardman
               Janie Bolger
               John Gleason

Copyeditor   Deb Robison

Cover Design by Matt Klepac
Layout Design by Julia Marsh
Printed by Morgan Printing, 900 Old Koenig Lane, Suite 135, Austin, Texas 78756

ISBN 0-9668649-0-5

On the Front & Back Cover:
Field of coreopsis photo courtesy of Texas Parks & Wildlife Department.

If you have any questions or comments concerning this book, please contact:
Xeriscape Garden Club of the Austin Area, Inc.
P. O. Box 5502
Austin, TX 78763

Information Hotline: (512) 370-9505
Website: http://www.zilker-garden.org/xgc.html

The **Xeriscape Garden Club of the Austin Area, Inc.** is a nonprofit organization formed in 1987 for the express purpose of teaching and promoting water conservation through creative landscaping. Meetings are held the third Wednesday of each month (except December) at 7:30 PM in the Zilker Garden Center, 2220 Barton Springs Road, Austin, Texas. These meetings are free and always open to the public. The XGC of the Austin Area is a member of the Austin Area Garden Council and a charter member of the Texas Waterwise Council, which coordinates activities between the "blue" and "green" (water and plant) industries. For information on upcoming XGC meetings, speakers, and field trips, visit the XGC website at http://www.zilker-garden.org/xgc.html or call the XGC information hotline at (512) 370-9505.

Contents...

	Acknowledgments	*v*
1	**Xeriscape**	**1**
	Xeriscape: A Method of Gardening	2
	The Seven Principles of Xeriscape	2
	Xeriscape for Central Texas	3
	Bibliography	5
2	**Planning and Design**	**7**
	Is Xeriscape a Style of Design?	8
	Planning	9
	Design Theory	14
	The Design Process	15
	Planting Design	22
	Using a Professional Landscape Architect or Designer	27
	Legal Checklist for Landscape Construction	31
	Useful Landscape Formulas	35
	Bibliography	36
3	**Soil Analysis**	**37**
	Soil Analysis	37
	Central Texas Soils	38
	Geological and Chemical Properties of Soil	39
	Amending the Soil	41

Mineral Requirements	42
Mulch Makes the Difference	43
Bibliography	43
Notes & Ideas...	46

4 Plant Selection   47

Trees	48
Shrubs	55
Ground Covers	63
Antique Roses	66
Herbs	74
Perennials	79
Annuals and Biennials	87
Bulbs	88
Climbing Plants	93
Ornamental Grasses	94
Bibliography	97

5 Turf Areas   99

Turf Grass and its Uses	100
The Xeriscape Concept of Practical Turf Areas	100
Types of Turf Grasses	101
How Turf Grass Spreads	102
Maintenance	103
Alternatives to Turf Grass	103
Sources of Turf Grass	103
Notes & Ideas...	106

6 Maintenance   107

Soil Maintenance and Management	108
Fertilizers	109
Disease Control	114
Pest Control	116
How to Clear Uncultivated Ground	119
Lawns	124
Trees	129
Shrubs	134
Ground Covers	137
Antique Roses	138
Herb Gardens	141
Perennials	142
Annuals and Biennials	144
Bulbs, Corms, Tubers, ...	145

Climbing Plants 147
Ornamental Grasses 148
Container Plants 149
Tools 151
Cultivation Methods 154
Seasonal Maintenance Guide 154
Bibliography 161
Notes & Ideas... 162

7 Efficient Irrigation — 163

Water in Central Texas 164
Planning for Efficient Water Use 166
Irrigation Equipment 173
Irrigation Management 177
Bibliography 185

8 Texas Wildscapes — 187

Texas Wildscapes: Backyard Wildlife Habitat ... 188
Attracting Wildlife 188
Food Sources 189
Providing Shelter 192
Water Sources 193
Wildlife Problems 194
Co-Existing With Deer 195
The Hummingbird Garden 199
Butterfly Gardening 203
The Texas Wildscapes Program 209
Acknowledgments 209
Bibliography 210

Appendices... — 211

A: Conversion of Existing Landscapes ... 212
B: Sustainability and Xeriscape 213
C: Color Throughout the Year 214
D: Shade Tolerant Plants 219
E: Perennials and Grasses 223
F. Hydrozone Coding 229
G. Water Harvesting 232
H: Central Texas Resources 233
I: Recommended Reading & References 239

Acknowledgments

Any author can attest to the fact that writing a book is no small feat. Rewriting our handbook was no different. Seven people from varying backgrounds, but with a shared belief in Xeriscape and how it can help gardeners and the community as a whole, worked together during the Fall of 1997 and on into the Spring of 1998 to put this manual together. Their efforts required sacrifices in the form of many late evening meetings and weekends spent researching, writing, and editing when sunny skies and family activities tempted them to abandon their assigned tasks. We'd like to express our appreciation to them and to their patient spouses and families. The following individuals deserve congratulations for a job well done, and sincere thanks for freely giving of their talents and time:

Brenda Barger   **John Gleason**

Gerre Boardman   **Julia Marsh**

Lyle Boardman   **Chuck Simms**

Janie Bolger

Special thanks also go to the Xeriscape Advisory Board, **Dick Peterson**, City of Austin Xeriscape Program Coordinator, who provided a lot of valuable information on the history and benefits of Xeriscape, and to **John Herron**, Program Director of the Texas Parks and Wildlife Nongame and Urban Program, who gave us permission to include some of the excellent information from their *Texas Wildscapes Information Packet* in Chapter Eight. **Jill Nokes**, **Chip Schumacher** of New Braunfel's *Hill Country Gardens*, and *Barton Springs Nursery* all shared their collected information and lists of deer resistant plants. Finally, thanks to our copyeditor, **Deb Robison**, for her assistance in pulling it all together, and to **Matt Klepac** for the beautiful cover design.

Chapter 1

Xeriscape

In This Chapter...

Xeriscape: A Method of Gardening

The Seven Principles of Xeriscape

- Planning and Design
- Soil Analysis
- Appropriate Plant Selection
- Practical Turf Areas
- Efficient Irrigation
- Use of Mulches
- Appropriate Maintenance

Xeriscape for Central Texas

- Difficult Soil Types
- Water Conservation
- Low Maintenance
- Sustainability

Bibliography

The definition of Xeriscape is quality landscaping that conserves water and protects the environment. This chapter discusses the value and principles of Xeriscape. Then, it looks at why knowing your soil type and the plants that will grow and prosper in it can save you both time and money. The remainder of this book is dedicated to presenting information and ideas to help you create a lush, green, beautiful landscape that is pleasing to the eye, water conserving, and easy to maintain.

Xeriscape...
  "quality landscaping that conserves water and protects the environment."

Xeriscape: A Method of Gardening

To the uninformed, Xeriscape means rocks and cactus, but *to those in the know* it means lush, green, beautiful landscapes that are both pleasing to the eye and water conserving. In the 1980s, the word Xeriscape was coined from the Greek word "xeros" for dry. The definition of Xeriscape is *quality landscaping that conserves water and protects the environment*. With the emphasis on quality, it is not a style of gardening, but rather a *method* of gardening.

Recently, a neighbor of an award-winning Xeriscape yard commented, "I've never seen a 'zeroscape' that I liked." What he didn't realize was that almost any landscape he found to his liking could be a Xeriscape. His neighbor simply preferred a more natural style. A very formal landscape, or even an oriental garden, can be a Xeriscape.

The Seven Principles of Xeriscape

Xeriscapes depend on seven basic principles. By using these principles, you can reduce yard maintenance, use less chemicals and synthetic fertilizer, and spend more time enjoying your yard.

Planning and Design

Developing a landscape plan is the first and most important step in a successful Xeriscape. A properly planned Xeriscape takes into account the regional and micro-climatic conditions of the site, existing vegetation and topographical conditions, the intended uses and desires of the property owner, and the zoning or grouping of plant materials by their water needs. A plan also allows landscaping to be done in phases. Many individuals can develop their own plan, but for best results, consult a landscape professional.

Soil Analysis

Soils will vary from site to site and even within a given site. A soil analysis based on random sampling provides information that enables proper selection of plants and any needed soil amendments. When appropriate, soil amendments can enhance the health and growing capabilities of the landscape by improving water drainage, moisture penetration, and the soil's water-holding capacity.

Appropriate Plant Selection

Plant selection should be based on the plants' adaptability to the landscape area, the effect desired, and the ultimate size, color, and texture of the plants. Plants should be arranged to achieve the desired aesthetic effect and grouped in accordance with their respective water needs. Most plants have a place in Xeriscape. Maximum water conservation can be achieved by selecting the plants that require a minimal amount of supplemental watering in a given area. Landscape professionals can be of assistance when selecting plant material.

Practical Turf Areas

The type and location of turf areas should be selected in the same manner as all other plantings. Turf shouldn't be treated as a fill-in material, but rather as a major planned element of the Xeriscape. Since many turf varieties require supplemental watering at frequencies different than other types of landscape plants, turf should be placed so it can be irrigated separately. While turf areas provide many practical benefits in a landscape, how and where it is used can result in a significant reduction in water use.

Efficient Irrigation

Watering only when plants need water—and watering deeply—encourages deeper root growth resulting in a healthier and more drought tolerant landscape. If a landscape requires regular watering and/or if an irrigation system is desired, the system should be well planned and managed. Water can be conserved through the use of a properly designed irrigation system. Consult landscape and irrigation professionals when planning irrigation for a Xeriscape.

Use of Mulches

Mulches applied and maintained at appropriate depths in planting beds will assist soils in retaining moisture, reduce weed growth, and prevent erosion. Mulch can also be used where conditions aren't adequate or conducive for growing quality turf or ground covers. Mulches are typically wood bark chips, wood grindings, pine straws, nut shells, small gravel, or shredded landscape clippings.

Appropriate Maintenance

Proper landscape and irrigation maintenance will preserve and enhance a quality Xeriscape. When the first six principles have been followed, maintenance of a Xeriscape is easier and less expensive. Because a Xeriscape is healthier and uses a minimal amount of water, less fertilizer, pesticides, and other chemicals are needed to maintain the plant material.

Xeriscape for Central Texas

The Central Texas region consists of several soil and climate combinations. Not knowing your soil and the plants that will grow and prosper on your lot can be costly both in time and money.

7 Principles of Xeriscape

- *Planning & Design*
- *Soil Analysis*
- *Plant Selection*
- *Practical Turf Areas*
- *Efficient Irrigation*
- *Use of Mulches*
- *Maintenance*

Difficult Soil Types

Distinct vegetation areas located throughout Central Texas have resulted in the following natural regions:

- Edwards Plateau.

- Blackland Prairie.

- Oak Woods and Prairies.

- Llano Uplift.

Each of these areas has different soil types with different planting requirements. The native and adapted plants that will thrive on these soils are also very different. *Adapted plants* are non-native plants that thrive in this climate. Figure 1.1 outlines the natural regions of Texas. Refer to the chapter on soils, Chapter 3, for greater detail about how each of these areas differs.

As a result of these different soil types, your homesite should be evaluated for its dominant soil type, not by its location on a map. Your site may be slightly different from that of your neighbor, both in soil and micro-climate. A *micro-climate* is an area that is warmer, cooler, or somehow different based on solar orientation, shade, moisture, or other factors.

Reasons to Xeriscape in Central Texas

- *Difficult Soil Types*
- *Conserve Water*
- *Low Maintenance*
- *Heat Tolerance*
- *Sustainable*

Water Conservation

Any landscape requires water to survive. Xeriscapes require less than most traditional designs, but *any* landscape can be encouraged to be more drought tolerant. Create zones in your landscape according to existing or improved soils. Group plants that have similar soil and water needs together. Keep high water use plants to a minimum and group these together to make a miniature oasis. These small distinct areas can be easily maintained if they are easily accessed and visible, such as near the front or back door.

Be aware of micro-climates that exist even within your own property. Central Texas author Scott Ogden writes in *Gardening Success with Difficult Soils* (Taylor Publishing), "Even the smallest gardens offer a series of micro-climates around the house or grounds that favor various plants and enable a wider variety to be grown." For example, reflected heat from walls or patios can create pockets of warmer temperatures for more tender plants, while plants exposed to cold north winds need to tolerate colder winter temperatures.

Low Maintenance

Native and adapted plants grow the best and are low maintenance. In Central Texas, with our hot, dry summers, native and adapted plants require very little water to thrive. While you can never totally eliminate maintenance, you can certainly reduce the time spent on maintaining your yard, which means more time to relax and enjoy your landscape. Additionally, Xeriscapes require less fertilizer and chemicals after they are established, and an efficient landscape that is sustainable and protects the environment benefits us all.

Sustainability

Sustainability means meeting our needs in the present without compromising the needs of future generations. It requires that you take a long term, "big-picture" view of things. It means balancing economical, environmental, and social concerns, whether you're creating (or managing) a city or a landscape. It pragmatically recognizes that our environment is our "life-support" system, and acknowledges that "What we do for the earth, we do for ourselves." A sustainable approach toward landscaping is one of the many ways that we as homeowners can soften our impact on the local environment. Thus, landscaping which meets our needs in the present without compromising the needs of future generations can be part of the cure for restoring health to our urban environment.

You can have a beautiful, efficient landscape that is friendly to the environment. Logical landscape choices will ensure that our children have a cleaner, greener planet. The future depends on you. The remainder of this book will provide you with guidelines and plant lists to help you to plan, design, install, and maintain a beautiful, lush green landscape which conserves water, is easy to maintain, and environmentally friendly. You and your family will enjoy your Xeriscape for many, many years.

Landscaping which meets our needs in the present without compromising the needs of future generations can be part of the cure for restoring health to our urban environment.

Bibliography

Gleason, John. *Sustainability and Xeriscape.* See article in Appendix B.

Ogden, Scott. *Gardening Success with Difficult Soils: Limestone, Alkaline Clay, and Caliche.* Dallas: Taylor Publishing Company, 1992.

Peterson, Dick. *Logical Landscapes for Green Living in Central Texas.* [On-line] Available: http://www.greenbuilder.com/general/articles/AAS.xeri.html.

The Definition of Xeriscape and Description of the Seven Principles. The National Xeriscape Council, Inc.

Xeriscape for Central Texas

Figure 1.1: Natural Regions of Texas

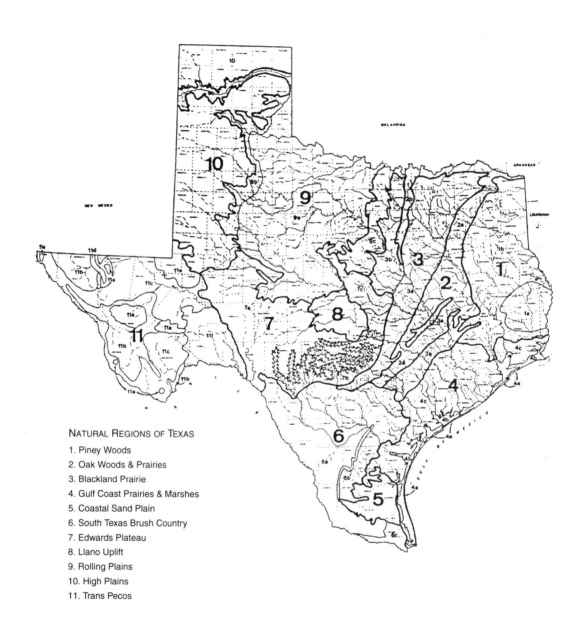

NATURAL REGIONS OF TEXAS
1. Piney Woods
2. Oak Woods & Prairies
3. Blackland Prairie
4. Gulf Coast Prairies & Marshes
5. Coastal Sand Plain
6. South Texas Brush Country
7. Edwards Plateau
8. Llano Uplift
9. Rolling Plains
10. High Plains
11. Trans Pecos

Chapter 2

Planning and Design

In This Chapter...

Is Xeriscape a Style of Design?

Planning

Design Theory

The Design Process

Planting Design

Using a Professional Landscape Architect or Designer

Legal Checklist for Landscape Construction

Useful Landscape Formulas

Bibliography

This chapter focuses on Xeriscape principle number one—how to plan and design a sustainable, as well as beautiful, landscape. Gardens are forms of personal expression that we build for our use and enjoyment. This chapter gives you some direction in exploring the full creative potential of your project.

Gardens are cultural forms designed to shape and control nature.[1]

It has been said that there are as many different types of gardens as there are gardeners. Not all gardens are created equally, however, especially when it comes to maintenance requirements. Gardens can be very resource-intensive especially in terms of *water*, *labor* (time and energy), and *money*. The Xeriscape approach to the planning, design, installation, and management of your landscape will help conserve resources in all of these areas.

Although Xeriscape planning is primarily concerned with water and resource conservation, this is rarely the sole interest or intention of the homeowner in planning a landscape project. Gardens are also forms of personal expression, and this chapter also hopes to give you some direction in exploring the full creative potential of your project.

While the nature and scale of your project will determine how comprehensive your own planning approach needs to be, even the smallest projects can benefit from the process described below. Every project can present unforeseen challenges, and for those of you who might need professional advice, there is also a section on what to expect in working with a landscape architect or designer.

Is Xeriscape a Style of Design?

There are still some popular misconceptions about what a Xeriscape "looks like." In fact, there is no certain "look" that characterizes a Xeriscape garden. Xeriscape is really not a *style* of landscape design at all, but a planning approach to structure how a garden functions ecologically. Like the natural landscape, Xeriscapes involve a unique response to such regional and local site conditions as climate, soil composition, topography, and solar orientation.

Unfortunately, many people still think Xeriscapes consist exclusively of desert plants in a dry, graveled landscape. However, even these highly *xeric* landscapes are not necessarily the best choice if they fail to consider specific site conditions and the local climate. The goal is not to convert gardens in semi-arid or temperate areas to dry desert landscapes in order to minimize water usage. It can be quite tricky to grow desert plants in Central Texas where our periodic and seasonally abundant rains can rot many plants unless perfect drainage is provided.

It does make sense, of course, to maximize the benefits of natural rainfall by choosing plants that are already well-adapted to the region. And although this strongly suggests the use of native plants, this does not mean that Xeriscapes necessarily mimic the native landscape. This brings up another frequent misconception—that Xeriscape gardens are naturalistic, unkempt "wildscapes." In fact, there are many formal Xeriscape gardens, such as the very drought-tolerant Italian and Mediterranean style landscapes, or even formal herb gardens which also qualify as Xeriscapes.

[1] Dean McCannell, "Landscaping the Unconscious," *The Meaning of Gardens*, Mark Francis and Randolph T. Hester, Jr., eds. Cambridge: MIT Press, 1990, pp 94-101.

Whatever *form* your garden takes—whether *formal* or *informal*—or whatever garden *style* you choose, following the Xeriscape principles will help you create a garden that is easier and less expensive to maintain and, which will endure the vagaries of our climate to thrive for many years to come.

Planning

The terms planning and design are often used interchangeably, yet there are some important differences. *Planning* involves defining goals and objectives, identifying opportunities and constraints, and then documenting and organizing this information in preparation for the design phase. The purpose of planning is *strategic*—to develop a method that will show you *how* to accomplish your goals.

Landscape Planning Procedures Checklist

1. **ESTABLISH PURPOSES AND GOALS**

   - *Define Purpose.* What are you trying to accomplish?

   - *Design Goals.* What vision do you have for this project? What do you want it to look like?

   - *Budget Goals.* What physical, financial, and creative resources do you want to invest?

   - *Maintenance Goals.* How do you intend to maintain the landscape?

2. **ESTABLISH THE PROGRAM**

   - Describe and diagram wants and needs for new use areas.

   - Address all critical *access* and *circulation* areas.

   - List needs of various family members and pets.

   - Create a diagram for all functional use areas.

3. **CONDUCT A SITE INVENTORY AND ANALYSIS**

   - Obtain a copy of your survey to enlarge as a base map.

   - Locate and map existing site features for your *site inventory*.

   - Analyze existing site conditions, and identify any opportunities and constraints. Diagram or record this information to create a *site analysis*.

   - Check for any deed and homeowner's restrictions or code requirements.

   - Analyze climate data for your area.

4. **PREPARE A PRELIMINARY MASTER PLAN**

   - Review all collected data.

   - Explore design concepts, and begin recording sketches and ideas.

Formal—
often characterized by symmetry, geometric regularity, or a strong sense of order, balance, and repose.

Informal—
irregular patterns having an unresolved or a complex, integrative order.

Xeriscape for Central Texas

Planning involves defining goals and objectives, identifying opportunities and constraints, and then documenting and organizing this information in preparation for the design phase.

- Create a conceptual master plan using all information and ideas.
- Refine conceptual master plan into a preliminary master plan.

5. **SCHEMATIC PLANTING DESIGN**

- Zone your landscape into water use zones.
- Designate turf areas.
- Diagram planting areas according to type of vegetation (i.e., groundcovers, evergreen trees, etc.).
- Create a plant selection list by categories.

6. **PREPARE PRELIMINARY COST ESTIMATES**

- Calculate areas and estimate quantities of plants and other materials.
- Obtain price quotes and cost estimates.
- Review and modify preliminary plan to conform to budget.

7. **DRAW THE FINAL MASTER PLAN/PLANTING PLAN**

- Draw the final plan with notes.
- Draw the detailed planting plan.
- Create a bill of materials.

8. **SCHEDULE THE WORK**

- Obtain final bids and schedule commitments from contractors.
- Arrange to have materials properly and conveniently stored on-site.
- Coordinate the work, and arrange to have site ready for each phase of the work.

Conducting the Site Inventory and Analysis

Once you have defined your project, conducting a thorough site inventory and analysis will help you discover the various *opportunities* and *constraints* your site offers.

STEP 1: SITE INVENTORY

Creating a base map. You will need a fairly accurate plan of your property to use as a "base map" for the site inventory and analysis and later for your design work.

If you no longer have a copy of your property's survey, contact your title company to find out the name of the surveyor for your property. They can provide you with an additional copy at minimal cost. You may want to have your copy of the survey enlarged to a scale easier to work with such as 1/8" = 1'0" for large properties or 1/4" = 1'0" for smaller residences or even 1/2" = 1'0" for very detailed design work. Any local blueprint company can handle this for you.

If you cannot obtain a copy of your survey, you can create your own base map by carefully measuring the site and drawing it to scale. You will need a 50' or 100' tape measure. It helps to have someone to hold the end of the tape for you, but you can pin it to the ground or place a rock on it to hold your starting point if necessary.

The following sketch illustrates how to use the baseline method to record your measurements.

Figure 2.1: Baseline Method

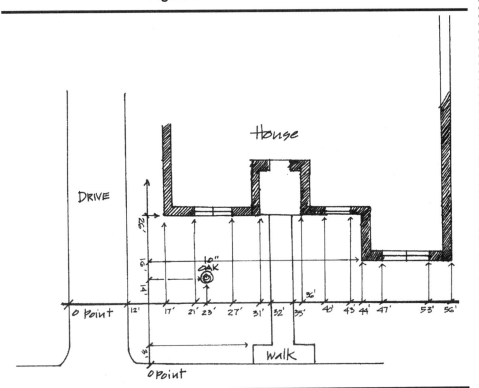

Creating a Base Map
You will need a fairly accurate plan of your property to use as a "base map" for the site inventory and analysis and later for your design work.

Locating existing features. Neither the photographs nor the survey will provide you with all the information you will later need. You will also want to record the following on your base map:

1. Locate all structures and outbuildings not shown on survey.

2. Locate all paths and sidewalks not indicated on survey.

3. Locate all water spigots, sprinkler systems, etc.

4. Locate all utility lines, meters, covers, and poles. Contact the City of Austin's "One Call" service if you do not know where your buried utility lines are. The number is (512) 472-2822.

5. Locate all major trees and existing vegetation.

Photodocument the site. It is very helpful to have a complete set of photographs of existing site conditions. Things show up in the two-dimensional objectivity of photographs that the casual eye sim-

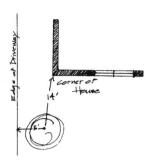

How to Locate Trees and Site Features by Triangulation

Using your base map and a 100' tape measure, you can locate and record any important vegetation such as major trees or hedges, utility lines, pathways, or any other significant features not shown on the original survey. It is easy to pinpoint these features by "triangulating" their location. This involves taking two measurements from a fixed point shown on the survey, such as a building corner. Using an architect's or engineer's scale, you can then transfer these measurements to locate the feature on your base map.

ply overlooks. And later when you have completed your new landscape, you will be glad to have the "before" shots.

You may want to create your own panoramic shots to record wider views. Just hold the camera level and rotate your entire body with your arms locked in position, overlapping the image in the viewfinder just slightly so you can re-assemble the prints later into a panoramic format. It is better to use a 50mm lens and avoid wide angle or telephoto lenses for this work since they greatly distort the spatial dimensions.

STEP 2: SITE ANALYSIS

In addition to locating the above site elements, you will also need to analyze or make *qualitative* observations about these and other relevant site conditions. You can diagram this on the base map or make written observations. Then, based on your analysis, begin to explore all the possible *opportunities* and *constraints* these various influences present:

1. *Regional character—both cultural and natural.* Does this suggest an appropriate character or style for your project? Are there unique local landscape features or materials you can utilize? Are there traditional building forms or patterns that inspire you? What qualities do you admire in the natural landscape?

2. *Architectural character of the house.* What style of gardens complements the architectural style of your house? What is the personality of your house? Are there colors, materials, or proportion and scale relationships that you want to reflect in your grounds?

3. *Character of adjacent buildings or other off-site influences.* Consider your immediate neighbors, your neighborhood, and even the part of the city you live in. How do adjacent uses and other visual impacts affect your decisions? How does your proposed design fit into the larger scheme of things?

4. *Light conditions, sun and shade patterns, solar orientation.* What kinds of vegetation will grow in the different light conditions throughout your site? What hydrozones (*For more information, see "Hydrozones" on page 168.*) would be best for these areas? What are the best uses considering the type of vegetation that can be grown in these spots? If siting a new house or other structures, try to maximize winter sunlight by planting mostly deciduous trees on the south and west facades.

5. *Identify special micro-climates and associated hydrozones.* Even a small house and garden will have many different micro-climates. South- or southwest-facing walls may retain and radiate enough solar energy to create warmer Zone 9 growing conditions. A shady north exposure subject to winter winds may function more like a cooler Zone 7. Study your landscape for any unique micro-climates that limit or expand growing

2—Planning and Design: Planning

opportunities or suggest different possible uses. Determine which of these areas are most appropriate to be:

- *Very low water use zones.* Areas that tolerate and thrive in drought conditions.

- *Low water use zones.* Areas that require little or no supplemental water.

- *Moderate water use zones.* A zone for plants that look best with some supplemental water five times a year or more.

- *High water use zones.* Areas suitable for turf tropicals and more thirsty annuals and perennials.

6. *Evaluate existing vegetation.* Try to observe the property for an entire year to make sure you have identified all desirable (and undesirable) species. Diagram tree canopy size and trunk diameter. The quality of your existing vegetation may offer some of your best design opportunities. You will want to take extreme measures, if necessary, to protect existing trees and other valuable vegetation from any construction activity.

7. *Soils.* Our soils (or lack of, in many cases) in this area rarely offer what most gardeners consider design opportunities, but by careful study of how local plants grow under natural conditions, you may find some inspiration. Take your shovel and investigate soil composition and depth in several different areas of the property. You may wish to submit soil samples for nutritional analysis. For those of you with heavy clay soils, you will want to learn which plants tolerate clay conditions. Scott Ogden's book, *Gardening Success with Difficult Soils,* is an essential reference on this subject.

For those of you about to begin construction of a new house, you will want to discuss with your contractor a plan to carefully remove and stockpile the existing topsoil over any areas to be excavated. Beyond the footprint—the area covered by the foundation—of the house, insist on protecting the soil and existing vegetation as much as possible from construction damage and any unnecessary soil compaction. You will also want to discuss where to fill or spread (or whether to haul off) the subsoil and rock unearthed during excavations. ***Do not allow the contractor to spread excavated subsoil back onto what will be finished grade for your future lawn or other planting areas.*** If you do not have anywhere to utilize this material on site, it is better to have it hauled off than try to later amend it for future planting.

Keep any boulders! Your contractor may also unearth large boulders in excavating your foundation. Ask him to carefully set these aside for future landscape use, trying not to scar the stone any more than necessary.

For those of you about to begin construction of a new house, you will want to discuss with your contractor a plan to carefully remove and stockpile the existing topsoil over any areas to be excavated. Beyond the footprint of the house, insist on protecting the soil and existing vegetation as much as possible from construction damage and any unnecessary soil compaction.

Xeriscape for Central Texas

8. *Topography/drainage patterns.* Indicate areas of steep slopes, rock outcroppings, swales, or depressions. Diagram drainage patterns and note any erosion problems, poor drainage, or flooding potential. Your careful analysis of existing terrain and drainage should indicate all kinds of opportunities and limitations. Try to develop a grading strategy that will allow you to minimize run-off and make maximum use of all rain your site receives. Grading can be quite a sculptural art. Be brave if you have the mechanical or musclepower available to creatively regrade. You may be severely limited in your grading opportunities, however, if you want to protect sensitive areas or existing vegetation.

9. *Prevailing and seasonal wind patterns.* You will want to maximize your enjoyment of our cool breezes from the southeast, just as you may want to minimize exposure to the north/northwest winds in the winter.

10. *Circulation and access.* Circulation and access are two of the strongest ordering factors in the planning process. They are two of the first things you diagram. Note any "desire lines" where footpaths indicate the need for a more permanent path. Circulation offers many different kinds of design opportunities. It guides people through your landscape, directing their views, slowing them down, or speeding them up. Use it as the basic organizing system for your plan.

11. *Views.* You will want to give great consideration to your view analysis. Much of your design efforts will involve screening undesirable views, creating or emphasizing focal points, opening up desirable vistas, and creating privacy. It can be very helpful to carefully clean and clear the site of undesirable brush and vegetation before you begin your design planning.

12. *Wildlife.* If deer have access to your site, this will present quite a few constraints. See the section on co-existing with deer in Chapter Eight for a fairly broad list of plants that may work for you. Entertaining wildlife in your garden can be fun for you, too, and you may want to devote considerable space and efforts to creating wildlife habitats in your garden.

Much of your design efforts will involve screening undesirable views, creating or emphasizing focal points, opening up desirable vistas, and creating privacy.

Design Theory

Design Influences

Issues of form and style often preoccupy all other design concerns, but what determines the stylistic decisions we make? How well do we understand the reasons behind our own tastes in design? As Joe Eck describes in the *Elements of Garden Design* (Henry Holt, 1996), we bring our entire history of evaluating other gardens to the making of a garden. And, as Eck points out, the more gardens one sees (whether actual or in books) and the more one analyzes them, the better one's own garden is likely to be. "Like any other art," he says "gardening begins with borrowing."

Regional Design Identity

Although there are many different *styles* of gardening evident throughout the country, it is hard to say if any certain *form* or *pattern* dominates contemporary garden design. If anything, one general trend seems to reflect a kind of nostalgic *Romantic Naturalism.* And like most romantic periods, this seems to be characterized by an eclectic borrowing of styles from the past, not just in landscape design but in architecture and in interiors as well.

There is much to borrow from in the long history of garden design. Many traditional patterns for gardens have developed over the centuries, most of them closely identified with a particular culture or nationality. Japanese, French, Islamic, English, or Italian gardens are all easily recognized by a consistent arrangement of certain elements.

There are also many proponents of *regionalism* as a design theory. Regional-based design takes advantage of the unique natural ecology and physical character of a particular place. It recognizes the natural ecology as a complex, integrated system to which humans have historically adapted, developing unique forms and patterns in their construction environment. Regionalism—with its respect and appreciation for the special qualities of time and place—holds great potential to help protect and preserve both our natural and cultural resources and traditions.

Unfortunately, unless appreciated and jealously guarded (i.e., heavily regulated), regional character is difficult to sustain in areas experiencing rapid changes in population that bring in diverse outside cultural influences and design traditions. Very few communities have been able to institute what are considered aesthetic regulations, and these have had very old and clearly identifiable design traditions. The benefits of such design controls, however, are easily seen in places like Santa Fe where the architecture and the landscape still seem to speak the same language.

The Design Process

Contrary to the analytical nature of planning, the design process is a *synthesis* of all the natural and cultural influences affecting a project. Based on your analysis, you will interpret all of the following design influences as part of your creative process.

Establishing an Identity for your Project

As you begin the design phase, your project should already have an initial identity or basic concept. Your interpretations of the natural and cultural influences should be able to suggest many pos-

Ecological/Natural Influences

- *Regional/Local Plant Communities*
- *Soils/Stone/Building Materials*
- *Solar Orientation/ Light Conditions*
- *Existing Vegetation on Site*
- *Climate/ Rainfall/ Prevailing Winds*
- *Topography/Drainage*
- *Wildlife*

Cultural Influences

- *Regional Identity*
- *Personal Expression*
- *Architectural Identity/ Existing Structures*
- *Economic, Labor, and Financial Resources*
- *User Needs/Functional Needs*
- *Movements in Art and Design*

sible concepts: Which ones carry more significance for your project? What design metaphors do they suggest? Whether poetic or prosaic, a concept can serve as a point of departure for exploring the design potentials of your project and guide you as your ideas expand and develop.

Even if your project is something as mundane as restoring the disturbed area over a new septic field, having a concept for it such as "Wildflower Meadow" or "Pocket Prairie" will help give you design direction.

Elements and Principles of Design

There are not too many rules of garden design, but the elements and principles of design are essential tools for composition.

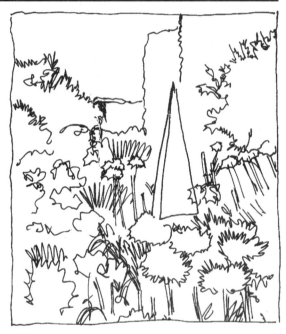

Line—
a simple steel-edged drainage channel accentuates the curvature of the adjacent slopes.

Emphasis—
a sculptural element is even more prominent when displayed amidst a solid mass of the same species.

Composition vs. Place-Making

Generally speaking, if a garden looks right in the plan, it will also feel well-designed in three dimensions. However, gardens that rely too much on two-dimensional geometries for their pattern and structure can be boring and predictable, particularly when all the design interest is focused on the ground plane.

Yet, gardens that *lack* sufficient clarity can make us feel frustrated and annoyed, as do gardens with awkward or unresolved geometries. The use of pure geometry in composition, however, should never substitute for a design theme or concept. No matter how perfect a garden's composition is in terms of the principles and elements of design, if it has failed to synthesize the natural and cultural influences in an interesting and meaningful way, it will fail to satisfy emotionally, intellectually, and perhaps even ecologically. One of your design goals should always be to express the special qualities and character of place, both site-specific and regional.

Creating a Framework

In order for a garden to cohere into something distinguishable from its surroundings, it must have a recognizable structure, form, or pattern. The pattern of this composition is determined by the arrangement of various structural elements. *Structural elements* of a garden include pathways, steps, stairs, bridges, terraces, buildings, walls, fences and hedges, arbors, planters, and water features, as well as certain kinds of woody vegetation, especially evergreens.

A garden is generally set off from its surroundings by some larger framework. This is often a fence or a distinct change in vegetation creating a sense of enclosure. This larger space is often subdivided into a series of outdoor "rooms" where different activities take place.

To create pleasing and harmonious structure, many people rely on historic or traditional garden forms or patterns. It may be true that formal gardens with their clearly recognizable structure are easier to maintain. It takes a skilled gardener to maintain an informal naturalistic garden over any length of time.

Detail Design and Construction

The decisions you make concerning your hardscape will determine not only how your garden looks, but how comfortable it is to experience and how easy or difficult it is to maintain. It may help for you to think of the construction of your outdoor hardscape areas as extensions of the house and its design and construction. Just as you carefully considered choices of patterns and materials for your kitchen floor, so should you weigh all your options for your outdoor "floors and hallways."

No matter how much you would like to cut costs, if you want to really enjoy your garden, you will have to invest in quality materials and construction. Unless you are an energetic and skilled do-it-yourselfer, you will need a good contractor and perhaps a designer to help you plan and construct the hardscape features of your garden. Do not be tempted to scrimp on your hardscape. If you are planning to build a new house or finance a major remodeling, you may want to budget for your landscape (10% of the cost of the house and lot is the average) and include this in your mortgage.

Design Options

Take time to observe, measure, sketch, or photograph similar structural elements or other garden features that will help you with your own design decisions. Clip photos from design magazines of

Design Elements
- *Point*
- *Line*
- *Mass/Form*
- *Texture*
- *Color*
- *Time*

Design Principles
- *Unity*
- *Harmony*
- *Emphasis*
- *Balance*
- *Scale & Proportion*
- *Rhythm*
- *Contrast*
- *Simplicity*

Hardscape—all elements of a garden other than the plants. Typically the pathways, patios, steps, retaining walls, driveways, etc.

Xeriscape for Central Texas

structural elements you like—study their materials and how they are constructed. If not for your own use, this will help you communicate your vision to a designer or a contractor.

Especially if you are new to the area, you might enjoy some of the local private home and garden tours. In addition to the City of Austin's Annual Xeriscape Garden Tour in October, the American Institute of Architects (AIA) also has an annual fall home and garden tour. The Austin Pond Society, Barton Springs Nursery, and the Austin Museum of Art at Laguna Gloria sponsor additional garden tours in the spring. The AIA also sponsors a tour of local craft studios every year, called the Artisan's Workshop Tours, and this is a great way to meet the blacksmith or the stone carver of your dreams.

Hardscaping Do's

- *Do* choose materials that complement your house and that will contribute to the overall design unity.

- *Do* consider using local materials which are often less expensive and help maintain a connection with the natural landscape.

- *Do* visit your local stone or brickyard and bring home samples of different materials to test against the colors and textures of your house.

- *Do* pay attention to the color of the mortar you select for mortared stonework; there are many shades of white and gray or other colors available to complement your choice of stone.

- *Do* make pathways wide enough for two people to walk side by side (4-6 feet); secondary paths can be smaller (2-3 feet).

- *Do* think of the entry and back terraces as additional rooms of your house and keep them in scale with the house. One suggestion is that they be similar in size to the adjacent interior room.

- *Do* minimize the amount of impermeable surfaces for large areas of hardscape or at least plan to retain and utilize all stormwater runoff on site.

Creating structure for your garden is the single most important act of garden design. It will not only affect the appearance of your garden, but how you experience it spatially as well.

2—Planning and Design: The Design Process

Some Hardscaping Treatments

Provide a mowing strip between your lawn and any planting beds. This can made of stone, brick, or concrete, but should be at least 8" wide and slightly lower than the mowing height for your turf. Steel edging is also available if its appearance is appropriate. If you are worried about Bermuda grass getting into your beds, you might want to have an extra deep, 10" to 12" concrete footing for this strip.

Cast concrete edging is an excellent way to retain a gravel path. It will also act as a mowing edge and prevent the mower's blades from slinging gravel.

Consider the utility of a "wheelbarrow ramp" for certain areas of your garden.

Drainage channels can be developed as attractive design features.

Break up large areas of gravel with focal points of stone or brick.

Here, a coarsely-textured concrete driveway with finely-brushed concrete at the edges borders a rough exposed aggregate center. Rustic or even crude materials contrast with the elegance of the adjacent plantings and emphasize their beauty.

Ready-made concrete pavers are used creatively to minimize the amount of turf in this small lawn area.

Use upright edging stones set in mortar to retain dry-laid stone or gravel paths and to serve as a mowing strip.

Paving patterns are particularly important for large patio areas.

Square granite sets (square pavers) are used in a gravel path.

Grading can sculpt the land.

Small hedge between path and outer row of stone edging emphasizes the curving lines of the path.

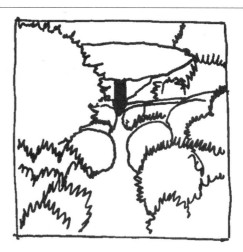

Formality can be softened by the loose forms and textures of plants.

Planting Design

In planting design, cycles of taste have always alternated between the formal and the informal, they often correspond to broader movements in art and architecture. Lucy Gent's highly recommended book, *Great Planting* (Ward Lock, 1995), presents an excellent history of the life of planting styles, including essays on 10 of the most influential landscape designers. Her insightful analysis of many well-known gardens is a superb example for us to study.

2—Planning and Design: Planting Design

Great planting design is an art unto itself, and certainly for many people, it is *the* most important component of garden design. However, like a great painting, great planting design also needs the appropriate frame and setting to show it to its best advantage. And just as with all other forms of construction, even a great planting scheme will not endure unless it is built to survive extreme conditions on occasion.

Xeriscape is really about making a garden that is well-suited to its environment. By choosing what Austin-area landscape professional Dick Peterson calls "bullet-proof" plants, placing them in the right location in the right kind of soil, and knowing a little bit about how to maintain them, you can create a long-lasting and drought-tolerant landscape.

The Xeriscape approach can help us plan our gardens so that they *function* well and be beautiful—full of glorious flowers and lush foliage.

Games Gardeners Play

Plants mean different things to different people. In his 1988 book, *The Poetics of Gardens,* the late Charles Moore, former Dean of Architecture at UT, described several "games gardeners play." We are probably most familiar with *the plant collector's game,* and many of us with strong horticultural interests fall into this category. (I am always reminded, however, as someone famous once said, that a mere collection of plants is not a garden, but a nursery.)

Plants are extraordinary designs unto themselves. That is why so many plant collectors continuously fall in love with just about every plant they see. Grouping plants together with other plants from their native plant communities can be a great approach to designing a collector's garden or a botanical garden. Plants from the same native habitat often share aesthetic as well as ecological affinities and combine well together visually.

Many famous designers have played what can be called *the painter's game*—Monet is the first to come to mind, but this is also how Gertrude Jekyll described herself, and, in Brazil, Roberto Burle Marx also worked in the manner of a painter, which he was, in fact. This is the intent of many home gardeners who strive to create beautiful compositions framed within a planting bed. While texture, form, and pattern are all important to these careful compositions, most painterly gardeners are primarily interested in color.

An increasing number of people seem to be playing *the wildlife game*, with both private and public butterfly gardens continuing to gain in popularity. While the design of a wildlife garden is still of some concern, it is the creation of the proper habitat to attract wildlife that is the gardener's real intention.

Xeriscape is really about making a garden that is well-suited to its environment. By choosing "bullet-proof" plants, placing them in the right location in the right kind of soil, and knowing a little bit about how to maintain them, you can create a long-lasting and drought-tolerant landscape.

While all of these games have their own unique set of rules which the players seem to understand and use in evaluating each other's gardening skills, they still do not provide the basic structure, form, or pattern for the garden's design.

The Design Elements in Planting Composition

Although tastes in planting design vary widely, designing with plants is simply another form of composition that relies on the basic elements and principles of design.

Design Elements
- *Point*
- *Line*
- *Mass/Form*
- *Texture*
- *Color*
- *Time*

Point—*small plants in massed plantings act as a series of points; brightly colored flower heads held aloft above masses of foliage act as points of color.*

Line—*many plants are characterized by line such as sotols, grasses, and tree trunks. Plants are frequently composed in a linear fashion.*

Mass/Form—*we all know many special plants we admire for their form and mass, such as prickly pear or bananas, and certainly there are many evergreen shrubs whose mass and form we rely on as a kind of "green architecture" to help create structure year-round in our gardens. It is also important to be conscious of the voids that mass and form create; voids act somewhat like white space in graphic design and can carry a lot of visual weight.*

Texture—*chiefly determined by the scale of a plant's foliage, it is usually described as coarse, medium, or fine. Texture is tremendously important in plant groupings and often underutilized.*

Color—*This is such a dramatic design element that it is easy to rely on it too much and possibly neglect the importance of other elements. Planning for year-round color is always an admirable goal, however, and surprisingly easy when using the full range of native perennials. Color is also a function of light, and the qualities of light at your site will greatly influence the color effects you achieve.*

Time—designing with seasonal changes is something unique to garden design. The daily changes in our gardens bring new surprises and delights throughout the year. Although this is what hooks many of us on gardening, seasonal change also presents many design challenges. Analyze and even photograph your garden at all seasons. Does your garden have sufficient structure to still look good at all times of the year?

The Principles of Planting Design

Unity in design is achieved when all the components of a composition contribute toward its identity or some desirable aesthetic effect. To achieve unity, the whole must take precedence over its parts. Although there may be a clear order or hierarchy among the individual parts of the design, they should appear well-integrated into a unified composition. A composition has achieved unity when removing any one of the elements destroys this sense of order and balance.

Harmony is achieved when a sympathetic relationship is achieved between the different components of a garden, or when things seem to belong together. This is functional as well as visual—plants must grow well in combination with each other as within their environment. Using native plants that associate with each other in nature is one easy way to achieve this harmony. Knowing a plant's growth habits is key to creating harmonious plant relationships.

Scale and Proportion requires plants to be in scale or relative size with each other and in scale with the overall garden. The scale of nature is grand, and most of our own efforts disappoint because they are not sufficiently dramatic in contrast to their surroundings. It can take a bold gesture (and lots of resources) to make a strong design statement with plants. This may mean planting 300 bulbs instead of just 30!

Emphasis is used to create excitement. Focal points and accents such as specimen plants or structural features are commonly used to create emphasis. Scale exaggerations are another way.

Balance involves the right quantities in the right scale and proportions. There is symmetry and asymmetry; and there is balance that depends on scale and proportion as well as color balance.

Rhythm is so important to the experience of a garden because it directs the flow of energy through the garden. Rhythm is achieved by repetition of elements, and this can be accomplished by repeating any of the design elements.

Principles of Planting Design
- Unity
- Harmony
- Scale & Proportion
- Emphasis
- Balance
- Rhythm
- Contrast

Xeriscape for Central Texas

Contrast—can be achieved through differences in colors, or light and dark, but plants are also shown to great advantage when juxtaposed with other structural elements. The contrast between soft and hard materials heightens the appreciation for a plant's living form, texture, and color.

Practical Hints and Conventional Wisdom in Planting Design

Practical Hints in Planting Design

- *Plant in odd-numbered groups.*
- *Follow plant spacing guidelines.*
- *Use form and texture for contrast.*
- *Provide year-round form and color.*
- *Make a statement.*
- *Study plant communities in nature.*
- *Keep a notebook.*

- Plant in odd-numbered groups of three or five. Using just two plants creates an awkward tension unless they are symmetrically balanced.

- Carefully follow plant spacing guidelines. Know the individual growth habits of plants and give them plenty of room to reach their mature form without crowding other plants. Use annuals if necessary to fill in the gaps while your shrubs and perennials grow to size.

- Contrast in form and texture can be more important than color contrasts.

- Provide sufficient quantities of evergreen shrubs and perennials with your herbaceous perennials to provide some structure and year-round form and color.

- Pay particular attention to the background of your planting compositions. Play plants against some structural element. Make the most of the contrasts between hard and soft materials.

- Make a statement of some kind—repetition, contrast, accentuated rhythms, strongly emphasizing some element, or exaggerating scale. Remember, simplicity is sometimes the most powerful statement.

- Study plant communities in nature. Notice what plants occur together as a combination of ground cover, shrub understory, and tree canopy. Analyze this relationship and re-create something similar in your own garden.

- Cut out plant photos from magazines and your old catalogs. Try out different plant combinations by holding the photos next to each other. It is surprising how quickly you can evaluate your plant choices using this trick. You may enjoy keeping a notebook of these experiments.

Some Favorite Plant Combinations

Gardeners are always searching for interesting and effective plant combinations, and listed below are a few we have found successful or exciting. However, as Marco Polo Stufano, garden director at New York City's Wave Hill, told Margaret Kennedy in a recent interview (*House Beautiful*, January 1998), it is better to

[P]ut together a palette of plants you feel drawn to and work with it. It should never be conscious. Don't worry about what anyone thinks. The minute we fall into the "we always put this with that" syndrome, it's not a living garden anymore.

The point is to feel free to try new planting combinations to suit your own eye, your own garden, and the spirit of the moment. Although there is no end of interesting combinations in the plant world, here are a few pairings you might like to try.

Favorite Plant Combinations

Morning Glories and Moonflowers

Texas Sage and Buddliea

Larkspur and White Lace Flower

Climbing Roses and Clematis

Russian Sage and 'Powis Castle' Artemesia

Blackfoot Daisy and Santolina

Pitcher Sage and Maximilian Sunflower

Dwarf Miscanthus and Oxeye Daisy

Purple Coneflower and Pine Muhly

Cherry Sage and Coral Yucca

Damianita and Mexican Wire Grass

Spineless Prickly Pear and Pavonia

Purple Oxalis, Ajuga, and Purpleheart

Bicolor Sage and Magic Carpet Flower

'Lipstick' Orange Cherry Sage and Texas Betony

Sedum 'Autumn Joy' and German Iris

Bluebonnets, Pink Evening Primrose, and Gulf Muhly

Shirley Poppies and Tall Bearded Iris

'Goldsturm' Rudbeckia and Indigo Spires Salvia

Yuccas and Firebush (Hamelia patens)

Crimson Pygmy Barberry and Blue 'Victoria' Salvia

Iberis 'Little Gem' and Grape Hyacinths

Mexican Mint Marigold and Mexican Bush Sage

Variegated Miscanthus and Bamboo Muhly

Pink Scullcap, Dwarf Hedging Germander, and Engelmann Sage

Feel free to try new planting combinations to suit your own eye, your own garden, and the spirit of the moment.

Using a Professional Landscape Architect or Designer

Choosing a Designer

Many people question the distinction between landscape architects and landscape designers. While they both offer many of the same services, including creating planting plans and hardscape designs, there are some differences between the two occupations. *Landscape architects* are currently licensed in 45 states, including Texas. To be a candidate for licensure, they must have a degree

Xeriscape for Central Texas

from an accredited school of landscape architecture or seven years of experience in the office of a licensed landscape architect. They must then successfully complete an intensive three-day examination to qualify for registration. Landscape architects are, by law, excluded from performing any services within the definition of the practice of engineering, public surveying, or architecture.

Although many *landscape designers* also hold degrees in landscape architecture or horticulture, they are not licensed by the state and may or may not have any formal training. It is not always the case, but many landscape designers are more adept at plantsmanship while landscape architects, by virtue of their extensive training, are more highly skilled at technical issues related to site planning and development, landscape construction, and solving grading and drainage problems.

Many landscape architects are employed by firms involved with large-scale public and private projects. Even individual practitioners may not be willing to take on small residential design work which is less lucrative and more time-consuming than commercial practice. Landscape designers, on the other hand, often specialize in residential design because they enjoy the more personal nature of the work.

Whether you use a designer or an architect, the most important thing is to find the individual who can best handle your needs or help fulfill your own vision.

Whether you use a designer or an architect, the most important thing is to find the individual who can best handle your needs or help fulfill your own vision. The only way to find this person is to do some searching: Start by asking the owner of your favorite nursery for recommendations, contact people whose gardens you like and find out who designed them, and go on local or regional garden tours to see different designers' work and to ask other gardeners for additional references.

You may have to let your fingers do the walking in the yellow pages. Contact several landscape architects and designers, describe the nature of your project and ask them if they do projects of this type. If they do not sound interested in your project, ask who they might recommend. If they express interest, you will want to interview the designer in person and get to know his/her work. Ask if there are any completed projects that you can visit. It is best to view actual gardens, but the designer may also have a portfolio of sample work that can save you some mileage. Ask what kinds of services are offered and what the fees are. Ask to see examples of the kinds of plans you will get at different phases of the design process.

Follow through in checking references to find out what it was like to work with the designer, what the design process entailed, and what actual services were provided. If the designer also supervised the installation of the project or was employed by a design/build firm that completed the work, you will want to know how well the project was managed and if it was completed on time and within budget.

2—Planning and Design: Using a Professional Landscape Architect or Designer

Working with a Designer

Not all designers do elaborate presentation drawings for their clients to review and approve. If this is important to you, you will want to find a designer whose methods of graphic communication are most effective for you. However, if you are familiar enough with a particular designer's work and are confident in your choice, you may want to set a budget and allow a free rein! Some of the very best projects result from this kind of open arrangement.

On the other hand, you may want to be more closely involved with certain aspects of the design. Most designers welcome client input as long as there is a feeling of trust and respect. If you want a more collaborative process, the chemistry between you and the designer really needs to be right. Good communication is the key to this relationship, and it helps for the designer to understand your desires and expectations from the very beginning. Some basic things your designer will need to know include:

Good communication is the key to this relationship, and it helps for the designer to understand your desires and expectations from the very beginning.

THE PROJECT AND DESIGN SERVICES

1. The scope of your project—what is involved, and what is your budget?

2. What design services do you need? Do you want a master plan for the entire property? Do you just want a planting plan and little or no hardscape? Will you need construction drawings for any structural elements?

3. What project management services will you need? Do you want the designer to act as project manager for you? Do you want assistance with the bidding and contracting phase? Who will supervise construction? Do you want a fixed fee contract, or are you comfortable with time-and-materials billing rates?

4. What construction services will you need? Do you want to do any of the work yourself?

5. What are your plans for maintaining your landscape? Would you like to consider a monthly or seasonal maintenance contract?

THE ACTUAL DESIGN

1. What are your design goals? What purposes do you want your garden to serve, or what do you want to accomplish? Provide a list of needs and desires. What are your design priorities?

2. What uses or activities will take place in various areas of your property? How often? What times of the day? What about special needs for children and pets (present or future)?

3. What styles are appropriate for your house, or what would you like to explore? What mood or character do you associate with different areas of your property? What design preferences or dislikes do you have? If you could cast yourself as a character in your landscape, what would it be?

4. What do you consider really important views? Which windows do you look out the most? What views are objectionable and need screening?

5. Are there any local gardens or landscapes you admire? Do you have any pictures you've been saving that illustrate the look you are after? Any that illustrate what you don't like?

6. What is your schedule for having the design work done? The project completed?

7. What plant material do you want to retain? What do you want to remove? What plant likes and dislikes do you have? What colors and textures do you like or dislike?

8. What opportunities do you see in your site? What kinds of limitations or problems do you see?

Client/Designer Consultations

It will be of great help to have the above questions answered before your first on-site meeting with your designer. After these issues are discussed, the designer can express any functional or aesthetic concerns that may have arisen. The designer will probably want to study your project for some time, typically several weeks, before presenting preliminary design ideas to you. Ask your designer to outline the client review process and what materials will be presented at each consultation.

After the preliminary or conceptual design review, the designer should have enough feedback from you to start the final master plan/planting design. This will be presented to you in the next (possibly final) meeting for your review and acceptance.

Some homeowners try to save money and hire a designer for just a few hours for a brief on-site consultation. If your design problem is small enough, you may obtain all the information or ideas that you need. However, much of the time may be spent with you doing most of the talking, requiring the designer to make an off-the-cuff response. Unless all you need are some verbal recommendations and a quick sketch, this may or may not be a good investment of your design dollars.

It is strongly recommended that, after you have given the designer final authorization on your project, you allow your designer the time needed to develop the best possible design for you. This may be anywhere from three weeks to a year or more, depending on the scope of the project.

It is strongly recommended that, after you have given the designer final authorization on your project, you allow *your designer* the time needed to develop the best possible design for you. This may be anywhere from three weeks to a year or more, depending on the scope of the project. The point is that one of the things you are paying for is the designer's time. If you are working on a fixed fee basis, don't cut yourself short just because you are eager or impatient to see the results. This does not mean, however, that you should not ask the designer for a time schedule for the design process. Find out how many meetings are included in the design fee, and go ahead and schedule them. If the designer seems to be falling behind schedule, additional input from you may put the project back on track. Good communication is essential throughout the design process.

Design Fees

Many designers can quote a flat fee for a residential landscape plan that includes all necessary site visits, client consultations, design work, and drawings. A simple planting plan for a small residential property may cost only a few hundred dollars, whereas a master plan for an estate-size property, complete with grading plans and hardscape construction details, may cost more in the neighborhood of $2,000 to $3,000. You will want to clarify exactly what is included in the designer's fee—how many site visits, how many consultations, and what kinds of drawings or services you will receive. Additional design work can be provided at an hourly rate, which may range from $50 to $100 per hour. Other services such as project management may be billed on a percentage basis, usually somewhere between 8% to 12% of the total construction cost. A simple design services contract should be drawn up to clarify the agreement between you and your designer.

Given the overall costs of an average new landscape, including hardscape such as walks and drives, you should figure roughly 10% of the cost of the house and lot. Good design is a little money very well spent.

Given the overall costs of an average new landscape, including hardscape such as walks and drives, you should figure roughly 10% of the cost of the house and lot. Good design is a little money very well spent.

Legal Checklist for Landscape Construction

Before undertaking certain landscape construction projects, you should consult the following sources of information for any restrictions on your project:

CONSULT YOUR PROPERTY DEED AND SURVEY

- Exact location of property pins (when in doubt of their actual physical location on your property, contact the survey company to come out and set some iron pins for your reference).

- Easements or rights-of-way.

- Building restrictions.

- Tree removal restrictions.

- Building setback requirements

CONSULT YOUR LOCAL PLANNING DEPARTMENT

- Any setback requirements not shown on your survey.

- Height limitations for fences, buildings, or other structures.

- Lot coverage guidelines.

- Safety codes for pools and spas.

- Open burning restrictions for firepits.

Xeriscape for Central Texas

- Building codes for all construction.
- Tree ordinances.
- Historic preservation ordinances.
- Permits for fences and retaining walls above a certain height, other garden structures, or electrical and plumbing work.

CONSULT YOUR LOCAL UTILITY COMPANY

- Location and depth of underground utilities.
- Contact Austin's One Call Service—(512) 472-2822—to locate all utility lines, cables, etc.

CONSULT YOUR WATER DEPARTMENT

- Restrictions or guidelines on water usage.
- Rebate or incentive programs for voluntary water conservation planning.

CONSULT YOUR NEIGHBORHOOD AND HOMEOWNERS ASSOCIATION

- Changes that affect views, mutual privacy, quiet, sunlight, and airflow.
- Any homeowner's association building or landscape restrictions, requirements, or guidelines.

2—Planning and Design: Legal Checklist for Landscape Construction

Table 2.1: Measurements for Price Estimates

Item	Unit of Measure
Design Fees	Hourly or Lump Sum
Grading	Hourly or Cu. Yd.
Drainage (Pipe and Inlets)	Linear Feet Pipe #Inlets Cu. Yds. Gravel
Drainage (French Drain)	Linear Feet Excavated Cu. Yds. Gravel
Utilities (Plumbing, Electric)	Hourly/Materials, Lump Sum
Sprinkler System	Lump Sum
Pavement	Square Foot
Fences	Linear Foot
Gates/Hardware	Per Gate
Walls	Linear Foot or Square Foot of Wall Face
Retaining Walls	Linear Foot or Lump Sum
Trellises and Arbors	Lump Sum
Pond	Lump Sum
Swimming Pool	Lump Sum
Garden Lighting	Lump Sum/Per Fixture
Outdoor Furniture	Each
Children's Playsets	Each
Tree Pruning	Lump Sum or Hourly
Shredding/Chipping	Lump Sum or Hourly
Trees	Each: five gallon; 10 gallon, 15 gallon, 20 gallon, 30 gallon, 50 gallon, boxed; or by trunk diameter (caliper)
Tree Staking	Each
Deer Tree Barriers	Each
Shrubs and Vines	Each: 4"; one gallon; two gallon, three gallon, five gallon, 10 gallon
Groundcover	Each: plugs; 2"; 4"; or 1 gallon
Perennials	Each: Flats of 18 or 20 -4"; one gallon; five gallon
Annuals	Each: Flats of 18 or 20 -4"; one gallon;
Grass	Seed, Plugs, Sprigs, Square Yard or Pallet (50 sq. yds. or 450 sq. ft.)
Annual Rye Grass	Pound
Topsoil	Cu. Yd.
Compost/Soil Amendment	Cu. Yd.
Decomposed Granite	Cu. Yd.
Sand	Cu. Yd.
Mulch	Cu. Yd.
Bed Preparation Labor	Hourly/ Materials or Square Foot
Jute Mesh Erosion Control	Sq. ft. or Roll
Steel Edging	10 gauge/16 ft lengths; 14 gauge/10 ft; 16 gauge/16ft
Steel Edging Stakes	Each
Plastic Edging	20-ft. lengths
Other Edging	Linear Foot
Concrete Pavers	Each
Brick	Each/Pallet
Stone	Ton
Gravel	Cu. Yd., Ton

Xeriscape for Central Texas

Table 2.1: Measurements for Price Estimates

Item	Unit of Measure
Mortar	Pounds
Tools	Each
Tool Rental	Half-Day, Daily, Weekly, Monthly
Fertilizers	Gallons or Pounds
Herbicide	Gallons
Fire Ant Killer	Gallon or Pound
Deer Repellents	Quart or Gallon
Garden Hoses	1/2" diameter, 5/8" diameter, 3/4" diameter in 25 ft., 50 ft., 75 ft., and 100 ft.
Manual Sprinklers	Each
Planters	Each
Potting Soil	Cu. Yd., Pounds, Pecks
Flower Seed	Per Packet/Pound
Greenhouse	Lump Sum
Storage Shed	Lump Sum
Rainwater Harvesting System	Lump Sum, Delivery Fees Per Truckload
Hauling/Debris Removal	Lump Sum, Truckload
Maintenance	Hourly, Weekly, Monthly, Annually

Useful Landscape Formulas

CALCULATING VOLUMES

Volume = length × width × height

Table 2.2: Soil Coverage Measurements

Depth (in Inches)	Coverage (in Square Feet)
1/8	2,592
1/4	1,296
3/8	864
1/2	648
5/8	518
3/4	432
1	324
2	162
3	108
4	81
5	67
6	54
8	40
10	33
12	27

It may be easy to remember that one cubic yard of soil materials covers a 10' x 10' area (100 s.f.) 3" deep.

EXAMPLE

Area to be covered is 2,160 sq. ft. to a depth of 4 inches. From Table 2.2, one cubic yard will cover 81 sq. ft. to 4 inches.

$$\frac{2160}{81} = 26.67 \text{ cu. yds. required}$$

Expressed another way:

$$\frac{L' \times W' \times D''}{324} = V$$

$V = Volume\ in\ Cubic\ Yards$
$L = Length\ of\ the\ Area\ in\ Feet$
$W = Width\ of\ the\ Area\ in\ Feet$
$D = Required\ Depth\ in\ Inches$

FORMULAS FOR AREA CALCULATIONS

- Area of a Square or Rectangle = length × width

- Area of a Right Triangle = $\frac{1}{2}$base × height

- Ellipse = π(long radius)(short radius)

- Circle = π(radius)^2

- π = 3.1416

Table 2.3: Measuring Materials

Cubic yard = 100 sq. ft. at a depth of approx. 3"

Cubic foot bag = 4 sq. ft. at a depth of 3" or 12 sq. ft. at a depth of 1"

2 cubic foot bag = 8 sq. ft. at a depth of 3"

1 pallet of sod will cover approximately 450 sq. ft.

1 ton of patio flagstone will cover approximately 70-80 sq. ft.

1 ton of decomposed granite = approximately .75 cubic yards

Table 2.4: Common Plant Container Sizes

6 pack	4 inch
1 gallon	2 - 3 gallon
5 gallon	10 gallon
15 gallon	30 gallon
50 gallon	Balled and Burlapped Trees (B&B) are usually sold by the caliper inch of trunk diameter

Bibliography

Brenzel, Kathleen N., Editor. *Sunset Western Garden Book.* Menlo Park: Sunset Publishing Corporation, 1995.

Brenzel, Kathleen N., Editor. *Sunset Western Landscaping.* Menlo Park: Sunset Publishing Corporation, 1997.

Duffield, M.R. & W. Jones. *Plants for Dry Climates: How to Select, Grow and Enjoy.* Tuscon: HP Books, 1981.

Eck, Joe. *Elements of Garden Design.* New York: Henry Holt & Company, 1996.

Gent, Lucy. *Great Planting.* London: Ward Lock, 1995.

Hogan, Elizabeth. *Waterwise Gardening: Beautiful Gardens with Less Water.* Menlo Park: Sunset Publishing Corporation, 1989.

Ogden, Scott. *Gardening Success with Difficult Soils: Limestone, Alkaline Clay, and Caliche.* Dallas: Taylor Publishing Company, 1992.

Paul, Anthony. *Creative Ideas for Small Gardens.* London: Harper Collins, 1994.

Wasowski, Sally and Andy Wasowski. *Native Texas Plants: Landscaping Region by Region.* Houston: Gulf Publishing, 1991.

Welch, Dr. William C. *Perennial Garden Color.* Dallas: Taylor Publishing, 1989.

Chapter 3

Soil Analysis

In This Chapter...

Central Texas Soils
    Our Soils Relate to the Local Geology

Geological and Chemical Properties of Soil
    Geological Soil Regions of Central Texas
    Soil Chemistry for Thriving Plants

Amending the Soil
    Say *No* to Sandy Loam
    How Often to Amend the Soil
    How Much to Amend

Mineral Requirements
    Symptoms of Shortages of Essential Elements

Mulch Makes the Difference

Bibliography

Soil provides the base structure for plants to grow. It holds water and nutrients until they are absorbed by the root hairs and allows carbon dioxide to escape from the growing roots. Soil also provides the oxygen necessary for the soil bacteria and fungi to complete the decay process of organic matter. This chapter will help you identify the type of soil in your garden and ways to amend it so you can grow bigger and stronger plants.

Central Texas Soils

Soil textures in Central Texas are distinctive and can differ by neighborhood. Soil structure varies from the coarse texture of sandy soils, to moderately fine loamy soils, or to the fine texture of clay soils. The soil types are well known by landscape professionals who almost always answer the question "How will this plant grow?" with another question "Where do you live?"

Our Soils Relate to the Local Geology

Our Central Texas area was formed some 60 million to 10 million years ago when this area was alternately covered by sea water and then exposed as a coastal plain.

Figure 3.1: Formation of Edwards Plateau

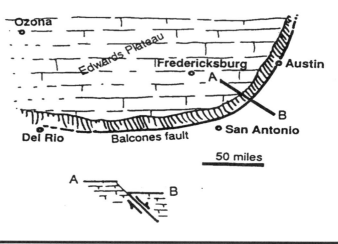

Source: Spearing, 1992.

Ten million years ago, the Edwards Plateau was uplifted along the Balcones fault.

Ten million years ago, there was a shifting of land masses which produced an upheaval of the Edwards Plateau creating an 800-foot-high ridge called the Balcones fault or escarpment. The fault makes a broad arc from the Red River area in the north, through Dallas, Waco, Austin, San Antonio, and Del Rio. In the Central Texas area, the Balcones fault is just west of IH-35. The land to the east of the fault is deep, lime-rich blackland soil with a mildly alkaline pH of 7.4 to 8.4 or higher.

The land west of the Balcones fault eroded over the years which, in turn, created the deep canyons. This erosion exposed different layers of limestone, chalk, and marl. The remaining hills characterize the uplands of the Edwards Plateau which have, at best, shallow soils. Depending on where you're located within Central Texas, you may have deep soil which is mildly alkaline or shallow limestone-studded soil which is strongly alkaline.

Figure 3.2: Formation of the Hill Country

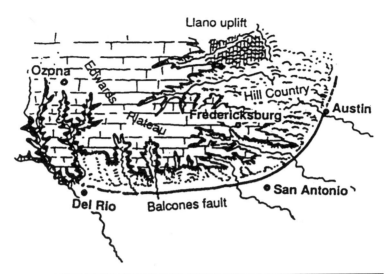

Stream erosion carved into the Edwards Plateau, exposing the Llano Uplift and creating the Hill Country.

Source: Spearing, 1992.

Geological and Chemical Properties of Soil

We have to concern ourselves with both the geology and the soil chemistry to be able to select the best plants to survive and thrive in this alkaline soil. The different soil types are easily identified by describing the woods, prairies, and plateaus in our Central Texas area. After describing the geological soil regions, we will discuss the chemical properties of the soil. Both properties affect the selection of plants and ultimately determine if the plants will prosper.

Geological Soil Regions of Central Texas

In Central Texas natural geological regions come together and produce the varied geography we enjoy *and struggle with*. A perfect example of this occurs in the Austin area where three different regions—Edwards Plateau, Blackland Prairies, and Oak Woods and Prairies—converge. Each of the three regions has identifying characteristics which can be replicated for healthy, natural looking landscapes.

REGION A: THE EDWARDS PLATEAU

Soils of the Edwards Plateau are usually shallow and dark-colored, and they typically develop under grassland vegetation with a variety of surface textures. These soils are slightly alkaline, with a pH of 7 to 8. These grassland areas have underlying layers of limestone.

Xeriscape for Central Texas

Geological Soil Regions of Central Texas
A. Edwards Plateau
B. Blackland Prairies
C. Oak Woods & Prairies

Our Central Texas soils are alkaline, with a pH ranging from 7.4 to above 8. In a nutshell, that is why acid-loving plants like azaleas, camelias, and most hollies will not do well here.

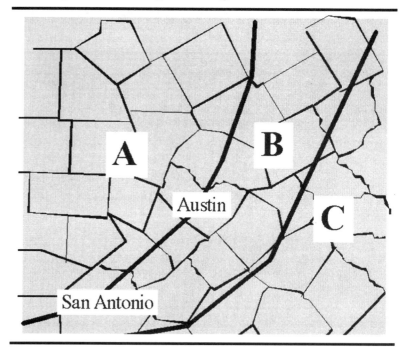

Figure 3.3: Geologic Soil Regions of Central Texas

REGION B: BLACKLAND PRAIRIES

Blackland prairies are gently-rolling to nearly-level, and they are well divided into hills and ridges for rapid surface drainage. Fairly uniform, dark-colored alkaline clays, often referred to as "black gumbo," are interspersed with some gray acid sandy loams. In Central Texas, most soils east of I-35 fall in this category.

REGION C: THE OAK WOODS AND PRAIRIES

The Oak Woods and Prairie soils are acidic sandy loam or sand. The soil of this region is often yellowish-brown in color due to accumulation of aluminum. Bottomland soils washed down by erosion may be light brown to dark gray and acidic, with textures ranging from sandy loams to clays.

Soil Chemistry for Thriving Plants

Some plants are known to be lime-hating, while others are lime-loving. The plant's range of tolerance for the soil's pH or the degree of acidity or alkalinity is the factor that determines this difference. The range of pH is from 0 to 14, with 7 considered neutral. Most plants thrive in a pH zone from 5.5 to 7. Northern United States peat bog soils have a pH of 4.5, which is very acidic. To make soil less acidic (more alkaline), limestone is added. Our Central Texas soils are alkaline, with a pH ranging from 7.4 to above 8. In a nutshell, that is why acid-loving plants like azaleas, camelias, and most hollies will not do well here. To make it even worse, our ground water has seeped through limestone rock into the wells and lakes, making the water alkaline also. As a result, watering plants

3—Soil Analysis: Amending the Soil

neutralizes the acid of the potting soil or peat moss even more, making it very difficult to grow acid-loving plants. This is one important reason for planting native plants that thrive on our alkaline soil with a minimum of supplemental feeding.

Feeding plants with fertilizers can help them thrive by providing the major elements of nitrogen, phosphorus, and potassium. The trace elements or micro-nutrients are discussed later in the chapter. For more information about our alkaline soil, see the excellent book by Scott Ogden, *Gardening Success With Difficult Soils*. The different ways to amend soil are described below.

Amending the Soil

While some native plants actually *prefer* poor, rocky soils (e.g., Mountain Laurel), most plants thrive in amended soil. Amended soils are mixtures of native soils and additives, which improve the soil's fertility, friability (ease of crumbling), and drainage, and provide a long-lasting and stable root zone for plants.

Amended soils are mixtures of native soils and additives, which improve the soil's fertility, friability (ease of crumbling), and drainage, and provide a long-lasting and stable root zone for plants.

Amendments can be purchased to add to your existing soil to provide faster and better plant growth. Amended soils are typically called a *rose mix*, a *garden mix*, or a *yard mix,* and they contain progressively less composted organic matter. Amended soil's basic components are native soil, compost (cotton burrs or 'Dillo Dirt), and grit (sand). Different mixes are available for use in planting:

- Mixes for trees and shrubbery (mostly compost).
- Lighter mixes for flower beds (additional sand for drainage).
- Mixes for turf grasses which need both compost and sand.

For new beds or turf areas, rototill or hand till and remove rocks and construction trash. Incorporate sand and compost. Do *not* use peat moss, as it makes the soil worse and doesn't last long. After planting, add 3 to 4 inches of organic mulch. Refresh the mulch periodically, and the soil texture will improve continuously.

Say *No* to Sandy Loam

There are *no* good reasons to purchase what is called sandy loam, because it contains none of the organic material that plants need. Even worse, it frequently contains lots of weed seeds that sprout and compete with your desirable plants. Sandy loam is used by the construction trade because it is cheap, and it is easily spread and worked. It is rarely appropriate for plants in the Austin area. Turf grass sod laid over sandy loam will require extra water, fertilizer, and compost, and you will always have weak grass. You can, however, improve this soil with a thin layer of 'Dillo Dirt applied twice per year—spring and fall—to build up the organic matter and slowly release nitrogen for growth.

How Often to Amend the Soil

- Conversion of problem soils is best done before planting.

- In general, to improve soils, add sand and composted material.

- After the first year, fertilize or spread a thin layer of composted organic matter such as 'Dillo Dirt in the spring and the fall.

- Periodically fertilize the plants based on coverage and the amount and type of mulch.

How Much to Amend

- Do not amend the existing soil when planting trees.

- Raised beds will drain better if they are filled with amended soil and sand.

- Old ranch land, which has been grazed short over time, will have been depleted of its natural organic matter. It will require heavy amendment by composted material like 'Dillo Dirt at least two times per year.

- Heavy mulching of beds will build up the texture of the soil over time.

The three most important elements to a plant's healthy growth are:

- *Nitrogen.*
- *Phosphorus.*
- *Potassium.*

Mineral Requirements

Plants, like humans, need to receive steady quantities of specific elements for healthy growth. These elements are divided into two groups: *essential elements* ("macro-nutrients") and *trace elements* ("micro-nutrients"). In a perfect world, our soils would contain proper amounts of both types of elements. However, few soils are perfect, and it is important to understand how plants can react when the soils surrounding them have deficiencies or larger-than-normal quantities of one type of element.

Essential elements are, for the most part, responsible for forming important plant structures and activation enzymes. Some essential elements perform one or the other of these tasks. Others combine both functions. The three most important elements to a plant's healthy growth are *nitrogen, phosphorus,* and *potassium* (the three numbers on fertilizers reflect the amount of each of these elements). To a lesser extent, the trace elements of *calcium, magnesium,* and *sulfur* also are needed for maximum growth. These trace elements are mostly responsible for enzyme activation.

Symptoms of Shortages of Essential Elements

Table 3.1 lists the deficiency symptom, the excess symptom, the deficient element, and the treatment.

Mulch Makes the Difference

Plants require several different elements to grow well, and mulch helps provide all of these elements:

- It simulates nature's way to encourage plant growth.

- Mulching with composted vegetable and animal refuse feeds plants nitrogen and loosens the soil. 'Dillo Dirt is especially effective.

- Mulching with pine bark lowers the pH-releasing minerals needed for growth.

- Mulching with organic matter shades and cools the soil thereby reducing water needs and increasing root growth. Use less mulch in the spring to warm the soil.

- Mulching chokes out moisture robbing weeds. More than 3 inches of organic mulch completely chokes weeds, but over 4 inches can reduce aeration of roots and slow plant growth.

- Mulch prevents the formation of a crust on the top of the soil thus allowing more rain water capture.

- Stone mulch conserves heat in the winter, minimizing damage from freezing temperatures.

Bibliography

Ogden, Scott. *Gardening Success with Difficult Soils: Limestone, Alkaline Clay, and Caliche.* Dallas: Taylor Publishing Company, 1992.

Spearing, Darwin. *Roadside Geology of Texas.* Missoula, Montana: Mountain Press Publishing Company, 1992.

Xeriscape for Central Texas

Table 3.1: Essential Elements

Deficiency Symptom	Excess Symptom	Deficient Element	Treatment
Plant light green; lower leaves yellowing, drying to light brown. Older leaves esp. affected. Location of deficiency can be generalized. Plants may appear stunted.	Growth rate too quick; abundance of "soft" foliage, appearing darker green than normal. Soft growth subject to insect, frost damage. Root system minimal.	*Nitrogen* (N) Responsible for vegetative growth.	Use a high-nitrogen fertilizer such as dried blood.
Plants appear dark green, stunted. May develop red and purple colors, affecting older leaves first. Stalks often stunted and slender if element deficient in later growth stages; root system underdeveloped.		*Phosphorus* (P) Responsible for good root growth & metabolic processes.	Apply a dressing of bone meal fertilizer.
Leaves mottled or yellowing with large and small spots of dead tissue; symptoms first appear on older leaves; spots usually small, found at tips and between veins. Later, leaves may become bluish or bronze in their entirety; stalks slender, flowers & fruits poor quality.	Inability to take up magnesium, causing imbalance with other elements.	*Potassium* (K) Responsible for fruit and flower quality. Activates many plant enzymes needed to form starch and proteins.	Apply a dressing of rock potash.
Leaves yellowing, mottled with symptoms beginning in between veins of older leaves. Leaves may redden or have dead spots; leaf tips, margins curved upward; stalks slender.		*Magnesium* (Mg) Needed for chlorophyll in leaves and to help activate many enzymatic reactions.	Apply a dressing of seaweed meal, liquid seaweed, or liquid animal manure. Check for a good soil structure and for adequate organic matter in the soil.
Twisted and deformed tissues; seen in areas of new growth; examples, blossom-end rot in tomatoes & tip-burn in lettuce.		*Calcium* (Ca) Neutralizes certain acid forms in plants; helps with protein manufacture; activates plant enzymes.	No specific cure. Careful use of lime & balanced nutrient level are helpful treatments.
Uncommon in plants; general chlorosis throughout entire leaf, including veins; deficiency first noted in young leaves.		*Sulfur* (S) Found in proteins and helps with chlorophyll production.	Apply a light application of gypsum over the soil surface

3—Soil Analysis: Bibliography

Table 3.2: Trace Elements

Deficiency Symptom	Deficient Element	Treatment
Pronounced chlorosis in between veins. Occurs first in young leaves; may be followed by yellowing of veins. Often symptomatic in alkaline soils; can be confused with magnesium deficiency. Often found in species of the rose family.	*Iron* (Fe) Helps form chlorophyll; aids in respiration.	Spray with liquid seaweed and afterward apply a dressing of seaweed meal and/or manure or compost.
Growth reduction of young leaves & between nodes of stems. Leaf margins may appear puckered; interveinal yellowing may occur. Causes disorders such as "little leaf" and "rosette" of apples, peaches, & pecans.	*Zinc* (Zn) Helps activate enzymes & aids in chlorophyll formation.	Apply a dressing of seaweed meal, well-rotted manure, or compost.
Young leaves dark green, twisted & misshapen, often with dead spots; rarely a problem in the U.S.	*Copper* (Cu) Helps activate enzymes.	Apply a dressing of seaweed meal, well-rotted manure, or compost.
Interveinal yellowing on younger or older leaves (species dependent), followed by lesions of dead tissue; not a common deficiency.	*Manganese* (Mn) Helps form proteins and chlorophyll; activates enzymes.	Spray with liquid seaweed and afterward apply a dressing of seaweed meal and/or manure or compost
Wide range of symptoms exist, depending on species & plant age. Earliest symptoms failure of root tips to grow outward; growth of leaf tips in young leaves inhibited.	*Boron* (B) Helps with tissue development.	Prevention is necessary since after deficiencies become apparent, it is too late to get a crop. Apply seaweed, manure, or compost for next crop if current one destroyed.
Yellowing between veins which occurs first on the older or mid-stem leaves, progressing to younger leaves. Deficiencies are rare but are normally associated with acid soils.	*Molybdenum* (Mo) Helps produce protein.	Add lime to raise soil's pH. Spray plants with liquid seaweed fertilizer & then apply seaweed meal and/or manure or compost to the soil.
Normally affects legumes of tropical origins. Leaf tips damaged when flowering begins.	*Nickel* (Ni) An essential part of an enzyme that helps remove toxic urea. Thought to be an essential element.	Unknown.

Xeriscape for Central Texas

Notes & Ideas...

Chapter 4

Plant Selection

In This Chapter...

Trees
Shrubs
Ground Covers
Antique Roses
Herbs
Perennials
Annuals and Biennials
Bulbs
Climbing Plants
Ornamental Grasses
Bibliography

Which plants do best in Central Texas? The answer is deceptively simple—almost any plant, if you use it properly. The key to success with Xeriscape plants is to know where the plants originated and to create a similar environment (or micro-climate) for them in your landscape. Alternatively, you can identify the micro-climates in your landscape and then place plants which will do well in that environment. The sections in this chapter will provide you with information on a variety of plants that do well in Central Texas.

Xeriscape for Central Texas

The key to success with Xeriscape plants is to know where the plants originated and to create a similar environment (or micro-climate) for them in your landscape.

Which plants do best in Central Texas? The answer is deceptively simple—almost any plant, if you use it properly. The key to success with Xeriscape plants is to know where the plants originated and to create a similar environment (or micro-climate) for them in your landscape. Alternatively, you can identify the micro-climates in your landscape and then place plants which will do well in that environment.

Austin, for example, has an average annual rainfall of 32 inches. A plant from a higher rainfall area will need additional watering. Conversely, a plant from an area which receives less rain should be placed in a spot that drains rapidly so water doesn't accumulate. Remember, too, that annual averages can be deceptive—does a plant comes from an area with distinct wet or dry seasons, or is it better adapted to uniform rainfall throughout the year?

In addition to moisture requirements, you need to know whether a plant prefers sun or shade and the type of soil it prefers. If you are using native plants, a walk through a natural area will yield much of this information. Take a look at how nature achieves its delicate balance of form, color, and texture in grouping plants together. By duplicating at home what you see in the wild, you will have placed the native plants in their proper habitat.

There are other considerations as well when using plants from other regions in your landscape. In addition to those already mentioned, you should know the temperature limitations for each plant. The average cold temperature determines plant hardiness. Most of Central Texas falls in zone eight where the average minimum temperature ranges from 10° to 20°. Just as important is a general knowledge of the altitude at which a plant typically grows.

The sections in this chapter will provide you with information on a variety of plants that do well in Central Texas.

Trees

Trees are perennial plants which bear a single woody stem at ground level. What we often call a tree is, in fact, a treelike shrub. Trees range in heights from 2' to 100' or more, depending on the species.

"That's Not a Tree...It's a Big Bush"

This comment is one of the most often repeated statements voiced by new residents moving here from cooler and moister climates. Yes, because of our dry climate, most of our local trees are definitely smaller than those to the north and east of us. However, after living here awhile, newcomers usually learn to appreciate the intimacy afforded by our smaller versions. The antics of birds and squirrels are easier to watch, our shade trees provide a cozy room-like effect because their spreading branches are so close, and our smaller trees are much easier to maintain because they are easier to reach.

Why Planting Trees Is Important

There are many reasons to plant trees on your property:

- You can potentially reduce your energy consumption by up to 30% when shade is provided for windows, walls, and roofs.
- In the world of real estate, according to TreeFolks (Austin, TX) trees can add from 13% to 21% to the value of your home.
- Trees help reduce air pollution and add beauty.
- Erosion and surface water runoff are significantly reduced by trees.
- Trees are natural wildlife habitats for birds and other animals.

Desirable Characteristics to Look for When Buying a Tree

First, try to find a tree with a single, strong central leader. Next, check out the bark and tree limbs. Do they look damaged in any way? Any signs of disease or fungus? Now, look at the bottom of the container. Are roots healthily contained within the container, or are they so bound up that they are squeezing out the drainage holes? Finally, if the tree is dormant, gently scratch a tiny section of the bark to make sure that it is alive. Healthy trees will have a green, moist appearance beneath the bark's surface.

When Is the Best Time to Plant a Tree?

The very best time for planting trees is between the months of October and March. Container types of trees can be planted at any time. Bare root trees (trees that are transported and transplanted with no soil around their roots) should be planted while they are dormant (usually December to mid-February). Balled and burlapped trees (trees that are purchased with a ball of soil around their roots that is tightly wrapped in burlap) can be transplanted any time. Try to avoid planting trees in July or August. The prolonged intense heat and lack of moisture during those months can really stress newly planted trees.

What Should You Consider before Planting a Tree?

The most important thing you can do before planting is to think about the ultimate height and spread of your tree and plan for it. Many people neglect to do this and live to regret it. Here are some questions to ask before planting a tree:

- Will the tree eventually grow into the overhead power lines? Look around surrounding neighborhoods and observe utility company pruning jobs when this happens. It's not a pretty

The most important thing you can do before planting is to think about the ultimate height and spread of your tree and plan for it.

sight. *When planting around power lines, avoid planting any trees that will have a mature height of over 25'.*

- Is the tree planted too close to a ground transformer. (At least 8' clearance is required.)
- Will the tree block safety features like traffic signs or corner views?
- Will the tree grow over into your neighbors yard?
- Will the tree roots eventually grow under pavement surfaces and cause damage? Remember, tree roots usually extend out further than the trees' final spread.
- Will the tree eventually block a view that you especially enjoy?
- Will the tree eventually cause deep shade where you don't want it?
- Are you making sure that you are not planning to plant your trees too close together based on their eventual spread?

How Far Away from My House Should I Plant a Tree?

This is an important consideration. Trees can cause damage to home foundations when planted too closely, and those which are planted too far away from the house can provide little energy conserving shade. Table 4.1 lists some general guidelines; however, if your home has a very strong foundation, you may consider planting closer than these distances..

Table 4.1: Spacing Guide for Trees

Tree Height	Minimum Spacing From Wall	Minimum Spacing From Building Corner
Up to 25 ft.	10 ft.	10 ft.
25 to 50 ft.	15 ft.	15 ft.
Over 50 ft.	20 ft.	15 ft.

What Is the Best Side of the House to Plant Trees?

Try to plant deciduous trees (trees that lose their leaves during the winter months) on the south and west sides of the house. When placed there, they will provide shade and a cooling effect in the summer and allow the sun to come through during the winter. Try to position evergreen (or semi-evergreen) trees on the north side of the house. When placed there, they will help block the cold north winds that howl through our area on-and-off during the winter.

What Is the Best Way to Plant a Tree?

For many of us, planting a tree is not an easy task because of shallow soils and underlying layers of limestone. If this is the case,

Balled and burlapped trees are purchased with a ball of soil around their roots that is tightly wrapped in burlap

4—Plant Selection: Trees

your best bet may be to buy a smaller tree rather than trying to dig through layers of rock. For larger specimens, hiring an experienced landscape contractor may be worth the extra money.

The Ten Steps to Planting a Tree

1. Plan, plan, plan. Make sure to select the correct tree for the space allotted.

2. Measure the rootball diameter and then lightly mark an area that is 5 times wider than that diameter. Loosen this area to an 8" depth.

3. Now, in the middle of this loosened area, dig a hole. Make the hole 3 to 4 times as wide as the rootball. Dig the hole just deep enough so that when the rootball is placed inside, it is at the same growing depth as it was to begin with.

4. Make the sides of the hole really ugly and uneven. This lets roots explore more readily.

5. Go ahead and place the tree in the hole and remove the container from the tree. (*Note: It is bad for the delicate tree roots to pull it out by the trunk when removing it from the container, so try to pull the container, not the tree.*) Settle the rootball into the hole, position the way you want it, and straighten it. Make sure that it is at the right level—neither higher nor lower—than the level at which it was originally grown.

6. If you are using a balled and burlapped tree, place the tree in the hole as above, making sure that it is at the correct depth and that it is straight. Then, remove any wires that might be binding it and just let the surrounding burlap fall away from the root ball into the hole. The burlap will eventually rot. Don't try to remove the burlap from the hole because it will damage the roots.

7. Try to backfill the hole with the original soil that you dug out. Avoid pampering your tree with special soil mixes. If you do this, then you may wind up with roots that don't try to explore into outlying areas, but rather grow round and round in that one small well-prepared hole.

8. Backfill the hole until it is half full of soil. Then, turn the hose on low and slowly fill until the water reaches the top of the soil. Lightly tamp the soil with your foot to close up any air holes. Backfill the hole with the rest of the soil and repeat the process of wetting and lightly tamping.

9. Make a small berm around the perimeter of the tree. This will help keep in the water when you water.

10. Cover the entire area that you originally loosened with 3" to 4" of mulch to help reduce water loss. Do not fertilize the newly planted tree until the following spring.

Note: Avoid the old-fashioned practice of pruning the tops of trees back when planting. Recent studies have shown that this does not help balance root loss. If pruning is necessary when planting, only prune to remove damaged wood, crossed or rubbing branches, narrow crotches, or multiple main stems.

Xeriscape for Central Texas

Table 4.2: Trees for Central Texas

Common Name	Botanical Name	Light	Water	Height × Spread	Features	Zone
Anacacho Orchid Tree	*Bauhinia lunarioides or B. Congesta*	S/PS	L-M	8'-15' × 6'-15'	Canopy small, branches short & crooked, bark grayish-silver. Blooms fragrant. Fast growth rate. Good understory or patio tree, preferring dappled shade. Not winter hardy north of Austin. White blooms Apr.-May. Deciduous. Native.	8
Ash, Texas	*Fraxinus texensis*	S	L-M	35'-45' × 20'-30'	Form broadly pyramidal. Foliage somewhat rounded. Good fall color. Growth rate rapid. Deciduous. Native.	6
Buckeye, Mexican	*Ungnadia speciosa*	S/PS	L	to 25' × to 25'	Form upright, broadly spreading. Foliage long narrow leaflets. Grows as a small tree or in shrub form. Pink blooms early spring. Deciduous. Native.	8-9
Carolina Buckthorn	*Rhamnus caroliniana*	S/PS	M	to 25'	Form upright, oval. Looks best grown at the edge of woodlands. Good fall color. Growth rate slow. Deciduous. Native.	6-10
Cherry, Escarp-ment Black	*Prunus serotina*	S/PS	M	25'-50' × to 25'	Form upright, narrow, oval. Foliage oval, smelling like almonds when crushed. Avoid use in heavy clay soils. Good fall color. Moderate growth rate. White spring blooms. Deciduous. Native.	3-10
Cherry Laurel	*Prunus caroliniana*	S/PS	M	25'-30' × 25'	Form upright oval. Foliage dark green, shiny, oblong. Good for screening, hedges. Good drainage necessary. Growth rate moderate. White, early spring blooms. Evergreen. Native.	7-10
Crepe myrtle	*Lagerstro-emia indica*	S	M	to 25' × to 25'	Form upright with irregular branching pattern. Foliage oval, with good autumn color. Plant where good air movement. Good specimen tree. Summer blooms.Various colors available. Growth rate moderate.	7-9
Cypress, Arizona	*Cupressus arozonica*	S	M-H	25'-50' × 25'-50'	Pyramidal shaped conifer with silvery foliage. Takes many soil types & will even do well in prolonged moisture. Good fall color. Growth rate fast. Evergreen.	8
Cypress, Bald	*Taxodium distichum*	S/PS	M-H	50' + × 25'-50'	Form conical to irregular. Foliage feathery, delicate. Good fall color. Growth rate fast. Deciduous. Native.	4-10
Cypress, Montezuma	*Taxodium mucronatum*	S	M	40'-60' × 30'-50'	Form pyramidal. Foliage fine, feathery. Growth rate fast. Good fall color. Does well in wet or dry sites. Semi-evergreen. Native.	8-10
Elm, Cedar	*Ulmus crassifolia*	S	L-M	25'-50' × 25'-35'	Form upright with thin trunk & rounded, top-heavy canopy. Good spring, fall color. Growth rate slow. Deciduous. Native.	7-10

LEGEND

LIGHT
S = Sun
PS = Partial Shade
SH = Shade

WATER
L = Low
M = Moderate
H = High

4—Plant Selection: Trees

Table 4.2: Trees for Central Texas (Continued)

Common Name	Botanical Name	Light	Water	Height × Spread	Features	Zone
Elm, Chinese	*Ulmus parvifolia*	S	M	40'-60' × 30'-40'	Form rounded or oval. Foliage dark, glossy green. Growth rate rapid. Deciduous.	7-10
Eve's Necklace	*Sophora affinis*	S/PS	L	to 25' × to 25'	Form upright, spreading, rounded. Foliage consists of small leaflets. Ornamental seed pods poisonous. Tolerates poor drainage. Growth rate moderate. Pink blooms in late spring. Deciduous. Native.	8-9
Golden Ball Lead Tree	*Leucaena retusa*	S/PS	L	15'-20' × 12'-15'	Form open, airy. Foliage fine-textured. Wood brittle—protect from heavy winds. Yellow blooms spring to fall. Growth rate moderate. Deciduous. Native.	8-9
Golden Rain Tree	*Koelreuteria paniculata*	S	M	to 25' × to 25'	Form broad, oval. Foliage compound with oblong leaflets. Needs certain amount of chilling hours for good bloom. Yellow fall blooms. Growth rate moderate. Deciduous.	8-10
Holly, Possumhaw	*Ilex decidua*	S/PS	L-M	to 25' × to 25'	Form upright, spreading, irregular. Foliage oval, bright green. Females have bright red berries fall to winter. White spring blooms. Growth rate moderate. Deciduous. Native.	5-9
Holly, Yaupon	*Ilex vomitoria*	S/PS	L-M	to 25' × to 25'	Form upright, oval, irregular. Foliage small, oval, dark glossy green. Females have red berries in winter. White spring blooms. Growth rate moderate. Evergreen. Native.	7-10
Maple, Big-tooth	*Acer grandi-dentatum*	S/PS	M	25'-50' × 25'-35'	Form oval to rounded. Growth rate moderate. Good fall color. Deciduous. Native.	8
Mesquite	*Prosopis glandulosa*	S	L-M	to 25' × to 25'	Form open, irregular. Foliage light-textured, airy with tiny leaflets. Good for light, filtered shade. White spring blooms. Growth rate slow. Deciduous. Native.	8-10
Mountain Laurel, Texas	*Sophora secundiflora*	S/PS	L	to 25' × to 25'	Form upright, narrow. Foliage bright green, dense with oval leaflets. Seed pods poisonous. Showy, fragrant purple spring blooms. Growth rate slow. Evergreen. Native.	8-10
Oak, Bur	*Quercus macrocarpa*	S/PS	L-M	50' + × 50'	Form rounded with dense canopy. Drought tolerant. Large, showy acorns. Growth rate fast. Deciduous. Native.	7-8
Oak, Chinquapin	*Quercus muehlenbergii*	S/PS	M	50' + × 25'-50'	Form narrow, upright. Foliage large, coarsely-toothed, bright green. Does well in limestone soils. Growth rate moderate. Deciduous. Native.	7-8

Xeriscape for Central Texas

Table 4.2: Trees for Central Texas (Continued)

Common Name	Botanical Name	Light	Water	Height × Spread	Features	Zone
Oak, Lacey	*Quercus glaucoides*	S/PS	L-M	20'-30' × to 25'	Form upright, small, multi-trunked. Foliage bluish. Good seasonal foliage color. Growth rate slow. Deciduous. Native.	7-9
Oak, Plateau Live	*Quercus fusiformis*	S/PS	L-M	25'-50' × 50'+	Form upright with irregular branching. Foliage simple, oval. Susceptible to oak wilt & Live Oak decline. Growth rate moderate. Semi-evergreen. Native.	7-8
Oak, Shumard	*Quercus shumardii*	S/PS	L-M	50' × 40'	Form upright, oval. Foliage dense. Leaves like TX Red Oak but larger with bristled tips. Native to canyons & narrow valleys. Growth rate moderate. Deciduous. Native.	7-8
Oak, Texas Red	*Quercus texana*	S/PS	L-M	25'-40' × 20'-30'	Form upright, oval. Looks like a Shumard Oak, but leaves are smaller with no bristles on tips. Native to limestone hills. Good fall color. Deciduous. Native.	7-8
Pear, Bradford	*Pyrus callery-ana 'Bradford'*	S	M	20'-30' × 20'-25'	Form pyramidal to oval. Foliage oval to oblong, leathery, glossy. Good fall color. Growth rate moderate. White spring blooms.	4-9
Pecan	*Carya illinoiensis*	S	M	50' + × 50' +	Form broad, oval. Foliage compound with long, narrowed leaflets. Native. Deciduous. Growth rate rapid. Native.	7-8
Persimmon, Texas	*Diospyros texana*	S/PS	L-M	to 25' × to 25'	Form upright, usually multi-trunked, open. Foliage oval, dark green, leathery. Deciduous. Native.	8-9
Pine, Eldarica	*Pinus eldarica*	S	L-M	25'-40' × 20'-30'	Form pyramidal. Foliage needle-like. Growth rate rapid. Drought tolerant.	6-8
Pistache, Chinese	*Pistachia chinensis*	S	L-M	25'-40' × 25'-40'	Form variable, but usually rounded or oval. Foliage neat, compound with small leaflets. Good fall color. Growth rate rapid. Deciduous. Native.	8-10
Plum, Mexican	*Prunus mexicana*	S/PS	L-M	to 25' × to 25'	Form upright, irregular, open. Foliage oval, shiny. Usually grows as an understory or woodland edge tree. Growth rate moderate. White, early-spring blooms. Deciduous. Native.	7-10
Redbud, Texas	*Cercis canadensis 'Texensis'*	S/PS	L-M	to 25' × to 25'	Form oval or rounded. Foliage large, heart-shaped, dull-green. Blooms rose colored in early spring. Growth rate moderate. Deciduous. Native.	4-9
Senna, Common Tree	*Cassia corymbosa*	S/PS	L-M	5'-8' × 3'-4'	Form irregular, leggy, upright, oval. Yellow summer blooms, sparse in shade. Semi-evergreen, but may freeze back. Growth rate moderate. Native.	8-10

4—Plant Selection: Shrubs

Table 4.2: Trees for Central Texas (Continued)

Common Name	Botanical Name	Light	Water	Height × Spread	Features	Zone
Soapberry	*Sapindus saponaria var. drummondii*	S/PS	L-M	15'-30' × 12'-20'	Form tall with erect branches. Canopy rounded. Good fall color. Fruit rounded, yellow, poisonous only to humans. Growth rate rapid. White spring blooms. Native.	5-9
Sumac, Prairie Flame Leaf	*Rhus lanceolata*	S/PS	L-M	10'-20' × 10'-15'	Form upright, irregular with broad, rounded canopy. Foliage long, narrow. Good fall color. Deciduous. Native.	7-8
Sycamore, Texas	*Platanus occidentalis var. glabrata.*	S	M	50' + × 50' +	Form upright, oval, or pyramidal. Foliage lobed, fuzzy. Native. Deciduous. Growth rate rapid.	7-9
Walnut, Texas	*Juglans major*	S/PS	M	40'-50' × 30'-40'	Form oval, open. Foliage oblong leaflets. Good fall color. Associated with moist bottomlands. Growth rate slow. Deciduous. Native.	7-9
Willow, Desert	*Chilopsis linearis*	S	L	to 25' × to 25'	Form irregular, willow-like (not related to willows). Foliage narrow, long. Growth rate rapid. White, lavender, burgundy blooms in summer. Deciduous. Native.	8-9

Shrubs

A *shrub* is a perennial plant which bears several woody stems at ground level. Shrubs range in size from a few inches in height, such as some of the dwarf varieties, up to 20' tall. Shrubs are often mistakenly referred to as trees because of their size and form, and many shrubs can be trained into treelike forms.

Without a doubt, shrubs are major players in setting the tone for a landscape. They can lend gardens a formal polished look, provide an informal eclectic setting, act as key elements in a shady woodland retreat, and provide stark form contrasts in dry desert landscape styles.

Why Foliage Is So Important

The texture, color, and shapes supplied by foliage provide the true heart of a garden. In fact, many of the world's most sophisticated gardens rely on foliage supplied from trees and shrubs, rather than the transient colors supplied by flowers. Foliage sets the stage for the rest of the garden and can certainly key viewers in to whether the garden is formal, informal, eclectic, or wild.

FOLIAGE-ONLY GARDENS: A GREAT CHOICE FOR BUSY HOUSEHOLDS

For many of us, achieving the extra time necessary for landscape maintenance can be a problem. If this is the case in your household, you might want to take a minute to look over the following reasons to design a landscape devoted solely to contrasting foliage textures, sizes, and colors.

REASONS FOR USING FOLIAGE-BASED LANDSCAPES

Foliage gardens (we aren't talking boring lines of hedges):

- Require less maintenance than gardens devoted to flowers.

- Promote a cooler look in our hot climate.

- Impart an innovative and elegant feeling within the landscape.

- Can include flowers with interesting foliage textures.

- Are adaptable to areas both close to and at a distance from the house.

- Impact viewers with great visual interest.

- Can be achieved by using countless combinations.

- Provide year-round interest.

- Make excellent backdrops for flowers.

- Tie the garden together by providing a cohesive force.

- Can hide unsightly views or objects.

- Provide support for other plants.

- Count on a multitude of textures with choices for every conceivable taste.

FOLIAGE COLORS—CHOICES ABOUND

Most people think of the color green when they conjure up a picture of foliage in their minds. Green is definitely one foliage color, but there are many other colors from which to choose. Like blooms of flowers, differing leaf colors, shapes, and textures, when arranged next to one another, can give a landscape an energetic feeling. Here are just a few leaf colors from which to choose:

Blue	Pale Green
Purple	Gray
Scarlet	Beige
Yellow	Brown
Orange	Variegated
Lime Green	Mottled
Emerald Green	Speckled
Dark Green	Striped

HOW TO ACCENTUATE YOUR LANDSCAPE WITH FOLIAGE COLOR

As a general rule, if you live in a home with a dark-colored exterior, paler-colored foliage will stand out best as a good contrast. If you live in home with a lighter toned exterior, try to use strong textures and vivid colors that don't wash out. The same rule goes for deciding what type of foliage choices to use with different lighting. If you live in a shady, woodland area, pale, airy-textured foliage will probably look best. For homes situated in a bright, sunny location, make sure to use strong foliage colors and strong textures.

As a general rule, if you live in a home with a dark-colored exterior, paler-colored foliage will stand out best as a good contrast. If you live in home with a lighter toned exterior, try to use strong textures and vivid colors that don't wash out. The same rule goes for deciding what type of foliage choices to use with different lighting.

4—Plant Selection: Shrubs

HOW TO DECIDE WHICH FOLIAGE COMBINATIONS ARE BEST

There are many ways to accomplish this feat. None are especially difficult.

- Do a little research: Read books, look at magazines, study plant charts.
- Look around and jot down great combinations that you notice.
- Go to a well-stocked nursery and play around with a few plants and note their leaf contrasts. Ask a well-trained nursery worker for help with ideas.
- Visit area botanical gardens and enjoy a leisurely stroll.

THINK HIGH-MEDIUM-LOW

To avoid monotony, try to picture the area of the garden that you want to transform into a foliage garden as a slate divided into three sections: high (6' and above), medium (2' to 6'), and low (ground level to 2'). Use these dividing lines as guides when choosing foliage plants. Try to make the taller plants interesting specimens which will catch the eye. When using a mixture of foliage types, mid-range plants at eye level should provide different colors and textures so that each plant is shown off to its best advantage. Dark against light, large leaves next to airy leaves, and bright blooms and berries will all be easily seen from this level. At ground level, use low-growing plants that will catch your eye as you walk by. Remember, when we walk, we usually glance down to make sure of our bearings. Why not make the glance down of interest? Try using interesting visual shapes and textures such as mounds, rosettes, or delicate sprawling carpets of tiny leaves.

Note: When making foliage plant choices, try to choose plants with similar soil, light, and water requirements. When grouped together, plants with similar environmental requirements make maintenance chores a snap.

Before You Choose Your Plants...

When planning shrub choices, do a little fun research work and visit nurseries or sites where a good selection of mature shrubs are on display before deciding on your final choices. You'll find that plants are available in many sizes, and the leaves of these plants provide a wide assortment of texture, shape and colors. At better nurseries, knowledgeable staff can answer questions. When visiting different growing locations, you can see how these plants actually grow and can decide for yourself whether certain choices are realistic sizes for the space you have allotted.

One of the first decisions to make when choosing a shrub is whether you want to use an evergreen shrub or a deciduous shrub, which loses its foliage during the winter months.

Xeriscape for Central Texas

Considerations When Selecting Shrubs

- *Height*
- *Hardiness*
- *Moisture requirements.*
- *Soil drainage.*
- *Location.*

Evergreen Or Deciduous—The Choice Is Yours

One of the first decisions to make when choosing a shrub is whether you want to use an evergreen type or if you prefer to use a deciduous shrub which loses its foliage during the winter months. Each type provides specific uses in landscapes.

Table 4.3: Landscape Uses for Shrubs

Evergreen Shrubs	Deciduous Shrubs
Key elements in foundation plantings.	Form borders.
Specimen plants.	Screens
Hedges.	Background plantings.
Corner plantings.	Special effect foundation plantings.
Along sidewalks.	Provide seasonal color.

What To Consider When Selecting Shrubs

- *Height.* Try to choose plants that will not block windows or require frequent pruning after they reach their mature height.

- *Hardiness.* Consider if the plant is hardy to our area. If it is not, you will probably be spending quite a bit of time pampering it when conditions are not favorable.

- *How much moisture it requires.* Try to select shrubs that are suitable for the area under consideration. For instance, if you have a shady, moist site, pick shrubs suitable for that condition. If, on the other hand, you have a site with full sun and reflected heat, avoid placing a moisture-loving plant in that site.

- *Soil drainage.* Most plants need adequate drainage to grow to their full potential. Others can exist on less than optimum conditions. Are you prepared to amend the soil to help soil drainage, or would you prefer to pick a plant that will grow well in poor drainage conditions?

- *Location—where the shrub will be planted.* Choose the right shrub for the right place. Does that plant like sun or shade, does it need good air circulation, does it prefer a good garden soil or will it get along quite nicely on native soils? All of these are questions that you should ask yourself before shopping.

The Best Time To Plant Shrubs

Bare root shrubs (shrubs that are transported and transplanted with no soil around their roots) should be planted while they are dormant (usually December to mid-February).

Balled and burlapped shrubs (shrubs that are purchased with a ball of soil around their roots that is wrapped tightly in burlap) can be transplanted anytime.

4—Plant Selection: Shrubs

Containerized shrubs (shrubs grown in pots, baskets, and tubs) can be transplanted anytime.

Tip: Try to avoid planting shrubs in July or August. The prolonged intense heat and lack of moisture during those months can really stress newly planted shrubs.

How To Plant Shrubs

When planting shrubs, follow the same basic planting procedures used for trees. Avoid the old-fashioned practice of pruning the tops of shrubs when planting. Recent studies have shown that this does not help balance root loss when planting. If pruning is necessary when planting, only prune to remove damaged wood or to provide a better shape.

The Best Soil For Shrubs

When planting shrubs, try to mix in at least half native soil with any outside soil mix that you are using. This will help get the plants used to the native soil in which their roots will be spreading. Using a special outside soil by itself may inhibit the roots from spreading into outlying areas.

Table 4.4: Evergreen Shrubs for Central Texas

Common Name	Botanical Name	Light	Water	Height × Spread	Features	Zone
Agarita	*Berberis trifoliolata*	S/PS	L-M	3'-6' × 4'	Spiny gray-green leaves, red fruit, yellow spring blooms. Nurse plant. Native.	8-9
Barbados Cherry	*Malpighia glabra*	S/PS	M-H	3'-4' × 2'	Multi-branched, good accent, dies back at 25 deg. F. Whitish-pink blooms spring to fall. Native.	9-10
Barberry, Texas	*Berberis swayseyi*	S/PS	L-M	3'-5' × 4'	Upright with compound spiny leaflets. Not common. Yellow spring blooms. Native.	8-9
Cenizo, Texas Sage	*Leucophyllum frutescens spp.*	S/PS	L-M	6'-8' × 6'	Upright-to-round; many var. & sizes available. Violet, purple, pink, white bloom types available. Native.	8-9
Cotoneaster, Horizontal	*Cotoneaster horizontalis*	S	L-M	2'-3' × 4'	Form sprawling with fishbone branching pattern.	5-8
Elaeagnus	*Elaeagnus pungens*	S	L-M	6'-8' × 6'	Broad with pendulous foliage. May have spines.	7-9
Germander, Bush	*Teucrium fruticans*	S	L-M	1' × 18"	Low, tidy foliage.	5-9
Holly, Burford	*Ilex cornuta 'Burfordii'*	S/PS	M	10' × 6'	Upright, oval, with dense foliage. May suffer from iron chlorosis in alkaline soils.	7-9
Holly, Dwarf Burford	*Ilex cornuta 'Burfordii Nana'*	S/PS	L-M	4'-5' × 3'	Glossy spine-tipped foliage. Avoid use in compacted soils. May suffer from iron chlorosis in alkaline soils.	7-9
Holly, Dwarf Chinese	*Ilex cornuta 'Rotunda Nana'*	S/PS	M	2' × 2'	Rounded form, yellow-green spiny leaves. May suffer from iron chlorosis in alkaline soils.	7-9

Xeriscape for Central Texas

Table 4.4: Evergreen Shrubs for Central Texas (Continued)

Common Name	Botanical Name	Light	Water	Height × Spread	Features	Zone
Holly, Nellie R. Stevens	*Ilex cornuta* 'Nellie R. Stevens'	S/PS	M	8'-10' × 6'	Conical with dense foliage in sun, sparser in shade. May suffer from iron chlorosis in alkaline soils.	7-9
Holly, Yaupon	*Ilex vomitoria*	S/PS/ Sh	L-M	10'-15' × 6'	Oval form with irregular branching & medium density. Native.	7-9
Indian Hawthorn	*Raphiolepis indica*	S/PS	M	3'-4' × 3'	Sizes low-medium with dense foliage. Performs best with a.m. sun. May suffer from iron chlorosis in alkaline soils.	7-9
Juniper, Shore	*Juniperus conferta*	S	L-M	12"-18" × 4'	Low, creeping with dense mass. Needs good drainage.	6-10
Laurel, Cherry	*Prunus caroliniana*	S/PS	M	15'-20' × 12'	Upright oval form with dense dark green foliage. Native.	7-9
Mahonia, Leatherleaf	*Mahonia bealei*	PS	M-H	4'-5' × 3'	Leathery hollylike leaves on low, broad form.	6-9
Mountain Laurel	*Sophora secundiflora*	S/PS	L-M	10'-15' × 8'	Upright, irregular form. Seed pods toxic. Fragrant purple spring blooms. Native.	8-9
Myrtle, Wax	*Myrica cerifera*	S/PS	L-M-H	8'-10' × 8'	Mounding, upright with irregular branching. Adaptable. Bluish berries. Native.	7-10
Nandina	*Nandina domestica*	S/PS	L-M-H	4'-6' × 3'	Upright, oval with fine-textured foliage on tall canes. Red berries.	7-9
Nolina	*Nolina lindheimeriana*	S/PS	L	2'-3' × 4'	Low, broad form with thin arching grayish leaves. Native.	8-9
Nolina/ Sacahuista	*Nolina texana*	S/PS	L	2'-3' × 4'	Grasslike, arching foliage. Native.	8-9
Oleander	*Nerium oleander*	S/PS	L-M	10'-15' × 12'	Rounded with canelike stems. All parts extremely toxic when ingested.	8-10
Prickly Pear	*Opuntia spp.*	S	L	2'-3'	Sprawling, upright with spiny pads. Native.	7-10
Rosemary	*Rosmarinus officinalis*	S	L	3'-6' × 4'	Form upright-to-sprawling with narrow leaves. Bluish spring blooms.	7-9
Sotol spp.	*Dasylirion texana or D. wheeleri*	S/PS	L	3'-4' × 4'	Dense, clumping with long, narrow leaves. Native.	8-10
Sumac, Evergreen	*Rhus virens*	S/PS	L-M	5'-6' × 6'	Form open, irregular, mounding. Good accent. Native.	8-9
Yaupon, Dwarf	*Ilex vomitoria* 'Nana'	S/PS	L-M	2'-3' × 2'	Broad, mounding with dense texture. Stress tolerant. Native.	7-9
Yucca spp.	*Yucca spp.*	S	L	2'-3' × 3'	Low, mounding form with rigid strapped leaves. Native.	7-10
Yucca, Red	*Hesperaloe parviflora*	S/PS	L-M	4'-6' × 4'	Not a true yucca, but yucca-like. Flower stalks topped with summer blooms of salmon-pink flowers.	7-10

4—Plant Selection: Shrubs

Table 4.5: Semi-Evergreen Shrubs for Central Texas

Common Name	Botanical Name	Light	Water	Height × Spread	Features	Zone
Abelia	*Abelia grandiflora*	S/PS	M	6' × 6'	Rounded, fountainlike. Sizes vary.	5-9
Aspidistra/ Cast Iron Plant	*Aspidistra elatior*	S	M-H	18" × 30"	Broad, arching leaves. Needs fertile soil.	7-10
Barberry, Purple Leaf Japanese	*Berberis thunbergii 'Atropurpurea'*	S/PS	L-M	3' × 2'	Multi-stemmed, thorny, maroon foliage.	5-9
Senna, Flowering	*Cassia corymbosa*	S/PS	M	8' × 6'	Upright, oval, leggy, tender. Yellow blooms.	9-10
Dalea, Silver	*Dalea bicolor var. argyraea*	S	L	1'-3' × 4'	Fuzzy silver foliage. Spreads.	8-9
Coralbean	*Erythrina x herbacea*	S/PS	M	6'-15' × 6'	Broad, spreading, multi-stemmed.	7-10
Hydrangea, Oakleaf	*Hydrangea quercifolia*	PS	M	6' × 4'	Rounded-to-upright. Large, showy leaves. Frost tender.	5-9
Jasmine, Primrose	*Jasminum mesnyi*	S/PS	M	8' × 8'	Dense, wide, sprawling. Yellow spring blooms.	7-9
Honeysuckle, White	*Lonicera albiflora*	S/PS/ Sh	M	5' × 5'	Rounded, oval, arching branches with tiny white spring flowers.	6-9
Pavonia, Rock Rose	*Pavonia lasiopetala*	S/PS	L	3' × 3'	Upright, woody, spindly. Showy pink blooms throughout summer.	8-9
Pomegranate	*Punica granatum*	S/PS	M-H	10' × 6'	Upright, oval with orange or white blooms.	7-9
Rosemary, Prostrate	*Rosmarinus offici- nalis'Prostratus'*	S	L	2' × 2'	Low, sprawling, tender. Light blue flowers in spring.	7-9
Sage, Cherry	*Salvia greggii*	S/PS	L-M	2' × 2'	Upright, irregular, loose.	8-10

Table 4.6: Deciduous Shrubs for Central Texas

Common Name	Botanical Name	Light	Water	Height × Spread	Features	Zone
Acanthus, Flame	*Anisacanthus wrightii*	S	L	3'-4' × 3'	Stiff, upright branches. Orange tube-like blooms. Native.	8-9
Althea/Rose of Sharon	*Hibiscus syriacus*	S	M	8'-12' × 10'	Upright with showy blooms.	6-10
Arrowwood	*Viburnum dentatum*	S/PS	M-H	8' × 4'	Upright, arching; white spring bloms; native	4-9
Beautyberry, American	*Callicarpa americana*	PS/Sh	M-H	3'-4' × 6'	Large, arching. Nice winter berries. Native.	6-9
Bird-of-Paradise	*Caesalpinia gilliesii*	S	L	8' × 4'	Open, irregular; tropical yellow blooms	9-10
Bird-of-Para- dise, Mexican	*Caesalpinia mexicana*	S	L	8' × 4'	Open irregular form. Showy orange blooms.	9-10
Buckeye, Red	*Aesculus pavia*	PS	M-H	8' × 6'	Oval, irregular. Tall, showy spring blooms. Native.	6-9
Buckeye, Yellow	*Aesculus glabra*	PS	L-M	20' × 10'	Irregular shape. Grows on north facing slopes. Native.	6-9

Xeriscape for Central Texas

Table 4.6: Deciduous Shrubs for Central Texas (Continued)

Common Name	Botanical Name	Light	Water	Height × Spread	Features	Zone
Butterfly Bush	Buddleia davidii	S	L-M	8' × 6'	Upright, broad, spreading, blooms many colors.	5-9
Button Bush	Cephalanthus occidentalis	S/PS	H	8' × 10'	Irregular form. Round white blooms. Native.	5-9
Chilie Pequin or Chilie Petin	Capsicum annuum or C. frutescens	PS/Sh	M-H	2'-5' × 2'	Slightly arching with ornamental berries. Frost tender.	8-9
Coralberry	Symphoricarpos orbiculatus	PS	M-H	2' × 3'	Erect, open, with sprawling branches. Native.	7-9
Dalea, Black	Dalea frutescens	S	L	1'-3' × 4'	Broad spreading, multi-stemmed. Native.	7-9
Dogwood, Roughleaf	Cornus drummondii	S/PS	L-H	20' × 15'	Upright, oval with flat flower clusters. Native.	4-9
Elbow Bush	Forestiera pubescens	S/PS/ Sh	L-M	5' × 6'	Sprawling, open, somewhat invasive. Native.	7-9
Holly, Possumhaw	Ilex decidua	S/PS	M	12' × 8'	Upright, spreading, winter berries. Native.	7-9
Indigo Bush, Texas	Amorpha roemeriana	S/PS	M-H	10' × 10'	Open form. Best in low areas. Native.	7-8
Kidneywood, Texas	Eysenhardtia texana	S/PS	L	6'-9' × 6'	Upright, oval, airy, fragrant blooms. Native.	7-9
Lantana, Texas	Lantana horrida or L. Camara	S/PS	L-M	18"-3' × 2'	Low sprawling, yellow-orange blooms; native	8-10
Lantana, Trailing	Lantana montevidensis	S/PS	L-M	2' × 4'	Low, mounding, profuse blooms.	8-10
Mistflower, White	Eupatorium wrightii	PS	L	1'-2' × 3'	Wide with irregular branching. White fall blooms. Native.	7-9
Saltbush, Four-winged	Atriplex canescens	S/PS	VL	3'-8' × 3'-8'	Silver leaves, open form, invasive.	7-9
Spicebush	Lindera benzoin	S/PS	H	6' × 8'	Upright, oval, spreading, irregular branching. Native.	4-9
Sumac, Aromatic	Rhus aromatica	S/PS	L-M	3' × 3'	Oval, upright, airy. Fall color. Native.	4-9
Turk's Cap	Malvaviscus arboreus var. drummondii	S/PS/ Sh	M-H	2'-3' × 3'	Open, irregular, sprawling red blooms. Can be invasive. Native.	1-9
Viburnum, Rusty Blackhaw	Viburnum rufidulum	S/PS/ Sh	M	12'-15' × 8'	Upright, glossy foliage. Fall color. White spring blooms. Native.	7-9
Vitex	Vitex agnus-castus	S	VL	10' × 8'	Upright, rounded, showy lilac spring blooms. Native.	7-9
Wedelia	Wedelia hispida	S/PS	VL	18"-2' × 2'	Daisylike orange blooms, sprawling woody stems. Native.	8-10
Yellow Bells	Tecoma stans var angustata	S/PS	L-M	3'-6' × 3'	Upright, lush, yellow blooms. Native.	8-10

Ground Covers

Ground covers are low-growing plants, which are often used in landscapes in place of turf. Ground covers can be evergreen or deciduous, and they perform a variety of functions such as providing continuity to plantings in the garden, helping with erosion control, providing color in shady areas, and filling in bare spots.

There are a variety of plants which can be used as ground covers—*ornamental grasses, low shrubs, ferns, bulbs, herbs, and roses.* All of these can be used to cover large expanses of ground.

Before Selecting a Ground Cover, Consider the Following:

- The type of soil you have and the type of ground cover that would work best in that type of soil.

- How well the type of ground cover you want to plant will acclimate to our harsh climate.

- How long it will take the plants to cover the entire area under consideration.

- The mature height of the plant.

- Whether the plant is prone to a specific disease or insect infestation.

- How expensive is that type of ground cover? Remember, you'll have to plant quite a few to get good coverage.

The Best Time To Plant A Ground Cover

The least stressful times to plant most ground covers in our area are during the spring and fall months. Not only will you get free moisture (hopefully) during each of our rainy seasons, the cooler temperatures will also help reduce the shock that the plants normally undergo during transplanting.

Soils and Ground Covers

Because most ground covers grow in close proximity to one another, they can deplete soil nutrients because of their crowded conditions. If possible, try to make sure you start out right by bringing in a good quality soil or amending your own soil. The extra effort will pay off with lusher foliage, healthier looking plants, and a quicker spread rate.

Ground covers can be evergreen or deciduous, and they perform a variety of functions such as providing continuity to plantings in the garden, helping with erosion control, providing color in shady areas, and filling in bare spots.

Xeriscape for Central Texas

Table 4.7: Evergreen Vines and Ground Covers

Common Name	Type Plant	Botanical Name	Light	Water	Height × Spread	Features
Artemesia	GC	*Artemesia ludoviciana*	S/PS	L	1'-3' × 1'	Silver foliage. Shaggy. Invasive. Native.
Damianita	GC	*Chrysactinia mexicana*	S/PS	L	1'-2' × 1'	Foliage tiny, fragrant. Blooms yellow from spring to fall. Native.
Fern, Holly	GC	*Cyrtomium falcatum*	PS/Sh	M	2' × 2'	Leathery, shiny leaves. Needs good soil & adequate moisture. Protect from direct sun.
Fig Ivy	V	*Ficus pumila*	S/PS	M	to 60'	Small, dull green, heart shaped leaves on clinging vine. Can be invasive.
Germander, Bush	GC	*Teucrium chamaedrys*	S	L	15" × 15"	Waxy green leaves. Trim for best effect.
Honeysuckle, Coral	V or GC	*Lonicera sempervirens*	S/PS	L-M	15'-20'	Orange to scarlet tubular blooms. Hummingbird attractor. Twinning. Native.
Horseherb	GC	*Calyptocarpus vialis*	PS/Sh	L	8"-10" × 1'	Semi-evergreen except in harsh winters. Mat forming. Native.
Ivy, English	V or GC	*Hedera helix*	Sh	M	to 30'-40' or 6"-10"	Self climbing. Needs good soil. Fairly well-behaved. Slow-medium growth.
Jasmine, Asian	V or GC	*Trachelospermum asiaticum*	S/PS/Sh	M	20'-25' or 10"-18"	Dense, matting. Glossy, leathery leaves.
Jasmine, Confederate	V	*Trachelospermum jasminoides*	S/PS	M	to 20'	Dense, glossy with white spring flowers.
Jessamine, Caroline	V	*Gelsemium sempervirens*	S/PS	M	to 20'	Dense, twinning. Toxic if swallowed. Yellow spring blooms. Native.
Liriope	GC	*Liriope muscari*	PS/Sh	L-M	12"-18" × 1'	Straplike, arching, dense foliage. Clump-forming. Blue blooms.
Liriope, Variegated	GC	*Liriope muscaro 'Variegata'*	PS/Sh	L-M	12"-18" × 1'	Variegated, straplike, arching foliage. Dense clumps. Purple blooms.
Monkey Grass	GC	*Ophiopogon japonicus*	PS/Sh	L-M	6"-12" × 1"	Clumping, dense, mat-forming. Narrow foliage.
Oregano	GC	*Origanum vulgare*	S	L	to 30"	Likes dry, gravelly soils. Shrubby to mounding form.
Periwinkle, Small-leaf	GC	*Vinca minor*	PS	M	10"-12"	Dwarf, glossy foliage. Tidy growth.
Rose, Lady Banks	V	*Rosa banksiae*	S/PS	L-M	to 20'	Thornless, climbing, arching. Yellow spring blooms. Native.
Ruellia, 'Katie Dwarf'	GC	*Ruellia brittoniana 'Katie'*	S/PS/Sh	L-M	8"-12" × 18"	Neat mounds with purple blooms. Reseeds. Native.
Santolina, Gray/Green	GC	*Santolina chamaecyparissus*	S	L	12"-18" × 2'	Short-lived (3-5 yrs). Broad. Mounding. Yellow spring blooms.
Sedum/ Stonecrop	GC	*Sedum spp.*	S/PS	L-M	4"-6"	Well-drained soil necessary. Many types available.
Setcreasea	GC	*Setcreasea pallida*	S/PS	M	15"	Dark purple foliage. Irregular, sprawling.
Yarrow	GC	*Achillea millefolium*	S/PS	L-M	1'-2' × 1'-2'	Delicate foliage. White spring blooms. Self sows. Can be invasive. Native.

4—Plant Selection: Ground Covers

Table 4.8: Deciduous Vines and Ground Covers

Common Name	Type Plant	Botanical Name	Light	Water	Height × Spread	Features
Clematis	V	*Clematis pitcheri*	S	M	20'-30'	Prefers fertile soil. Various colors available. Autumn blooms.
Dead Nettle	GC	*Lamium maculatum*	S/PS	M-H	1' × 6'	Can be invasive. Plain or variegated types available.
Flame Vine, Mexican	V	*Senecio confusus*	S	L	to 20'	Bright orange blooms. Butterfly attractor. Frost tender. Native.
Frogfruit	GC	*Phyla nodiflora*	S/PS/Sh	L-M	3"-4" × 1'	Low-growing with tiny verbena-like blooms. Do not mow it. Native.
Horseherb	GC	*Calyptocarpus vialis*	PS/Sh	L-M	2"-8" × 1'	Colonizes by stolons. Low, mat-forming. Native.
Iris spp.	GC	*Iris spp.*	S/PS	L-M	2'	Upright straped foliage. Spring blooms. Hardy.
Lantana, Trailing		*Lantana montevidensis*	S/PS	L-M	18" × 48"	Purple blooms, aromatic foliage. Drought tolerant. Native.
Mint	GC	*Mentha spp.*	S/PS	M-H	24"	Spreads by stolons. Invasive. Keep contained. Needs loose, well-drained soil.
Passionflower	V	*Passiflora incarnata*	S	L-M	15'-20'	Intricate, exotic purple blooms. Native.
Periwinkle, Bigleaf	GC	*Vinca major*	PS	L-M	10"-12"	Sprawling. Roots where it touches the ground. Semi-dormant in mid-summer. Violet spring blooms. Native.
Plumbago, Burmese	GC	*Ceratostigma plumbaginoides*	S/PS	M	8"-12" × 15"	Bloom period long lasting. Bloom color deep blue.
Plumbago, Blue	GC	*Plumbago auriculata*	S/PS	L-M	3'-4' × 2'	Sprawling. Not frost hardy. Long blooming. Blue flowers.
Potato Vine	V	*Solanum jasminoides*	S/PS	M	to 20'	White blooms. Deer resistant.
Spiderwort	GC	*Tradescantia spp.*	S/PS	M-H	2'-3'	Grass-like foliage. Blue spring blooms. Needs fertile soils. Native.
Tumpet Vine	V	*Campsis radicans*	S	L-M	30'-50'	Blooms yellow & red-orange trumpet shaped. Attracts humming-birds. Growth rampant. Native.
Virginia Creeper	V	*Parthenocissus quinquefolia*	S/PS/Sh	L-M	to 25'	Fast growth. Invasive. Good bronze fall color. Native.
Widow's Tears	GC	*Commelina spp.*	PS	L-M	1'-2' × 1'	Aggressive growth. Bright blue spring blooms. Native.
Wisteria	V	*Wisteria macrostacha*	S/PS	M-H	to 30'	Twining vine. Purple spring blooms. Fragrant. Bright green leaves. Native.
Wood Fern	GC	*Thelypteris kunthii*	S/PS	M	3'	Delicate fronds. Will tolerate drier soils than most ferns. Native.

Spacing Plants

Plants should be spaced equidistantly in a triangular pattern as shown above. Choose the proper spacing between plants based on your plant selection, then multiply the square footage by the decimal number under the "Number of Plants" column in Table 4.9. The product of this multiplication will tell you how many plants to purchase.

The Scourge of Newly-Planted Ground Covers—Weeds

Nothing can reduce the looks of a ground cover quicker than a good crop of weeds. And weeds can creep into the open spaces between new plants quickly. There are several things that can be done to combat this problem. (See weed control in Chapter 6.)

- Start out with quality, weed- and grass-free soil.
- Just after planting start a weekly vigil to look out for any weeds. Remove intruders quickly.
- Apply a thick layer of mulch (3" to 5") after planting.
- Talk to extension agents or knowledgeable nursery workers to learn about herbicides which may safely help reduce weeds while not harming the plants.

How To Plan For Spacing With Ground Covers

Once you know which ground cover you want to plant and the total square footage of the area to be planted, you can use Table 4.9 to help you determine how many plants to purchase. (See sidebar.)

Table 4.9: Spacing Requirements for Ground Cover

Spacing Between Plants (Inches)	Number of Plants
6	4.61
9	2.00
10	1.66
12	1.25
18	.512
24	.290
30	.185
36	.128

Antique Roses

Roses are excellent additions to any landscape. Versatile and attractive, roses add a touch of romance and a hint of fragrance when in bloom. Because of their low maintenance qualities, we will limit our discussion to the old varieties. William Welch in his book, *Perennial Garden Color*, provides us with this definition of old garden roses: They are typically 75 or more years old and display "old rose" characteristics—rich fragrance, muted or pastel colors, and an inherent beauty of form. More importantly, they do not require hours of fertilizing, spraying, and care as do the hybrid types.

Site and Soil Requirements

Roses are sun lovers, and most roses (with the exception of Hybrid Musk types) require six hours of sun each day (preferably with morning sun). In addition, roses resist disease and grow healthier when they receive good air circulation. Try to locate your rose bed in an open, sunny location.

Even though many antique roses were located in abandoned sites with poor soils, they will grow much better when they are planted in soils which are amended with organic materials. If possible, prepare your beds a couple of months prior to your scheduled planting time. This will allow the soil to settle in and will also provide newly-planted roses easy access to micro-nutrients. In our area, the best time to prepare rose beds is during the spring or summer months.

Planting Roses

The optimum time to plant roses in our area is during the fall and winter months. When planting, follow these suggestions for best results:

- Plant bare root roses as soon as you receive them. If you can't do this, dig a shallow trench, place the roses in the trench, and cover the rose roots loosely with soil. You can also plant them in containers and place them in a protected area for a short time.
- Before planting, soak the roots for approximately one hour in a bucket of water.
- Dig a hole that is just large enough to place the roots in and allow them to spread out naturally. Place a mound of dirt at the base of the hole.
- Check the rose roots for damage. Carefully prune away any damaged roots.
- Set the roses in the hole on top of the soil mound. Lay the roots across the mound. Make sure that the plants are set close to the same growing level at which they had previously been growing.
- Add soil to cover the roots. Gently tamp the soil down and then water this portion of the soil well. Add more soil and make a slight mound (for settling purposes) around the base of the plant, trying not to cover too much above the original growing level. Tamp down and water again.
- Cut back any damaged canes.

Apply a 3" to 4" layer of mulch around the circumference of the plant to aid in moisture retention and to prevent weeds.

Old Garden Rose

Most old garden roses require six hours of sun each day (preferably morning sun). They resist disease and grow healthier when they receive good air circulation. Therefore, try to locate your rose bed in an open, sunny location.

Table 4.10: Rose Classifications

Type	Description and Possible Use
Found Roses	Consists of a wide range of unknown varieties with varying growth habits, colors, and fragrances. These roses with unknown lineage have been discovered in many different settings.
Species Roses	Consists of a variety of native climbers, mounding, and naturally bushy types of shrubs. Terrific blooms once a year. Good in naturalistic settings.
Old European Roses: • Albas • Centifolias • Damasks • Gallicas • Mosses	Known for their cold-hardiness • White or pale pink. Foliage blue-green. • Pink shades. Also known as "Cabbage roses." • Rich pink, sometimes white. • Red tones. Produce many rose hips. • Pink shades. Tiny prickles on flower bud.
China Roses	Ever-blooming plants with lush, bushy foliage. Good as specimen plant or as hedges.
Noisette Roses	Long-blooming with large flowers and pale shades of cream, pink, and yellow. Used on fences, pillars, or as climbers.
Bourbon Roses	Shrub-type roses in a range of heights. Flowers a deep, rich color and fragrant. Good spring show with slight blooming later on. Cold hardy. Susceptible to black spot.
Tea Roses	Form lush bushes with new foliage a reddish color. Fragrance like that of the crushed leaves of freshly harvested tea plants. Shades are rich and soft. Good spring and fall bloom. Flowers larger than Chinas. Good cut flowers.
Hybrid Perpetual Roses	Bush type roses with long canes with limited foliage. Not a good choice for a shrub rose unless you are willing to prune it back frequently. Good rose fragrance. Heavy spring and fall bloom with intermittent blooms in between. Good cut flowers.
Early Hybrid Tea Roses	Bush type roses with thick stems and upright (as opposed to drooping) flowers. Fragrance good. Not an especially hardy type due to inbreeding.
• Polyanthas • Floribundas • Miniatures	• Ever-blooming, bushy, compact, care-free. Clustered flowers. • Profuse blooms of clustered flowers. Bushy growth habit. • Tiny profuse blooms top small bushes.
Rugosa Roses	Bushy plants with thick, wrinkly leaves. Stems prickly. Flowers large-petaled. Fragrance clove-like. Late spring blooms followed by orangish-red hips. Tendency to clump and form suckers.
Shrub Roses	Both modern and old rose types are in this miscellaneous category. Grown primarily as specimen plants, these roses can also be grouped in the landscape. Colors are primarily reds and pinks.
Hybrid Musk Roses	Large sized plants with growth habits ranging from arching, cascading, single specimen, weeping, hedge-like (when pruned), and climbing (when trained). Fragrance musky. Will take some shade (can thrive on 4 hours of sun a day). Blooms heavily in spring and fall, with a few blooms in between.
Climbing Roses	Vines which repeat or spring bloom. Profuse single or clustered flower blooms in the spring. Good used for covering walls or buildings and for growing up into trees.
Rambling Roses	Foliage small. Profuse clusters of flowers in the spring. Very cold hardy. Growth more horizontal than vertical. Good used for covering walls or buildings and for growing up into trees. Can also be used for pillars, trellises, and as ground covers.

Training Climbing Roses

Climbing roses are great vertical subjects for landscapes. When using a trellis for climbing roses, fan out the canes and attach them to the trellis with a stretchable material like gardener's stretch ties.

If a climber is used to cover a wall or grow up a chain link fence, use the same fanning out technique so that the rose can flower to its fullest potential. For walls, special staples and attachment tools are available at nursery centers. Climbing roses can also be trained up posts by either braiding or wrapping them around a post. The eventual effect is a spectacular rose pillar.

Roses As Hedges

Certain types of roses are best suited for hedges, and rose hedges can be created with either a formal or an informal look. For an informal hedge, try one of the following with the growing characteristics you are seeking: shrub roses, one of the Hybrid Musk types, certain Species roses, and certain types from the China and Rugosa classes. When forming a formal rose hedge, use one variety of an ever-blooming type of rose to attain a look of sophistication and continuity. If you want a 4' to 6' formal hedge, try using a China or a tea rose. If you'd like a lower formal hedge, try using one of the lower growing Polyanthas.

Table 4.11: Climbing Roses

Climbing Roses	Height	Class	Bloom	Comments
American Beauty. Cl.	12'/15'	Hybrid Perpetual	spring	deep pink fragrant
American Pillar	12'/20'	Rambler	repeat	reddish-pink white center
Anemone	6'/10	Species	spring	pink fragrant
Cecile Brunner. Cl.	15'/20'	Polyantha	repeat	pink fragrant
Cherokee	15'/20'	Species	spring	pure white single fragrant
Clotilde Soupert, Cl.	8'/10'	China	repeat	crimson fragrant
Cramoisi Superieur, Cl.	8'/10'	China	repeat	crimson fragrant
Dr. W. Van Fleet	15'/20'	Wichuraiana	spring	pink fragrant
Dortmund	15'/30'	R. Kordesii	repeat	crimson red yellow stamens hips
Fairy, Cl.	10'/12'	Polyantha	repeat	rose-pink sprays glossy foliage
Fortune's Dbl. Yellow	10'/15'	Species	spring	apricot yellow fragrant
Lamarque	12'/20'	Noisette	repeat	creamy yellow fragrant
Lavender Lassie	10'/15'	Hybrid Musk	repeat	lilac-pink fragrant

Xeriscape for Central Texas

Table 4.11: Climbing Roses (Continued)

Climbing Roses	Height	Class	Bloom	Comments
Madame Alfred Carriere	15'/20'	Noisette	repeat	pale pink to creamy white fragrant
Maggie	5'/7'	Found	repeat	carmine-rose erect fragrant
Mermaid	15'/20'	Species	repeat	creamy yellow single fragrant
New Dawn	15'/20'	R. Wichuraiana	repeat	soft pink fragrant
Old Blush, Cl.	8'/12'	China	repeat	light pink upright fragrant
Pinkie Cl.	8'/12'	Polyantha	repeat	rose pink fragrant nearly thornless
Red Cascade	12'/18'	Miniature	repeat	crimson red fragrant
Russelliana	6'/12'	Hybrid Multiflora	spring	rich purple-lilac orange hips fragrant
Seven Sisters	15'/20'	R. Multiflora	spring	pink blend fragrant
Skyrocket	10'/12'	Hybrid Musk	repeat	red yellow stamens light fragrance
Sombreuil	8'/12'	Tea	repeat	creamy-white pink blush fragrant
Veilchenblau	10'/15'	Multiflora	spring	crimson purple fragrant nearly thornless
Will Scarlet	5'/7'	Hybrid Mush	repeat	scarlet orange-red hips fragrant
Yellow Lady Banks	10'/20'	Species	spring	yellow fragrant
Zephirine Drouhin	8'/20'	Bourbon	repeat	medium pink fragrant thornless

Table 4.12: Shrub Roses

Shrub Roses	Height	Class	Bloom	Comments
Amazone	4'/6'	Tea	repeat	buttery yellow fragrant
Anna de Diesbach	4'/5'	Hybrid Perpetual	spring	deep rose-pink fragrant
Applejack	8'/10'	Shrub	spring	pink apple fragrance trained climber

70

4—Plant Selection: Antique Roses

Table 4.12: Shrub Roses (Continued)

Shrub Roses	Height	Class	Bloom	Comments
Archduke Charles	3'/6'	China	repeat	deep red-pink fragrant
Ballerina	5'/6'	Hybrid Musk	repeat	light pink small single hips fragrant
Baronne Prevost	4'/5'	Hybrid Perpetual	repeat	medium pink erect fragrant
Basye's Blueberry	6'/8'	Dr. Robert Basye	repeat	bright pink yellow stamens fragrant fall foliage thornless
Belinda's Dream	4'/6'	Shrub	repeat	medium pink fragrant
Bermuda's Kathleen	5'/6'	Found	repeat	apple pink to dusty rose
Blush Noisette	4'/8'	Noisette	repeat	pale pink fragrant
Bryan Friedel Pink Tea	4'/6'	Found	repeat	pink blend compact fragrant
Caldwell Pink	3'/5'	Found	repeat	lilac-pink clusters
Cecile Brunner	3'/5'	Polyantha	repeat	pink fragrant
Champney's Pink Cluster	4'/8'	Noisette	repeat	pink fragrant
Chestnut	5'/7'	R. Roxburghii	spring	medium pink bristly hips light fragrance
Clotilde Soupert	3'/4'	Polyantha	repeat	pale pink to ivory quartered fragrant
Cramoisi Superieur	3'/6'	China	repeat	crimson silvery reverse fragrant erect
Duchesse de Brabant	4'/7'	Tea	repeat	light pink cupped fragrant
English Dawn	4'/5'	David Austin	repeat	lavender-pink single white eye fragrant
English Yellow	5'/7'	English	repeat	golden yellow fragrant
Eutin	4'/6'	Floribunda	repeat	dark red clusters
Fairy	3'/4'	Polyantha	repeat	pink sprays glossy foliage
Felicia	4'/6'	Hybrid Musk	fall	apricot pink to cream salmon fragrant

71

Xeriscape for Central Texas

Table 4.12: Shrub Roses (Continued)

Shrub Roses	Height	Class	Bloom	Comments
Fellenberg	3'/5'	Noisette	repeat	rose scarlet
Flower Carpet	2'/3'	R. Noatrum	repeat	hot pink
Fuschia Meidiland	3'/5'	Meidiland	repeat	vivid fuschia-red
General Jacqueminot	4'/6'	Hybrid Perpetual	repeat	dark red white reverse fragrant
Georgetown Tea	3'/5'	Found	repeat	dark salmon pink to lavender pink fragrant
Green Rose	3'/4'	China	repeat	bronzy-green fragrant
Highway 290 Pink Buttons	1'/2'	Found	repeat	miniature lilac-pink
Honorine de Brabant	4'/8'	Bourbon	repeat	soft pink splashed violet cupped fragrant
John Franklin	2'/4'	Floribunda	repeat	medium red fragrant clusters
Katharina Zeimet	3'/4'	Polyantha	repeat	white fragrant
Katy Road	3'/5'	Found	repeat	pink fragrant
Kirsten Poulsen	3'/5'	Floribunda	repeat	cerise pink single erect
Lafter	4'/6'	Hybrid Tea	repeat	pink/yellow/orange blend fragrant
Lamarne	4'/6'	Polyantha	repeat	pink/white fragrant
Louis Philippe	3'/5'	China	repeat	dark crimson fragrant
Madame Antoine Rebe	4'/6'	Tea	repeat	scarlet-pink single fragrant
Madame Isaac Pereire	6'/7'	Bourbon	spring	bright rose fragrant
Marchesa Boccella	3'/5'	Hybrid Perpetual	repeat	bright pink powder puff fragrant
Marie Pavie	3'/4'	Polyantha	repeat	white thornless fragrant
Martha Gonzales	2'/3'	China	repeat	bright red red tinted foliage single
Mary Manners	5'/6'	Hybrid Rugosa	repeat	pure white fragrant
Mlle. Franziska Kruger	3'/5'	Tea	repeat	coppery yellow to apricot fragrant

4—Plant Selection: Antique Roses

Table 4.12: Shrub Roses (Continued)

Shrub Roses	Height	Class	Bloom	Comments
Moroccan Rose	4'/5'	Found	spring	pink fragrant
Mrs. B. R. Cant	5'/8'	Tea	repeat	pale silver-pink with dark rose fragrant
Nearly Wild	3'/5'	Polyantha	repeat	rose-pink single fragrant
Nur Mahal	5'/8'	Hybrid Musk	repeat	birght crimson climber/pillar fragrant
Old Blush	4'/6'	China	repeat	lilac-pink fragrant
Old Gay Hill	4'/6'	China	repeat	deep red
Pam's Pink	3'/5'	Found	repeat	pink blend
Paul Neyron	3'/5'	Hybrid Perpetual	repeat	rose-pink cabbage thornless fragrant
Penelope	4'/5'	Hybrid Musk	repeat	salmon-pink pink hips fragrant
Petite Pink Scotch	2'/3'	Found	spring	pale pink ground cover
Pink Meidiland	3'/4'	Meidiland	repeat	clear pink
Pink Parfait	5'/6'	Polyantha	repeat	pink blend
Prosperity	4'/5'	Hybrid Musk	repeat	creamy white with pink fragrant climber
Puerto Rico	4'/6'	Found	repeat	creamy white with apricot pink fragrant
Roberta	4'/5'	English	repeat	soft pink "Heritage Rose" fragrant
Rouletti	1'/3'	China	repeat	lilac pink
Safrano	4'/6'	Tea	repeat	apricot/beige fragrant
Sarah Van Fleet	6'/8'	Rugosa	repeat	rose pink cupped fragrant
Scarlet Meidiland	3'/5'	Meidiland	repeat	vivid red
Sir Thomas Lipton	6'/8'	Rugosa	repeat	thick cream cupped fragrant
Smith's Parish	4'/6'	Found	repeat	white, red streaks deep pink or red

Table 4.12: Shrub Roses (Continued)

Shrub Roses	Height	Class	Bloom	Comments
Spice	3'/5'	Found	repeat	pale pink fragrant
Swamp Rose	6'/8'	Species	spring	soft pink weeping thornless fragrant

Herbs

Types of Plants Classified as Herbs

Herbs or *'erbs* are difficult to classify since they can be annuals, biennials, or perennials. Like perennials, most are plants which lack woody stems and die back after flowering. However, herbs have a singular distinction that sets them apart from regular flowering plants in that they are used for specific tasks. Those tasks range from providing flavors to foods, acting as natural medicines, serving as fragrances, and providing dyes for clothing. And they have been doing these things for at least 5,000 years. No wonder that many gardeners are fascinated with herbs—they are a solid link with our past.

Rosemary

Herbs can be planted in a formal garden style, they can be arranged to ramble about in an informal cottage garden style, or they can be tucked in between other plants.

Planning Herb Gardens

Like any other type of garden, herb gardens should be carefully thought out before planting. Many herbs will live in the same garden space for a number of years and will not enjoy being moved. Herbs can be planted in a formal garden style, they can be arranged to ramble about in an informal cottage garden style, or they can be tucked in between other plants. There are many arrangements and themes possible.

Note: When planning your herb garden, try to group plants with similar water and nutrient requirements. Some herbs prefer a drier soil and little fertilizer. Examples of these are rosemary, lavender, sage, thyme, and many salvias. Other herbs prefer rich soil and plenty of water. Examples of these herbs are chives, mint, basil, and parsley. Try to plan borders and beds with low-growing plants closest to the front and the taller ones in the rear.

Four Essential Elements for Healthy Herbs

ADEQUATE SOIL

Even though many herbs originate in rocky, inhospitable climates, most herbs appreciate a certain amount of soil preparation. Try not to go overboard when enriching the soil. Herbs do best in an average soil that is neither too rich nor too poor. In the Central Texas area, raised beds are often the best solution for establishing

4—Plant Selection: Herbs

herb gardens. Our soils are often too shallow or contain a high clay content which does not allow the plants the necessary nutrients or good drainage necessary for healthy growth.

GOOD DRAINAGE

Try to take steps to improve soils used for herbs with amendments such as composted organic materials. If your soil drains too quickly, these amendments will help the soil to retain moisture for a longer time. If your soil is tightly packed, they will help loosen the soil and promote good drainage.

SUNLIGHT

With a few exceptions, most herbs need at least six hours of sun each day to grow well. Sunlight helps them attain lush growth and develop their essential oils.

MULCH

During times of temperature extremes, nothing helps herb gardens retain their fresh appearance better than a thick layer of mulch. During the summer, mulch keeps the soil cooler, and during our intermittent winter freezes, it will protect plants from cold damage.

In addition, mulch will help reduce weeding time, and organic types will break down and provide additional nutrients to your plants. Compost is an excellent choice for a mulch since it protects and slowly feeds plants as well as permits herbs to self sow.

One of the key elements for success with herbs is good air circulation and good drainage.

Why Terra Cotta Containers Are Best for Herbs

While it is tempting to use attractive glazed ceramic pots or sturdy plastic pots, try to resist the temptation. One of the key elements for success with herbs is good air circulation and good drainage. Neither ceramic nor plastic pots can do this. Try to stick with a terra cotta variety for the best growing success.

When using containers, remember to provide:

- Frequent watering using a *weak* solution of liquid fertilizer with each application.

- A good potting soil mix.

- Half-day of sun each day.

Whiskey Barrel Herb Gardens

A larger, less moveable alternative for terra cotta containers are whiskey barrels. Before purchasing a barrel, make sure the bottom isn't warped so that water will not build up. After you get home, measure up 1" to 2" from the bottom, and then drill 1" or larger holes in the sides. An advantage to using whiskey barrels is that more plants can be grown together than when using terra cotta.

Harvesting Herbs

Mid-morning is the best time of day to harvest herbs. When harvesting leaves, try not to get overly enthusiastic and harvest more than you are capable of using in one day. Plants can safely be cut back by 1/3. If plants are dirty and need to be rinsed or if plants are somewhat damp, go ahead and harvest them and then hang them upside down in an open shady area to dry.

Uses For Herbs

Here are a just a few of the many uses for herbs:

- Companion planting to keep bugs away.
- Sprays and powders.
- Herbal oils.
- Teas.
- Baths, rinses, and body lotions.
- Dyes.
- Medicines.
- Vinegars, butters, and food flavorings.

Table 4.13: Herbs for Central Texas

Common Name	Botanical Name	Light	Water	Height × Spread	Features	Plant Type
Allium	*Allium spp.*	S	M-H	varied	Onionlike odor. Provide richer soil.	P
Aloe Vera	*Aloe barbadensis*	S/PS	M	2' × 1'	Succulent. Best grown in containers. Tender.	P
Anise Hyssop	*Agastache foeniculum*	S	M	3' × 2'	Lavender or blue spikes.	P
Artemisia	*Artemisia spp.*	S	M	2' × 2'	Many types available. Avoid invasive types.	P
Basil	*Basil spp.*	S	M	2' × 2'	Many varieties available. Easily grown. Deters certain insects. Attracts bees.	A
Bay	*Laurus nobilis*	S/PS	M	10' × 5'	Shrub form. Frost tender. Grow in containers.	P
Betony	*Stachys officinalis*	S/PS	M-H	4' × 2'	Many hybrids. Spreads by stolons.	P
Borage	*Borago officinalis*	S/PS	M	2' × 1'	Dainty blue flowers. Vigorous self-sower. Attracts hummingbirds. Attracts bees.	A
Bouncing Bet	*Saponaria officinalis*	S/PS	M	2' × 3'	Evergreen. Good ground cover. Pink or white blooms. Attracts hummingbirds.	P
Burnet, Salad	*Poterium sanguisorba*	S	M	1' × 1'	Clump-forming. Cucumber-flavored leaves. Evergreen.	P
Capsicum	*Capsicum spp.*	S/PS	M	2' × 1'	Good ornamental plant. Colorful.	A
Caraway	*Carum carvi*	S	M	3' × 1'	Unusual seed heads.	B

4—Plant Selection: Herbs

Table 4.13: Herbs for Central Texas (Continued)

Common Name	Botanical Name	Light	Water	Height × Spread	Features	Plant Type
Catnip	*Nepeta cataria*	S/PS	M	2' × 3'	Self sows. Prune to keep neat. Attracts cats, hummingbirds, and bees.	P
Chamomile	*Chamaemelum nobile*	S/PS	M-H	6" × 1'	Fades away in heat. Attracts bees.	A
Chervil	*Anthriscus cerefolium*	PS	M	2' × 1'	Start from seed in fall. Will reseed.	A
Chives	*Allium schoenoprasum*	S/PS	M-H	1' × 6"	Light onion flavor from foliage.	P
Columbine	*Aquilegia spp.*	PS/ Sh	M	2' × 2'	Spurred spring blooms. Provide good drainage. Attracts hummingbirds.	P
Comfrey	*Symphytum officinale*	S	M-H	3' × 2'	Develops deep tap root. Do not move.	P
Coriander	*Coriandrum sativum*	S	M	2' × 1'	Grow from fall-sown seeds. Vigorous reseeder.	A
Costmary	*Chrysanthemum balsamita*	S/PS	M	2' × 1'	Attractive leaves.	P
Dill	*Anethum graveolens*	S	M	3' × 1'	Plant seeds in fall. Prefers cool weather.	A
Dittany of Crete	*Origanum dictamnus*	S	L	2' × 1'	Avoid planting in clay. Good in containers.	P
Elderberry	*Sambucus canadensis*	S/PS	M-H	12' × 5'	Vigorous shrub.	P
Fennel	*Foeniculum vulgare*	S	L-M	4' × 2'	Sow seed in spring or fall. Anise-flavored seeds. Attracts bees.	A
Fenugreek	*Trigonella foenum-graecum*	S	M	2' × 2'	Cloverlike leaves with yellow-white blooms.	A
Feverfew	*Chrysanthemum parthenium*	S	M	1'-3' × 2'	White or yellow blooms. Self sows.	P
Foxglove	*Digitalis spp.*	PS/ Sh	H	4' × 1'	Needs rich, moist soil. Showy flower spikes. Attracts hummingbirds.	B
Garlic	*Allium sativum*	S	M	3' × 1'	Plant cloves in fall. Harvest following summer.	P
Geranium, Scented	*Pelargonium spp.*	S/PS	L-M	1' × 1'	Many types available. Frost tender.	P
Germander	*Teucrium spp.*	S	L-M	1' × 18"	Good for low borders when pruned. Attracts bees. Evergreen.	P
Ginger	*Zingiber spp.*	PS	M-H	2' × 1'	Tender. Needs rich soil.	P
Horehound	*Marrubium vulgare*	S	L-M	3' × 3'	Nice blue-gray foliage. Evergreen.	P
Hyssop	*Hyssopus officinalis*	S	L-M	1' × 1'	Can be trimmed to form low border. Attracts bees. Evergreen.	P
Lamb's Ears	*Stachys byzantina*	S	L	1' × 1'	Furry, silver leaves. Will turn mushy with overhead irrigation or hard rains.	P

Xeriscape for Central Texas

Table 4.13: Herbs for Central Texas (Continued)

Common Name	Botanical Name	Light	Water	Height × Spread	Features	Plant Type
Lavender	*Lavandula spp.*	S	L	2' × 1'	Needs excellent drainage—try raised beds. Some kinds frost tender. Deters certain insects. Attracts bees.	P
Lemon Balm	*Melissa officinalis*	S/PS	L	3' × 1'	Fragrant, bright green, lemon-scented leaves. Attracts bees.	P
Lemon Verbena	*Aloysia triphylla*	S	M	4' × 2'	Sprawling shrub. Leaves emit lemony aroma when rubbed.	P
Lemongrass	*Cymbopogon citratus*	S/PS	M	2' × 2'	Large grassy hummocks. Leaves lemon-flavored. Frost tender—protect.	P
Lovage	*Levisticum officinale*	PS	M	2' × 2'	Celery substitute. Provide rich soil.	P
Marjoram	*Origanum spp.*	S/PS	M	3' × 1'	Treat as an annual. Try O majoricum. Attracts bees.	A or P
Mint	*Mentha spp.*	S/PS	M-H	3' × 1'	Very invasive. Grow in contained spaces. Scented leaves. Attracts bees.	P
Mint Marigold	*Tagetes lucida*	S	M	2' × 1'	Abundant foliage with bright yellow blooms. Attracts bees.	P
Mugwort	*Artemisia vulgaris*	S	M	2' × 3'	Trim to keep neat. Invasive.	P
Mustard	*Brassica spp.*	S	M	3' × 1'	Sow seed in fall. Self-sows.	A
Nasturtium	*Tropaeolum majus*	S	M	2' × 1'	Grows best in fall or winter along a south wall.	A
Oregano	*Origanum spp.*	S/PS	M	2' × 1'	Many types available. Attracts bees.	P
Parsley	*Petroselinum crispum*	S/PS	M-H	2' × 2'	Shelter from p.m. sun. Mulch well.	B
Pennyroyal	*Mentha pulegium*	PS	M-H	2' × 1'	Low, creeping mint.	P
Perilla	*Perilla frutescens* 'Crispa'	S/PS	M	2' × 2'	Burgundy foliage. Invasive self-sower.	A
Poliomintha	*Poliomintha longiflora*	S	L-M	3' × 2'	Tubular lavender blooms. Attracts hummingbirds.	P
Pot Marigold	*Calendula officinalis*	S	M	1'-2' × 1'	Grow in fall or winter.	A
Rosemary spp.	*Rosmarinum officinalis spp.*	S	L-M	1'-6' × 2'-4'	Upright or prostrate forms available. Evergreen. Deters certain insects.	P
Rue	*Ruta graveolens*	S	L	2' × 1'	Great butterfly plant. Attractive blue-green leaves. Evergreen.	P
Sage & Salvia spp.	*Salvia spp.*	S	L	3' × 2'	Many types available. Provide good drainage. Deters certain insects. Attracts hummingbirds and bees.	P
Santolina	*Santolina chamaecyparissus*	S	L	1' × 3'	Provide great drainage. Raised beds best. Deters certain insects. Evergreen.	P
Savory, Winter	*Satureja montana*	S	M	1' × 3'	Good border plant. Evergreen.	P

78

4—Plant Selection: Perennials

Table 4.13: Herbs for Central Texas (Continued)

Common Name	Botanical Name	Light	Water	Height × Spread	Features	Plant Type
Society Garlic	Tulbaghia violacea	S	M	1' × 2'	Clump-forming. Attractive blooms.	P
Southern-wood	Artemisia abrotanum	S/PS	M	3' × 2'	Sprawling, delicate foliage. Deters certain insects. Semi-evergreen.	P
St. John's Wort	Hypericum perforatum	PS	M	2' × 2'	Best grown in a good soil. Bright yellow blooms.	P
Tansy	Tanacetum vulgare	S/PS	M	2' × 2'	Fernlike foliage. Yellow blooms.	P
Thyme	Thymus vulgare	S/PS	M	1' × 2'	Many types available. Keep pruned to retain vigor. Deters certain insects. Evergreen.	P
Violet	Viola odorata	PS/S	H	1' × 1'	Low, mounding. Needs rich soil.	P
Yarrow	Achillea millefolium	S/PS	L-M	2' × 1'	Can spread easily. Delicate appearance. Several types available.	P

Perennials

What Is A Perennial?

A *perennial* is any plant (tree, shrub, flower) that continues to live year after year and which has a growing and a dormant season. Despite the fact that certain herbaceous perennials are short-lived, they are considered permanent residents in the garden. This section will discuss herbaceous flowering perennials as well as flowering plants with non-woody stems. Instead of using the lengthy name *herbaceous perennial*, they will be referred to simply as perennials.

Perennials Are Versatile

Perennials are extremely versatile and there are many good reasons to incorporate them into a garden. Here are a some ideas you might want to consider:

Table 4.14: Using Perennials in the Garden

Decorate outside living spaces.	Convert a steep bank into a terraced showplace.
Add seasonal color.	Hide unsightly views.
Accentuate favorite plants.	Convert landscape trouble spots like overly damp or rocky areas.
Add interest to boring fences, walls, and hedges.	Bring added drama to a woodland area.
Increase privacy.	Fragrance near the house.
Create special views from windows.	Create visual interest when used with vegetable, fruit, or herb gardens.

Xeriscape for Central Texas

Why Perennials Aren't Necessarily Low Maintenance

Before deciding on a large perennial garden, make sure you are willing to put in the time it takes to keep it looking attractive. Many perennials spread by underground runners, reseed prolifically, become leggy during the growing season, require deadheading (bloom removal) to look their best, and require division every few years. In addition, many perennial beds require special irrigation practices and require a good layer of mulch applied twice a year. If your lifestyle is such that you don't want to put in this amount of work, you might want to consider large expanses of form and texture through the use of shrubs with a few splashes of annual or perennial color tucked in for drama.

Different Types Of Perennial Gardens

There are many types of perennial gardens. The following list details the different types and gives an explanation.

- *Mixed Borders.* A mixture of perennials, annuals, and flowering or evergreen shrubs. Plantings are close with little bare ground showing. This type of bed is designed to be seen from two or three sides.

- *Cutting Gardens.* Perennials and annuals grown in profusion and in long rows. Not meant to be a focal point in the landscape.

- *Cottage Garden.* Good used in landscapes where space is limited, this type of garden is usually small, enclosed, and individualistic in design. This type of garden incorporates many types of flowers in a small space, often with narrow pathways leading visitors from one point to another.

- *Island Beds.* Like a mixed border with a twist. It is usually irregular in shape and placed in a position with grass growing around its complete perimeter, and it is designed to be seen from all sides. For that reason, the tallest perennials are placed in the center of the bed and the shortest along the edges.

- *Container Gardens.* The container can be anything—whiskey barrels, funky old bathtubs, or ornate terra cotta containers. The choices are limited only by your imagination. Container gardens should be located close to the house, however, as they require frequent watering to look their best.

- *Pathway or Patio Gardens.* Plants can be grown between the cracks in stones to create a whimsical feeling.

- *Rock Gardens.* Gardeners often forget that rock gardens are excellent choices to show off low-growing perennials that prefer harsher climates. Rocks are arranged in varying heights and arrangements, and low-growing plants are situated in crevices to accentuate the different textures. An excellent choice in our area with our abundance of rocks.

*A **perennial** is any plant (tree, shrub, flower) that continues to live year after year and which has a growing and a dormant season.*

4—Plant Selection: Perennials

The Best Place to Locate a Perennial Garden

Perennials are meant to be admired. For that reason alone, a perennial border should be situated so that it can be easily seen throughout the growing season. This view may be from the street, your living room, a second story deck, or a breakfast nook. If space allows, try to plan for a fairly large border (but one that you can maintain). This will allow you to plant your perennials in large groupings or drifts so that the garden gives a big visual impact.

Soil Preparation for Perennial Gardens

While some plants can made do in just about any soil, most perennials will perform best if they are grown in an improved soil. Try to begin bed preparation long before you are ready to plant. This will allow you to really and truly get rid of that grass ahead of time, as well as allow you to amend the soil and improve drainage problems at an unhurried pace. Digging and planting beds in a couple of days is a recipe for future problems.

Columbine

Note: The type of soil used should match the plants' needs. Some plants like a moist, rich soil, while some prefer drier and leaner soils. Always place plants with similar soil, moisture, and light needs together.

Perennial Selection: What Is Your Purpose?

Before randomly selecting perennials to stick in the ground, consider the purpose of your choice. For example:

- Do you want a low edging plant?
- Are you looking for a long-lasting burst of color?
- Does the plant need to be one that will work well in rock gardens?
- Should the plant be able to take reflected heat?
- Do the choices need to be able to survive in dry shade?

Thinking about the specific job you want that perennial to perform will help make your decision much easier. Jot down your requirements before going to the nursery. Then, you can look through your perennial list or ask qualified nursery workers, extension services, or workers at a botanical gardens to help you make a decision. As a general rule, follow these guidelines when planting perennials:

Table 4.15: Perennial Planting Table

Bloom Time	Best Planting Time
Late Summer or Fall	Spring
Spring	Late Summer or Fall

Note: Try to avoid planting perennials shortly before the onset of extremes in weather—our normal extreme times are January through February 15, July, and August.

Planting Perennials

Your tiny little perennial may look forlorn and alone when first planted in the garden, and the natural tendency is to plant it closer than the recommended spacing. Don't! Instead fill in the space with annuals or mulch. That plant will grow, most likely to the size indicated. It is going to need the space, both above and below the ground, to grow to its full potential.

Plant Placement Strategies For Showy Perennial Beds

- Mass enough of the same type of perennial to produce single-color drifts that are several feet long and at least a foot wide *or* clumps that are from 2 to 3 feet around.

- Make drifts thin toward the front edge of a border where low-growing plants are placed.

- If you use oblong drifts, try to get them to follow the contour of the border.

- Be sure to plan for foliage at the same time as planning for color.

- Use tall, spiked plants as accents. Place the same spiked plant in 2 or 3 widely-separated places in the garden to relieve the flatness and to create a sense of rhythm.

- In island beds, tall plants should be placed in the center. In borders, they should be placed at the back.

- To exaggerate the depth of a bed, emphasize the differences in height between the little plants in front and the taller ones in back.

Color Strategies for Perennial Beds

Ever seen a garden whose colors just seem to click? That arrangement, most likely, did not come about by chance. There was probably a bit of thought put into the effort as well, as some moving around of plants until just the right harmony was achieved. Books are devoted solely to color theory, but within the garden, with its many three-dimensional considerations, achieving harmonious color arrangements is an ever-evolving and fascinating experiment with nature.

HOW TEXAS LIGHT AFFECTS COLOR

We live in an area of strong, intense light. For that reason, soft colors that predominate in the quieter sunlight of northern gardens

Our strong Central Texas light demands heavy use of intense colors softened with accents of softer tones, grays, creams, and blues, as well as foliage colors.

4—Plant Selection: Perennials

will not show up well in our sunlight. Our strong light demands heavy use of intense colors softened with accents of softer tones, grays, creams, and blues, as well as foliage colors (see Table 4.16).

Table 4.16: Psychological and Visual Effects of Certain Colors

Color	Effect
Red	Arouses and advances. When used at the end of the garden, it will square a long narrow space.
Blue	Calming, contemplative, receding. Widens a garden when planted on the long side.
Yellow	Arouses and advances. When used at the end of the garden, it will square a long narrow space.
Green	Yellow-green is casual in feeling. Dark green imparts a rich, luxurious feeling. Good with white. Relieves eye strain.
White	Pacifies and relays a tidy and precise feeling—white is a good evening color. Will impart a zesty feeling when positioned within monochromatic (same color) themes.
Pink	Soothing. Good around patios.
Gray	Promotes creativity. Has no after-image.

TIPS TO ACHIEVE BALANCE WITH COLOR

Balance is an important aspect of color harmony within the garden. Here are a few tips to help you achieve balance in your landscape.

1. A strong color throughout the garden can create an energetic feeling. When using a strong color, however, try to balance it by also using less strong colors.

2. When viewers stand back to appreciate your garden, it is appealing if they are able to visually roam from place-to-place, enjoying the different associations. Eventually, viewer's eyes should be led toward one feature area, whether it be a piece of art, a grouping of rocks, or a spectacular plant association.

3. If you want to exaggerate the depth of a border, try using bright, strong colors up close to the viewer and then use progressively bluer, grayer, and lighter tones toward the back.

4. If you want to really exaggerate the depth of a border, make sure that there is a strong emphasis on height differences between the shorter plants in the front of the border and the tall ones in back.

5. When drifts of color of ever-increasing height are used, more of each color can be seen.

6. If you have an area that is partly in shade or that is in a shadow all afternoon, using a closely grouped association of strong tones will create a harmonious blending of color.

7. Try to mass color drifts that are several feet long and at least a foot wide, or use clumps that are 2' to 3' around.

8. When planning your garden for color, try the following: Make a rough sketch of your landscape and its permanent features

Black-eyed Susan

Xeriscape for Central Texas

Annuals are temporary plants in that they grow from seed to flower, flower, and then die back all in one year. In other words, annuals complete their entire life cycle in one year.

like trees, shrub groupings, etc. Then, mark your plan with circles where you'd like to see some color and mark those circles with the word "bloom." Decide what color you want those blooms to be and when you want the blooms to occur (the same or different times). Check to see if those circles allow a viewer's eye to move from place-to-place and visually appreciate the blooms. Decide on appropriate plants to use in the areas (flowering trees, flowering shrubs, perennials, annuals, etc.).

POSSIBLE COLOR THEMES

Dominant color mixed with lighter shades. Choose a dominant color for your bed first. Then, plan large masses of flowers that are a lighter shade of the dominant color. Add in a few spots of a darker shade and a lighter tint of that same dominant color.

To make a bed seem deeper, use bright colors toward the front and lighter, grayer colors toward the back.

Table 4.17: Possible Color Combinations

Major Colors	Single Accents
Blues:	
Blue, Purple, White	Yellow, Silver
Blue, Silver, Apricot	Maroon, Yellow, Silver
Reds:	
Clear Crimson, Pink, White	Maroon, Silver
Strong Red, Orange	Maroon, Silver
Purple, White, Maroon, Dark Pink	Yellow-Green Variegated Leaves
Rich Pink, Pale Pink, Maroon	Silver
Green, Grays & Whites:	
Green, White, Gray	Maroon, Yellow
Dark Green, Light Green	Green with Yellow, White
Silver, White	Pale Yellow, White-Silver Variegated
Yellows:	
Pale Yellow, Gray	----------------------------
Pale Yellow, Light Blue, Med. Blue	Purplish Blue, Pale Purple
Gold, White	Variegated (yellow-green or white silver)
Mixtures of Unrelated Colors:	
Pink, Purple, Gray	White, Yellow
Maroon-Green Mass of Texture	Red, Orange-Red, Pink
Clear Blue & Clear Pink Shades	Maroon, Yellow Green, White, Silver
Cloudy Blues & Cloudy Pinks	Bright Pink, Silver, Maroon

Once-a-year impact. Colors can be related or complementary. The main goal here is a big visual smorgasbord one time each year.

Seasonal dominant colors. Plan for a particular dominant color in spring, another in summer, and another in fall.

4—Plant Selection: Perennials

Year-long dominant color. Two clashing dominant colors in bloom at the same time can cancel each other out.

Related colors as a dominant factor with complementary color accents. Complementary colors will lead the eye forward from one spot to another. Try to place complementary colors in syncopated rhythm. Examples: Yellow accenting violet or purple; red accenting blue-green, blues, and yellow-greens; bright blue accenting pale yellow-orange.

Different shades of the same color family planted close together. This achieves a good color balance (example: light yellow, dusty gold, burnt orange, green foliage). This will allow a single bright color to stand out better.

Monochromatic (same color) themes. One color used in a garden, such as white, will often create a dramatic impact.

Table 4.18: Perennials for Central Texas

Common Name	Botanical Name	Light	Water	Height × Spread	Color	Bloom Period
Bicolor Sage	*Salvia sinaloensis*	S/PS	L	12" × 18"	blue	April-Sept
Big Red Sage	*Salvia penstemenoides*	PS	L	36" × 24"	magenta	June-Sept
Black Dalea	*Dalea frutescens*	S/PS	L	24-36" × 36-48"	purple	July-Oct
Blue Mist Flower	*Eupatorium coelestinum*	PS	L/M	18" × 36"	blue	July-Oct
Brazos Penstemon	*Penstemon tenuis*	S/PS	L	24" × 24"	purple	Mar-June
Buchanan Sage	*Salvia buchaninii*	PS/SH	L	18" × 24"	magenta	April-Sept
Butterfly Weed	*Asclepias tuberosa*	S/PS	L	18-24" × 24"	orange	April-Sept
Calylophus	*Calylophus drummondianus var. berlandieri*	S	L	12" × 24"	yellow	April-June
Cedar Sage	*Salvia roemeriana*	PS/SH	L	12" × 12"	red	April-Sept
Chi-Chi Ruellia	*Ruellia brittonia 'Chi-Chi'*	PS/SH	L	36-48" × 24"	pink	April-Oct
Chile pequin	*Capsicum annuum*	PS/SH	L	24" × 24"	white/red berries	April-Nov
Yellow Columbine	*Aquilegia chrysantha*	PS/SH	M	24" × 24"	yellow	Feb-May
Coreopsis	*Coreopsis lanceolata*	S/PS	L/M	18-24" × 12"	yellow	April-June
Damianita	*Chrysactina mexicana*	S	L	18" × 24"	yellow	Mar-Sept
Fall Aster	*Aster oblongifolius*	S/PS	L	36" × 48"	pink, purple	Sept-Dec
Fall Obedient Plant	*Physostegia virginiana*	S/PS	M	36-48" × 24"	purple or white	July-Oct
Flowering Maple	*Abutilon pictum*	S/ PS	M	36" × 36"	yellow, pink	July-Nov
Four Nerve Daisy	*Hymenoxys scaposa*	S	L	8" × 12"	yellow	Feb-Nov
Fragrant Mist Flower	*Eupatorium havanense*	S/PS	L	36" × 48"	white	Aug-Sept
Gregg's Mist Flower	*Eupatorium greggi*	S/PS	L/M	18" × 36"	blue or white	Mar-Nov
Heartleaf Hibiscus	*Hibiscus martianus*	S	L/M	36" × 24"	red	May-Nov

85

Xeriscape for Central Texas

Table 4.18: Perennials for Central Texas (Continued)

Common Name	Botanical Name	Light	Water	Height × Spread	Color	Bloom Period
Hill Country Penstemon	*Penstemon triflorus*	S/PS	L	18-24" × 12-18"	magenta	April-May
Indian Blanket	*Gaillardia pulchella*	S/PS	L	12-24" × 12"	yellow/red	May-July
Lantana hybrids	*Lantana hybrid*	S	L	18-30" × 24-48"	various	Mar-Oct
Lavender Lace Dianthus	*Diathus superbus*	PS	L/M	12-18" × 24"	lavender	May-Nov
Lavender Scullcap	*Scutellaria wrightii*	PS	L	6-8" x 6-12"	purple	Mar-Nov
Lindheimer's Cassia	*Cassia lindheimeriana*	S	L	18-36" × 24"	yellow	Aug-Sept
Lyre-Leaf Sage	*Salvia lyrata*	PS	L	12" × 12"	blue	Feb-April
Magenta Dianthus	*Dianthus sp.*	PS	L/M	6-12" × 24"	magenta	Mar-May
Majestic Sage	*Salvia guaranitica*	PS/SH	L	48" × 24"	blue or purple	April-Oct
Mealy Blue Sage	*Salvia farinacea*	S/PS	L	36" × 24"	blue	Mar-Nov
Mexican Marigold Mint	*Tagetes lucida*	S/PS	L	24" × 36"	yellow	Oct-Nov
Mexican Oregano	*Poliomentha longiflora*	S/PS	L	36" × 48"	pale lavender	May-Aug
Missouri Violet	*Viola missouriensis*	PS/SH	L/M	4-6" × 8-12"	purple	Feb-Mar
Oxalis	*Oxalis spp.*	PS/SH	L	10-12" × 12"	pink	Mar-April
Oxeye Daisy	*Chrysanthemum leucanthemum*	S/PS	L/M	6-24" × 12"	white/yellow	April-June
Pacific Chrysanthemum	*Chrysanthemum pacificum*	S/PS	L/M	24-36" × 36"	yellow	Fall
Pink Lantana	*Lantana camara*	S	L	36" × 48"	pink/yellow	Mar-Oct
Pink Rock Rose	*Pavonia lasiopetala*	S/PS	L	24-36" × 36-48"	pink	April-Sept
Pink Scullcap	*Scutellaria suffrutescens*	S/PS	L	12" × 24"	pink	April-Nov
Pringle's Bee Balm	*Monarda pringlei*	PS	L/M	12-24" × 24-30"	scarlet red	April-July
Purple Coneflower	*Echinacea purpurea*	S/PS	L/M	24" × 18"	purple	May-July
Purple Leaf Sage	*Salvia blepharophylla*	PS/SH	L/M	24" × 30"	red	April-Oct
Rock Penstemon	*Penstemon bacharifolius*	S/PS	L	18" × 18"	red	June-Sept
Skeleton Leaf Goldeneye	*Viguiera stenoloba*	S/PS	L	3' × 3'	yellow	May-Sept
Spring Obedient Plant	*Physostegia angustifolia*	S/PS	M	36-60" × 24"	lavender	Mar-June
Standing Cypress	*Ipomopsis rubra*	S/PS	L/M	48" × 8"	red	April-June
Texas Betony	*Stachys coccinea*	S/PS	L	18" × 30"	coral	Mar-Oct
Texas Lantana	*Lantana horrida*	S	L	48" × 48"	orange/yellow	Mar-Oct

4—Plant Selection: Annuals and Biennials

Table 4.18: Perennials for Central Texas (Continued)

Common Name	Botanical Name	Light	Water	Height × Spread	Color	Bloom Period
Texas Star Hibiscus	Hibiscus coccineus	S/PS	L	5-6' × 3-6'	red	June-Sept
Trailing Lantana	Lantana montevidensis	S/PS	L/M	12-24" × 24-30"	lavender white	Mar-Oct
Turk's Cap	Malvaviscus arboreus var. drummondii	S/PS	L	36-48" × 36-48"	red	June-Nov
Whirling Butterflies	Gaura lindheimeri	S/PS	L	18-48" × 24-48"	white/pink	Apr-Nov
Winecups	Callirhoe involucrata	S/PS	L	6-12" × 24-36"	magenta	Feb-June
Yarrow	Achillea millefolium	S/PS	L	12" × 24"	white	Feb-May
Zexmenia	Wedelia hispida	S/PS	L	2-3' × 24"	yellow	May-Nov

Annuals and Biennials

Annuals are temporary plants in that they grow from seed to flower, flower, and then die back all in one year. In other words, annuals complete their entire life cycle in one year. *Biennials* are also temporary plants. They grow from seed, produce leaves and stems in the first season, and then go on to produce a flower and seed out in the next season. After flowering, biennial plants usually die. Both annuals and biennials are great additions to the garden. Since they can both be raised from seed, they are good ways to achieve masses of color at affordable prices. Many of these types of plants are vigorous self-seeders and will return year after year.

How Annuals and Biennials Can Be Used in the Landscape

Easy-to-grow annuals and biennials serve a variety of purposes in the home landscape. They can be used to:

- Fill in spaces between plants which haven't reached their mature size.
- Give bursts of color when perennials are not in bloom.
- Provide color in bulb beds and disguise bulb leaves as they die down.
- Provide a good supply of cut flowers.
- Give masses of color when thickly planted in flower beds.
- Accent fences or walkways.
- Brighten hanging baskets or other containers.

Considerations Before Purchasing Annuals and Biennials

Before purchasing annual and biennial seeds or plants, take a few minutes to consider some things. What is the purpose of the plants, and where are you going to place them? Think about height and make sure that you are purchasing smaller plants for the front of the bed and taller ones for the back of the border. Also, consider color combinations. Try to select plants that have colors that blend well.

Warm and Cool Season Annuals and Biennials

Because of our long growing season, we are lucky in that we can have masses of annual or biennial color at any time of the year. Some of these plants have their growing season during the cooler months of October through March and are termed cool season plants. Others are vigorous growers during the heat of the warmer months and are termed warm season plants. Because of our extended warm months, many plants can undergo a second seeding to give an additional fall show after the end of their spring and early summer bloom time.

Soil Preparation For Annuals

Most non-native types of annuals and biennials enjoy well-prepared garden soil. They are happiest when they have plenty of nutrients available for their use. Those which are native will thrive in conditions which mimic their native habitat.

Color Strategies for Annual and Biennial Beds

See Perennial section above.

Bulbs

This section includes discussion on bulbs, corms, tubers, tuberous roots, and rhizomes.

Bulbs are underground storage organs characterized by overlapping, fleshy, scalelike leaves attached to a stem base.

Corms are enlarged underground stems which grow upright. They do not have fleshy scalelike leaves like bulbs.

Tubers are horizontal underground stems with very enlarged tips. They do not have a covering of dry leaves, nor do they have a bottom plant from which the roots can grow. They reproduce by growing roots from an eye or bud.

Tuberous roots are thick, horizontal underground stems, with the stem portion located at one end and true roots located at the other end.

Rhizomes are fleshy, horizontal underground stems that produce roots on the lower surface, and extend leaves and flowering shoots above ground.

Iris

Note: When selecting bulbs, corms, tubers, tuberous roots, or rhizomes to use in your garden, make sure they are drought tolerant. Avoid buying the tempting selections offered in out-of-state catalogs. Most of the advertised selections simply will not withstand our severe climate. Check with a reputable garden center, local garden club, or landscape professional to learn what varieties are best for our area.

4—Plant Selection: Bulbs

Table 4.19: Annuals and Biennials

Common Name	Bloom Season	Common Name	Bloom Season
Alyssum, Sweet	Spring	Copper Plants	Summer
Bluebonnets	Spring	Cosmos	Summer
Butter & Eggs	Spring	Cut-And-Come Again (Helianthus)	Summer
Chamomile, German	Spring	Cypress	Summer
Cornflower	Spring	Daisy, Arkansas Lazy	Summer
Cypress, Standing	Spring	Daisy, Dahlberg	Summer
Dianthus	Spring	Daisy, Gloriosa	Summer
Flax, Scarlet	Spring	Daisy, Tahoka	Summer
Foxglove	Spring	Datura	Summer
Golden Wave	Spring	Geranium	Summer
Honesty	Spring	Gomphrena/Globe Amaranth	Summer
Indian Blanket	Spring	Hibiscus	Summer
Larkspur	Spring	Hyacinth Bean/Purple Pea	Summer
Love-In-A-Mist	Spring	Impatiens	Summer
Maltese Cross	Spring	Moss Rose	Summer
Mullein, Pink	Spring	Penta	Summer
Phlox, Drummond	Spring	Perilla	Summer
Poppy, California	Spring	Periwinkle	Summer
Poppy, Dorn	Spring	Petunias	Summer
Poppy, Double Opium	Spring	Salvia, Scarlet	Summer
Sage, Clary	Spring	Spider Flower	Summer
Stocks	Spring	Tobacco, Flowering	Summer
Sweet William	Spring	Torenia	Summer
Verbascums	Spring	Zinnia	Summer
Ageratum	Summer	Cabbage, Flowering	Fall/Winter
Amaranth spp.	Summer	Calendula	Fall/Winter
Basil	Summer	Daisy, English	Fall/Winter
Begonias	Summer	Dianthus	Fall/Winter
Blue Daze	Summer	Kale, Flowering	Fall/Winter
Caladiums	Summer	Pansy	Fall/Winter
Cockscomb	Summer	Snapdragon	Fall/Winter
Coleus	Summer	Viola	Fall/Winter

What to Look for When Purchasing Bulbs

When selecting bulbs, try to pick bulbs of the highest quality. The bulbs should not be shriveled. Rather, they should have a firm, plump appearance. Avoid bulbs that have a mushy feel to them. Avoid purchasing bulbs from out-of-state catalogs. The pictures are beautiful, but many of these bulbs require certain climatic conditions which we do not have. It is better to buy bulbs that are known winners in our part of the country.

Where to Plant Bulbs

For the most part, bulbs require a great deal of sun. For that reason, bulbs that are planted and dug up each year should be situated in spots that receive 5 to 6 hours of sun a day. Those which stay in the ground all year will normally need 8 to 10 hours of sun each day. There are always exceptions to this rule, with some bulbs doing quite well under deciduous trees. Ask a reputable nursery professional or extension service for help if you are in doubt.

The Best Time to Plant Bulbs

Plant spring-flowering bulbs in late summer and early fall. Plant summer-flowering bulbs in spring after frost danger is past.

The Proper Depth for Bulbs

Different types of bulbs require different depths of planting. Check with a reliable source for accurate information.

How to Plant Bulbs

Before planting bulbs, bone meal and a small amount of 5-10-5 fertilizer should be added to the bottom of the hole or bed. Cover the fertilizer with approximately 1" of soil before placing the bulb into position. Avoid placing the bulb directly on top of the fertilizer. Bulbs that are in the shape of a teardrop should be planted with the pointed portion of the bulb up. The pointed portion is where the leaves and flower stalks emerge. Clawlike and flatter bulbs should be planted with their root side down. Plant each type of bulb at its recommended planting depth, replace the soil, and water the planting well. A layer of mulch added on top of the newly-planted bulb will help retain the moisture.

Planting Tip: When planting large numbers of bulbs, lay them all out on top of the soil before digging a single hole. This will avoid confusion as to where you've planted the last bulb. For a more random look in a naturalistic setting, toss a handful of bulbs on the ground and plant them where they land.

Why Bulbs and Fruit Do Not Mix

Sometimes people store bulbs in the refrigerator for a short time to trick them into thinking they have experienced a dormant period. When doing this, avoid storing bulbs and fruit in the refrigerator at the same time. When fruit ripens, it produces ethylene gas. This type of gas inhibits bulb flowering.

Before planting bulbs, bone meal and a small amount of 5-10-5 fertilizer should be added to the bottom of the hole or bed. Cover the fertilizer with approximately 1" of soil before placing the bulb into position.

4—Plant Selection: Bulbs

Table 4.20: Bulbs for Central Texas

Common Name	Botanical Name	Bloom Time	Best Soil Type	Light	Best Planting Time	Features
Allium, Giant	*Allium giganteum*	Spring	Deep, rich, drier areas	Sun	Fall	Large, ball-like clusters of bright lilac flowers. Stems 3'-5' tall.
Allium, Ornamental	*Allium aflatnense*	Spring	Deep, rich, drier areas	Sun	Fall	Large, ball-like clusters of lilac blooms. Stems 3'-5' tall.
Amarcrinum	*Crinodonna corsii 'Fred Howard'*	Late Summer	Any	Morning sun/ evening shade	Spring	Fragrant, long-lasting. Pink blooms.
Amaryllis, Hardy Red	*Hippeastrum x johnsonii*	Spring	Any	Sun or part sun	Fall	Long, strap-shaped foliage. Bright red lily-like blooms.
Canna, Common	*Canna x generalis*	Summer-Fall	Good soil	Sun	Early Spring	Varied colored blooms & sizes. Hardy. Easily grown.
Chives, Chinese	*Allium tuberosum*	Summer	Any	Sun	Fall	Leaves garlic-flavored. White blooms.
Elephant Ear	*Colocasia esculenta*	N/A	Good soil	Shade	Spring/ Early Summer	Grown for large showy leaves. Shelter from wind.
Garlic, Society	*Tulbaghia violacea*	Spring-Fall	Good, well-drained	Sun or part sun	Fall-Early Spring	Clump forming & grass-like foliage. Airy purplish-pink blooms. Hardy.
Gayfeather	*Liatris spicata*	Late Summer	Dry	Sun or part shade	Early Spring	Short, narrow foliage. Bloom spikes of purples or white. Do not water or plants become leggy.
Ginger, Butterfly	*Hedychium coronarium*	Summer	Heavy (if watered) to normal	Part shade	Fall or Early Spring	Various colors available. Usually tall.
Gladiolus, Byzantine Jacob's Ladder	*Gladiolus byzantinus*	Spring	Clay to well-drained	Sun or part Sun	Late Winter or Very Early Spring	Blooms purple. Foliage, tall, narrow. Good in cottage gardens. Corms need to be dug up, dried, & stored after plants die back.
Gladiolus, Parrot	*Gladiolus psittacinus*	Spring	Heavy	Sun or part sun	Late Winter or very early Spring	Hooded orange & yellow blooms. Foliage, tall, narrow. Sturdy. Corms need to be dug up, dried, & stored after plants die back.
Hyacinth, Roman	*Hyacinthus orientalis albulus*	Early Spring	Any/ well-drained	Sun or part sun	Fall	Blooms white, fragrant. Graceful.
Hyacinth, Starch	*Muscari racemosum*	Early Spring	Any	Sun or part sun	Fall	Foliage grass-like with purple blooms that look like bluebonnets.
Iris, Early or 'Cemetary Whites' or Early Purple'	*Iris albicans*	Early spring	Any	Sun or part sun	Fall	White or purple blooms. Drought tolerant. Hardy. Dependable.

Xeriscape for Central Texas

Table 4.20: Bulbs for Central Texas (Continued)

Common Name	Botanical Name	Bloom Time	Best Soil Type	Light	Best Planting Time	Features
Iris, Spuria	*Iris spuria hyb.*	Mid-Spring	Neutral to slightly alkaline	Sun	Fall	Foliage narrow & tall. Delicate blooms in varied colors. Hardy & adaptable. Will go dormant in late summer.
Jonquil Hybrid	*Narcissus jonquilla x odorus 'Campernelle'*	Early Spring	Any	Sun or part sun	Fall	Adaptable. Foliage rush-like. Blooms yellow, fragrant.
Jonquil Hybrid	*N. jonquilla x 'Trevithian'*	Mid-Spring	Any	Sun or part sun	Fall	Adaptable. Blooms yellow. Good planted in masses.
Lily of the Field	*Sternbergia lutea*	Fall	Good garden soil	Su or part sun	Aug-Sept.	Bright yellow cup-shaped blooms. Good in rock gardens or in drifts.
Lily, Aztec	*Sprekelia formosissima 'Orient Red'*	Spring & Fall	Well-prepared. Good drainage	Sunny	Fall	Cool-weather performer. Good in drifts. Blooms dark red. Foliage like daffodils.
Lily, Canna	*Canna spp.*	Summer-Fall	Moist, rich.	Sun	Early Spring	Blooms red or yellow. Easy, vigorous.
Lily, Crinum	*Crinum cvs.*	Spring/Summer	Any	Morning sun/p.m. shade	Fall or Early Spring	Arching foliage. Blooms trumpet-shaped. Hardy. Many hybrids available. Colors vary.
Lily, Madonna	*Lilium candidum*	Mid-Spring	Any	Part sun	Late Summer or Early Fall	Blooms white, fragrant. Foliage dies back after blooms & goes dormant. Keep mulched & avoid overhead watering.
Lily, Oxblood	*Rhodophiala bifida*	Early Fall	Any	Sun or part sun	Spring	Red amarylis-like blooms rise on single stalks before foliage appears.
Lily, Rain	*Zephranthes spp.*	Summer	Well-prepared	Sun	Any, but Fall best	Different types available. Blooms in shades of pink, yellow, or white.
Lily, Spider	*Hymenocallis liriosme*	Spring	Any	Sun or part sun	Fall or Early Spring	Large, showy straped foliage. White exotic blooms. Best in damp soils.
Lily, Spider	*Lycoris radiata*	Fall	Normal or heavy clay	Sun or part sun	Late Spring	Foliage appears in fall followed by spidery red blooms. Good with well-behaved ground covers. Use more water with heavy clay.
Montbretia	*Crocosmia pottsii*	Spring/Early Summer	Somewhat fertile	Sun or part sun	Fall or Early Spring	Straplike foliage. Blooms bright orange-red, airy. Can be invasive. Too much water, fertilizer causes weak growth.
Narcissus Hybrid	*N. tazetta 'Grand Manarque'*	Spring	Any	Sun or part sun	Fall	White blooms. Good impact in masses.

4—Plant Selection: Climbing Plants

Table 4.20: Bulbs for Central Texas (Continued)

Common Name	Botanical Name	Bloom Time	Best Soil Type	Light	Best Planting Time	Features
Onion, Wild	*Allium neopolitanum*	Early Spring	Deep, rich, drier areas	Sun	Fall	Try under deciduous trees. Large white flowers.
Orchid, Chinese	*Bletilla striata*	Spring	Richer soil	Shade or part shade	Late Summer/Fall	Blooms purplish-pink.
Oxalis, Pink	*Oxalis crassipes*	Fall-Early Summer	Rich, sandy but adaptable	Part shade	Fall	Foliage clover-like. Blooms pink, rose, or white. Prefers additional moisture.
Spring Star	*Ipheion uniflorum*	Early Spring	Sandy	Sun or part sun	Fall	Onion fragrance. Blooms star-shaped & in blue shades.
Star of Bethlehem	*Ornithogalum umbellatum*	Spring	Any	Sun or part sun	Fall	Foliage & bulb looks like Muscari. Blooms star-shaped, white.
Summer Snowflake	*Leucojum aestivum*	Spring	Heavy clay, moist	Sun to part sun	Fall	Striped foliage with small, white, bell-shaped blooms.
Tuberose, Mexican	*Polianthes tuberosa*	Late Summer	Well-drained	Morning sun & p.m. shade	Mid-Spring	Foliage grass-like. Blooms white, tubular. May suffer from north of Zone 9.
Tulip, Golden	*Tulipa chrysantha*	Spring	Good, well-drained	Sun or part Sun	Fall	Small, naturalizing. Blooms yellow & red.
Tulip, Lady	*Tulip aclusiana*	Spring	Good, well-drained	Sun or part Sun	Fall	Small, naturalizing. Blooms red & white.
Windflowers	*Anemone heterophylla*	Late Winter Early Spring	Upland & calcerous clays	Sun	Fall	Self-sows in lawns. Colors in blue to violet.

Climbing Plants

Climbers are plants that use various parts of their anatomy to cling to a support. They may cling by tendrils, twining, leaf stalks that curl, or adventitious roots (roots growing in unexpected places).

Uses For Vines

- Softening effect for bare walls and fences.
- Fill in gaps within a landscape.
- Shading patios and walls.
- Windbreaks.
- Color, texture, and visual interest.

Soil Preparation For Climbers

Climbers will perform best if they are grown in improved soil. Treat climbers the same as you would a shrub. Providing a good planting bed will make a noticeable difference in the vigor of your plant.

Special Needs When Planting Climbers

Plant climbers just as you would other plants. When planting them, remove their supporting stake when placing them in the ground. When climbers are planted, however, make sure they quickly receive the type of support appropriate for the type of climber you've purchased. They will grow quickly. If the climber clings, make sure it is planted close enough to a wall so that it can begin to grab hold. If, on the other hand, the climber requires a support, make sure to provide adequate support.

For Quick Cover Solutions

With the exceptions of certain overly-enthusiastic types of vines (wisteria, grapes, and trumpet vines), climbers can be planted from 3' to 5' for quick cover. Vigorous vines should be spaced further apart at 6' to 10' between plants.

Clematis

Ornamental Grasses

Ornamental grasses are clumping types of grasses and grass relatives used to provide color, texture, and visual interest in a garden. They come in a variety of forms, such as tufted, mounding, upright, upright divergent (up and out), upright arching, and arching.

Warm-Season Versus Cool-Season Grasses

One major distinguishing factor between grasses is whether they are warm-season or cool-season types. Most of the ornamental grasses which grow in our area are classified as warm-season grasses. They begin to green up in the spring, attain their growth during the hot months, and then set seed and begin to go dormant during fall and winter. Cool-season grasses, on the other hand, grow best in cool temperatures and require much more water than warm-season grasses.

Some Common Uses for Ornamental Grasses

- Backdrops.
- Space dividers.
- Hedges and screens.
- Windbreaks.

4—Plant Selection: Ornamental Grasses

- Ground covers.
- Accentuating other plants.
- Adding vertical interest to beds.
- Slope stabilizers.

Important Considerations in Selecting an Ornamental Grass

1. Try to select a grass that is suitable for our climate. Native grasses are abundant, attractive, and extremely well-adapted to our seasonal water and temperature extremes.
2. Think about the job you want the grass to perform and whether or not it will fit in your landscape plans. What shape will it be? How about its eventual size (very important)? What color foliage, flowers, and seed heads are you seeking?
3. Water considerations are also important. Some grasses require very little water while others require moist conditions at all times.
4. Finally, consider the growth behavior of the grass. Is it invasive or a prolific self-sower, or does it behave itself and stay contained in one place?

The Best Time to Plant or Sow Ornamental Grasses

Warm-season grasses appreciate being planted in the early spring. This allows them to establish a good root system in the cool, damp months of spring to better take on the harsh conditions of summer. Cool-season grasses should be planted in early fall. If you want to try to start ornamental grasses from seed, try seeding them during the cool, damp months of early spring.

Before Planting Ornamental Grasses, Make Sure to...

Try to get rid of all traces of weeds and invasive grasses like Bermuda long before you purchase your ornamental grasses. Remember, all it takes is a couple of active stolens or roots to allow these invaders to grow again. It is extremely difficult to get rid of these pests after your ornamental grasses have been planted, and these rampant invaders can quickly take over and destroy the looks of a well-executed plan. Patience, persistence, and a little extra time will pay off in the complete eradication of these pests.

Ornamental grasses *are clumping types of grasses and grass relatives used to provide color, texture, and visual interest in a garden.*

Soil Requirements for Ornamental Grasses

Avoid using soils that are too rich when using this type of grass. A balanced soil is appreciated, but one that is too rich may cause the foliage to be somewhat weak. Ornamental grasses (especially native types) grow quite well in less-choice soils. This makes them ideal candidates for many challenging landscape situations.

Xeriscape for Central Texas

How to Plant Ornamental Grasses

Use the same planting techniques that you'd normally use with perennials. Avoid planting grasses at a depth different than that of the container in which they were purchased. This may cause them to receive too much or too little water.

After planting, be sure to give your grass regular waterings until it has established a good root system. Then, ease back on the water and adjust your watering schedule to the needs of individual grass types. After their first year of establishment, many grasses are very drought tolerant and may need little additional irrigation other than what Mother Nature supplies.

Table 4.21: Ornamental Grasses (and Grass-Like Plants) for Central Texas

Common Name	Botanical Name	Light	Water	Height × Spread	Features	Zone
Gramma, Side Oats	*Boutelous curtipendula*	S	L-M	1'-2' × 1'-2'	Purple tinted flowers.	4-9
Buffalo Grass	*Buchloe dactyloides*	S	L	Varied	Good low-water turf grass. Poor growth in shade.	3-9
Sedge, Berkeley	*Carex tumulicola*	S/PS/Sh	H	1'-2' × 1'-2'	Good with ferns. Tolerates traffic.	8-10
Sea Oats, Inland or Wild	*Chasmanthium latifolium*	PS/Sh	M-H	2'-3' × 2'	Cool season gras. Good as accent or in groupings.	5-9
Pampas Grass	*Cortaderia selloana*	S	L-M	Varied	Dense, clumping. Many sizes, types available.	8-10
Lemon Grass	*Cymbopogon citratus*	S/PS	M-H	2'-3' × 2'-3'	Subtropical, clumping. Frost tender.	9-10
Umbrella plant	*Cyperus alternifolius*	PS	H	2' × 3'-5'	Good in water gardens.	9-10
Reed, Horsetail	*Equisetum hyemale*	S	H	3'-6'	Slender, vertical stems. Invasive.	4-10
Lovegrass, Weeping	*Eragrostis curvula*	S	L-M	2"-3"	Foliage fine-textured.	7-10
Lovegrass, Purple	*Eragrostis spectabilis*	S	L-M	1'-1.5' × 1'-1'5'	Reddish flowers. Clumping.	5-9
Fescue, Blue	*Festuca cinera 'Elija Blue'*	PS	M-H	8" × 1'	Powder blue foliage. Evergreen. Cool-season grass.	4-9
Maiden Grass/Silver Grass 'Gracillimus'	*Miscanthus sinensis 'Gracillimus'*	S	M-H	5'-6' × 2'	Leaves with silver midrib.	5-9
Maiden Grass/Silver Grass 'Morning Light'	*Miscanthus sinensis 'Morning Light'*	S	M-H	4'-5' × 2'	Narrow band of white on leaf margins.	5-9
Maiden Grass/Silver Grass 'Variegated'	*Miscanthus sinensis 'Variegatus'*	S	M-H	4'-6' × 2	White-striped leaves.	5-9
Muhly, Gulf or Hairy Awn	*Muhlenbergia capillaris*	S	L-M	2'-3' × 2'	Arching foliage with pink blooms.	8-10
Muhly, Pine	*Muhlenbergia dubia*	S/PS	L-M	2'-3' × 2'	Clumping with stiff, wiry, pinelike foliage.	8-10

4—Plant Selection: Bibliography

Table 4.21: Ornamental Grasses (and Grass-Like Plants) for Central Texas (Continued)

Common Name	Botanical Name	Light	Water	Height × Spread	Features	Zone
Muhly, Weeping	*Muhlenbergia dubiodes*	S/PS	L-M	2'-3' × 2'	Low, weeping with long, narrow foliage.	8-10
Muhly, Bamboo	*Muhlenbergia dumosa*	S/PS	L-M	3'-5' × 4'	Bamboo substitute. Open, airy foliage.	8-10
Muhly, Lindheimer's or Big	*Muhlenbergia lindheimeri*	S/PS	L-M	3'-6' × 3'	Arching clumps with blue-green foliage.	7-9
Muhly, Seep	*Muhlenbergia reverchonii*	S/PS	L-M	18"-24" × 2'	Compact, tufted. Wiry, with twisted narrow leaves.	8-10
Muhly, Deer	*Muhlenbergia rigens*	S/PS	L-M	3'-4' × 2'	Broad, dense clumps with gray-green evergreen foliage.	7-9
Fountain Grass, Purple-leaved	*Pennisetum setaceum* 'Rubrum'	S/PS	M	2'-3' × 2'	Narrow, arching, purple leaves. Frost tender.	9-10
Little Bluestem	*Schizachyrium scoparium*	S/PS	L-M	3'-5' × 1'	Upright, vertical clumps. Foliage blue-green turning rust.	3-10
Alkalai Sacaton	*Sporobolus airoides*	S	L-M	2'-3' × 2'	Arching gray-green foliage with pinkish flowers.	7-9
Feather Grass, Mexican	*Stipa tenuissima*	S/PS	L	12"-18" × 1'	Bright green, needle-thin leaves.	7-10
Gamma, Eastern	*Tripsacum dactyloides*	S/PS	M-H	1'-3' × 2'	Lush, upright, arching leaves.	5-10

Bibliography

Cox, Jeff and Marilyn Cox. *The Perennial Garden.* Emmaus, Pennsylvania: Rodale Press, 1985.

Dimond, Don and Michael MacCaskey. *All About Ground Covers.* San Francisco: Ortho Books, 1982.

Greenlee, John. *The Encyclopedia of Ornamental Grasses.* Emmaus, Pennsylvania: Rodale Press, 1992.

Hamilton, Geoff. *The Organic Garden Book.* London: Dorling Kindersley Limited, 1987.

Harper, Pamela J. *Color Echoes.* New York: Macmillan Publishing Company, 1994.

Hessayon, Dr. D. G. *The Tree & Shrub Expert.* Herts, England: pbi Publications, 1983.

Hill, Madalene, Gwen Barclay, and Jean Hardy. *Southern Herb Growing.* Fredericksburg, Texas: Shearer Publishing, 1987.

IPM Plans (City of Austin packet).

Keen, Mary. *Gardening With Color.* New York: Random House, 1991.

Meltzer, Sol. *Herb Gardening in Texas.* Houston: Lone Star Books, 1987.

Murphy, Wendy, Joanne Pavia, and Jerry Pavia. *Beds and Borders. Traditional and Original Garden Designs.* Boston: Houghton Mifflin Company, 1990.

Native Texas Nursery, Austin, Texas. Wholesale Catalog.

Odenwald, Neil G. and James R. Turner. *Southern Plants.* Baton Rouge, Louisiana: Claitor's Publishing Division, 1996.

Ogden, Scott. *Gardening Success with Difficult Soils: Limestone, Alkaline Clay, and Caliche.* Dallas: Taylor Publishing Company, 1992.

Xeriscape for Central Texas

Olkowski, William, Helga Olkowski, and Shelia Daar. *What Is IPM?* Michigan State University Cooperative Extension. Common Sense Pest Control IV(3), 1988 (Article).

Overy, Angela. *The Foliage Garden.* New York: Harmony Books, 1993.

Reiley, H. Edward and Carroll L. Shry, Jr. *Introductory Horticulture.* Albany, New York: Delmar Publishing, 1991.

Salisbury, Frank B. and Cleon W. Ross. *Plant Physiology.* Belmont, California: Wadsworth Publishing Company, 1992.

Shirey, Trisha. *Culinary Herbs For The Xeriscape,* 1997 (Handout given at a past XGC meeting).

Sperry, Neil. *Neil Sperry's Complete Guide to Texas Gardening.* Second Edition. Dallas: Taylor Publishing Company, 1991.

The Antique Rose Emporium, Brenham, Texas. 1996 Reference Guide (Mail-order catalog).

Tree Growing Guide For Austin and The Hill Country. TreeFolks. (Brochure)

Wasowski, Sally and Andy Wasowski. *Native Texas Plants: Landscaping Region by Region.* Houston, Texas: Gulf Publishing, 1991.

Welch, William C. *Perennial Garden Color.* Dallas: Taylor Publishing Company, 1989.

Woody Landscape Plants. (Chapter 14 in a reference book that Master Gardeners used as a reference guide in past years).

Welsh, Douglas F., Everett E. Janne, and Calvin Finch. *Fertilizing Woody Ornamentals.* Bulletin L-1097. Texas Agricultural Extension Service (A&M handout).

Westin Gardens, Fort Worth, Texas. *Antique & Old Roses* (Free selection list handout).

What's Bugging You? A Guide For Managing Lawn & Garden Pests (City of Austin brochure).

Chapter 5

Turf Areas

In This Chapter...

Turf Grass and its Uses

The Xeriscape Concept of Practical Turf Areas

Types of Turf Grass

    Turf Grass for Shady Areas

    Turf Grass for Sunny Areas

    Turf Grass for High / Low Traffic

    Turf Grass for Decoration

How Turf Grass Spreads

Maintenance

Alternatives to Turf Grass

    Decks, Patios, and Walkways

    Ground Covers, Mulches, and Wildflowers

Sources of Turf Grass

This chapter addresses the plant that is typically the most prevalent in our Central Texas landscapes—turf grass. The Xeriscape approach is to have "practical turf areas." A corollary to this approach is to use turf grasses that require fewer resources—water, fertilizer, and manpower—to maintain.

Xeriscape for Central Texas

Turf Grass and its Uses

Turf grasses are one of the six main groups of grasses. The common feature of turf grasses is that they build a dense layer of plants and roots. Other grass groups include grazing, ornamental, cereals, sugar cane, and woody grasses. In this section, we will discuss the turf grasses.

Most new homes, built to local and federal guidelines, include at least a front lawn, which generally consists of some variety of turf grass. For many owners of a new home establishing a green carpet of lawn becomes an almost immediate obsession.

This probably stems from the great pleasure humans get from views of meadows, green hillsides, or golf courses. Grass also is cleaner than bare dirt, and fills in areas between plantings of flowers and trees. As a result, in most landscapes, the predominant plant used is some kind of turf grass. Consequently, by virtue of its size, the lawn area is the largest water user in the landscape.

Planning Lawn Areas
- *Limit the size.*
- *Choose appropriate grass.*
- *Consider alternatives.*

The Xeriscape Concept of Practical Turf Areas

Using Xeriscape concepts in planning lawn areas can help you conserve water and money. There are several items you should consider when planning turf grass areas for your Xeriscape:

- Limit lawn areas to just the size required by the proposed use.

- Choose the most appropriate grass for the location and intended use.

- Consider lawn alternatives, such as flower beds, mulches, ground covers, patios, and decks.

Consider Your Purpose in Using Turf Grass

Lawn areas are useful for certain types of recreation, entertainment, and pets. Lawn grasses can also be used for erosion and dust control because of their quick growth. Think about what you will use your lawn area for, and then size it accordingly. Consider limiting the use of lawn areas to small recreation and entertainment areas close to the house. This also helps create a cool green space around your home and reduces the amount of time spent mowing.

Limiting turf grass areas is also beneficial in times of drought. A large, expansive lawn that has gone dormant due to drought is an unattractive landscape feature. To keep the lawn green requires large amounts of water. On the other hand, if your lawn is just one of several features in your landscape, the fact that it has gone dormant is less obvious if you have drought-tolerant plants as other elements.

Some grasses will die if left unwatered. Dormant grasses will respond to rain or watering, whereas dead grass will not. Table 5.1

100

at the end of this chapter identifies turf grasses that are more heat tolerant and require less water.

Types of Turf Grasses

Turf Grass for Shady Areas

ST. AUGUSTINE

If your yard is heavily shaded, your primary choice for a lawn grass is one of the varieties of St. Augustine. However, St. Augustine grass is only water-efficient in the shade. In sunny areas, heavy water use is required during the summer months, especially if there is limited soil depth. St. Augustine is usually established using the "solid sod" method or by using "plugs" and letting them spread.

ZOYSIA

In addition to being shade-tolerant, Zoysia grass is resistant to wear and, to some degree, periods of drought. It is a slow grower and, because the sod can be expensive, requires a larger investment than St. Augustine. It also requires a reel mower to properly maintain the grass.

FESCUE

Fescue is a high user of water because of its low heat tolerance. It is grown from seed and germinates in the cool seasons of spring and fall. It is not drought tolerant and will die if not watered during high temperatures.

Keep in mind that, once established, most lawns consist of a variety of grasses and other plants. Birds, stormwater runoff, and the wind have a big impact on the spread of most plants, including weeds. By knowing the needs of the turf grass of your choice, you can minimize the impact of invading plants.

Turf Grass for Sunny Areas

BERMUDA GRASS

Bermuda grass is drought tolerant and wears better than St. Augustine, but will not grow in the shade. There are many varieties of Bermuda grass, and it can be established by seed or sod. Bermuda grass has a much finer texture than St. Augustine. It spreads rapidly and will invade any adjacent flower beds.

BUFFALO GRASS

Buffalo grass is a native turf grass available in seed, sod, or plugs. In recent years, new varieties have been developed that grow more densely than the native varieties. It is drought tolerant, cold hardy, and insect and disease resistant. The seeded variety is slow to establish. Vegetative varieties (see the table at the end of this section) can establish from plugs on 12" centers in approximately 16

Consider limiting the use of lawn areas to small recreation and entertainment areas close to the house. This also helps create a cool green space around your home and reduces the amount of time spent mowing.

weeks. These varieties are more shade tolerant than Bermuda but less than St. Augustine. Since it is slow-growing, it cannot take a lot of traffic. Depending on your particular circumstances, Buffalo grass may not be very competitive against weed invasion. It can be left unmowed or require infrequent mowing; some varieties are low growing and may never need to be mowed.

Turf Grass for High / Low Traffic

The grasses most suitable for high traffic areas are Bermuda and Zoysia. The better approach for high traffic areas is to replace the grass with a stone, mulch, or wooden walkway (see "Alternatives to Turf Grass").

The grasses most suitable for low traffic areas are Buffalo grass and St. Augustine. Use of each should also include considerations of shade versus sun, maintenance requirements, and the desired look of the area.

Turf Grass for Decoration

Ornamental grasses go beyond the ones mentioned to this point, and include several native varieties. Examples include Muhly and Purple Fountain Grass, etc. (See the section on Ornamental Grasses in the "Plant Selection" chapter.) Use of turf as a decorative or ornamental area is often done to set off a backdrop of other plants, or to provide a color contrast to stones or other plants.

Generally, using grasses for decoration is limited to small areas, so the considerations become different than for a larger, lawn-type area.

How Turf Grass Spreads

Turf grasses use two primary methods for reproduction: *seeds* and *creeping stems*. Lawns that are mowed on a regular basis don't have an opportunity to go to seed, and some of the more desirable turf grasses are all female and rarely go to seed.

The creeping stems are either *rhizomes* (grow under the ground) or *stolons* (grow above the ground). Bermuda grass uses both methods, which accounts for its invasiveness and allows it to grow under and over rocks and other barriers. St. Augustine and Buffalo grass send out stolons and are to some degree less invasive and easier to control. How and where you will be using turf grasses should include some consideration of the growth method and pattern of the grass.

Table 5.1 also gives more information on the growth habits of several grasses.

Maintenance

Chapter 6 on Maintenance gives quite a bit of detail on maintaining turf grasses.

Alternatives to Turf Grass

Decks, Patios, and Walkways

Decks, patios, and walkways are excellent alternatives to lawn areas. Consider them when you want to:

- Create more space for entertaining.

- Enlarge children's play area.

- Replace paths worn in the lawn.

  Materials available include:

- Redwood, cedar, and treated wood.

- Native limestone as flagstones and cut stones available in several colors.

- Concrete in smooth, aggregate, or colored surfaces, or marked like tile. Concrete provides a permanent, low-maintenance surface.

- Patio tiles (concrete pavers, bricks, etc.) are available in many colors and shapes.

- Gravel, decomposed granite, and mulch are useful for walkways or patios, but some edging is required to contain the material during use and heavy rains.

  Your choice of materials will depend on the particular situation, including ground slope, aesthetics, and adjacent areas.

Ground Covers, Mulches, and Wildflowers

Other good lawn substitutes are ground covers, mulches, and wildflowers. These provide color and texture, while requiring less maintenance than lawns. Ground covers include low-growing plants and shrubs. A good selection of these types of plants is listed in Chapter 4—Plant Selection. Chapter 8 on "Texas Wildscapes" discusses alternatives to turf areas.

Sources of Turf Grass

In the local area, most nurseries carry turf grass to some degree. Others specialize in turf grass and offer delivery and installation. Check the yellow pages before you head out.

Most of the turf grass installed in yards around Central Texas is grown to the east or south in large fields. Some varieties are limited in availability, so planning ahead is vital. Discovering that the turf grass you desire is not available until next season may lead to solutions that prove unsatisfactory later.

Table 5.1: Attributes of Turf Grass for Central Texas Lawns

CHARACTERISTICS	Native Buffalo grass*	Prairie Buffalo grass*	609 Buffalo grass*	Stampede Buffalo grass*	Common Bermuda grass*	Baby Bermuda (S/Dwarf)	Texturf 10 Bermuda	328 Tifgreen Bermuda	419 Tifway Bermuda	Tifway II Bermuda	Emerald Zoysia	Meyer Z-52 Zoysia	El Toro Zoysia	ZoyBoy Zoysia	Common St. Augustine	Raleigh St. Augustine	Floratam St. Augustine	Rebel II Tall Fescue	K-31 Tall Fescue	Houndog Tall Fescue
ADAPTATION																				
Drought tolerance (Low, Medium, High)	H	H	H	H	H	H	H	M	M	M	M	M	M	M	M	L-M	L-M	M	M	M
Heat tolerance (Low, Medium, High)	H	H	H	H	H	H	H	H	H	H	H	H	H	H	H	H	H	L	L	L
Wear resistance (Low, Medium, High)	M	M	M	M	M	H	H	H	H	H	H	H	H	H	M	H	H	M	M	M
Water requirements (Low, Medium, High)	L	L	L	L	L	L	M	M	M	M	M	M	M	M	M-H	M-H	M-H	H	H	H
Weekly water requirements in summer	.5"	.5"	.5"	.5"	1"	1"	2"	2"	2"	2"	1-2"	1-2"	1-2"	1-2"	1-2"	1-2"	1-2"	2"	2"	2"
Minimum hours of sun per day	6	6	6	6	8	8	8	8	8	8	4	4	4	4	4	4	4	2	2	2
Shade tolerance (Low, Medium, High)	L	L-M	L-M	L-M	L-M	L-M	L-M	L-M	L-M	L-M	M-H	M-H	M-H	M-H	M-H	M-H	M-H	H	H	H
Cold tolerance (Low, Medium, High)	H	H	H	H	M	L-M	L-M	L-M	L-M	L-M	M	M	H	M	M	M	M	H	H	H
CULTURE																				
Mowing Height (in inches)	N/A	N/A	N/A	N/A	3"	2"	.75"	1"	2"	.75"	1.5"	1.5"	2"	2"	3.5"	3.5"	3.5"	3"	3"	3"
Mowing frequency (in days)	N/A	N/A	N/A	N/A	5-7	14	5	5	5-7	5	4-5	4-5	4-5	5-7	5-7	5-7	5-7	5-7	5-7	5-7
Mower type (Standard rotary, Reel type)	S	S	S	S	R	S	R	R	R	R	R	R	R	S	S	S	S	S	S	S
Nitrogen per year per 1,000 sq.ft. (in lbs.)	0-2	0-2	0-2	0-2	2-3	2-3	3-4	3-4	3-4	3-4	2-5	2-5	2-5	2-5	3-6	3-6	3-6	2-6	2-6	2-6
Thatching tendency (Low, Medium, High)	L	L	L	L	M	M	H	H	H	H	H	H	H	M	M	M	M	L	L	L
PESTS																				
Insect problems (Low, Medium, High)	L	L	L	L	L-M	L-M	M	M	M	M	M-H	M-H	M-H	H	H	H	H	L	L	L
Disease problems (Low, Medium, High)	L	L	M	L	M	M	H	H	H	H	M-H	M-H	M-H	M	H	H	H	M	M	M
Fungal problems (Low, Medium, High)	L	L	L	L	L	L	H	H	H	H	M-H	M-H	M-H	H	H	H	H	M	M	M
Weed problems (Low, Medium, High)	M	M	M	M	L-M	M	M	M	M	M	M-H	M-H	M-H	M-H	M-H	M-H	M-H	H	H	H
ESTABLISHMENT																				
Seed per 1,000 sq.ft. (in lbs.)	1-2	N/A	N/A	N/A	.5-1	N/A	N/A	N/A	N/A	N/A	N/A	N/A	N/A	N/A	N/A	N/A	N/A	10	10	10
Sod/1,000 sq.ft. for 2" Plugs (in yards)	N/A	N/A	N/A	N/A	3.3	3.3	3.3	3.3	3.3	3.3	5	5	5	5	3.3	3.3	3.3	N/A	N/A	N/A
Sod/1,000 sq.ft. for 4" plugs (in yards)	15	15	15	15	N/A	N/A	N/A	N/A	N/A	N/A	N/A	N/A	N/A	N/A	N/A	N/A	N/A	N/A	N/A	N/A
Rate of Spread (Slow, Medium, Fast)	M	M	M	M	F	F	F	F	F	F	S	S	S	M	M	M	M	F	N/A	N/A
Leaf texture (Fine, Medium, Coarse)	F	F	F	F	F	F	F	F	F	F	F	F	M	M	C	C	C	F	M	M

* Indicates turf types that are recommended in Xeriscape and Green Builder guidelines.

This chart is a compilation of information from the Green Builder and Xeriscape programs along with research from a multitude of sources and comments from members of the Xeriscape Advisory Board.

Xeriscape for Central Texas

Notes & Ideas...

Chapter 6

Maintenance

In This Chapter...

Soil Maintenance and Management
Fertilizers
Disease Control
Pest Control
Weed Control
Lawns
Trees
Shrubs
Ground Covers
Antique Roses
Herbs
Perennials
Annuals and Biennials
Bulbs, Corms, Tubers, ...
Climbing Plants
Ornamental Grasses
Container Plants
Tools
Cultivation Methods
Seasonal Maintenance Guide
Bibliography

There is no such thing as a maintenance-free home landscape, despite our fantasies that our carefully Xeriscaped gardens will eliminate the need for hard physical labor once they are installed. Our gardens are always growing and changing, even during the dormant season. Effective and appropriate maintenance is key to keeping your landscape in its healthiest condition. The following sections are designed as a guide to help you with your maintenance questions.

Xeriscape for Central Texas

Soil Maintenance and Management

Soil Conditioners

Ask several landscape professionals about conditioning the soil, and you are likely to get several differing opinions. One person may comment that plants should make it in unamended soil because plants need to be able to withstand Texas' tough growing conditions. Another person may say that plants should be set in half amended, half native soil. Another may comment that it is often best to provide as much freshly amended soil as possible to the garden, since our local soils are either thin and alkaline or dense with a claylike consistency.

The Fact Is...

To improve drainage, add nutrients, and increase the water-holding capacity of the soil consider mixing in organic matter to "condition" your soil.

The need for soil amending varies from one site to the next. Gardeners should take into consideration the following factors before plotting a course of action:

- Current soil conditions.

- Types of plants desired.

For example, if you have a clay soil with poor drainage and are using plants that are known to prosper in that type of environment, soil conditioners may not be necessary. However, if you plan to use plants that require good drainage, it might be best to improve the soil structure by adding organic matter to hold the particles apart so the roots and water can pass through.

Types of Organic Conditioners

MANURE AND COMPOST

To improve drainage, add nutrients, and increase the water-holding capacity of the soil consider mixing in organic matter to "condition" your soil. The two best types of conditioners are well-rotted manure and compost.

Well-rotted compost or manure can be used either as a soil amendment or as a mulch. If used as an amendment, work it into the top layers of the soil (preferably during the autumn months). If used as a mulch, they can be applied over the surface of the soil or in between plants in thick layers. These amendments will eventually break down and work themselves into the soil.

'DILLO DIRT

Another type of compost which can be used as a soil amendment is made from treated sewer sludge and shredded yard wastes. Despite the unattractive picture this description conjures in the mind, this amendment (sold in Austin as 'Dillo Dirt) is a safe and effective product. The Hornsby Bend Wastewater Treatment Facil-

108

6—Maintenance: Fertilizers

ity in East Austin produces it, and it is designated by the EPA for unrestricted use with its "Class A" designation. This means that it contains extremely limited amounts of heavy metals. Because the original permit granted the city did not allow it to be recommended for use on edible plants and because Hornsby Bend cannot change their recommendation without a very costly permit change, 'Dillo Dirt cannot legally be recommended for use in vegetable and fruit gardens.

Alternative Soil Conditioners

Beside manure and compost, additional soil conditioners can be mixed into the soil to help improve its drainage or water-holding capacity. Please note that these materials will not necessarily improve the nutrient content of the soil, and not all of them are available in our area.

USED MUSHROOM COMPOST

A mixture of horse manure, peat moss, and other organic materials, this is used by commercial mushroom growers.

COMPOSTED PINE BARK

Normally sold in a partly composted condition, this is best used as a mulch. It contains virtually no nutrients.

PEAT

Peat moss has very few nutrients in it. Its main function is to increase water retention in the soil; however, it disappears rapidly in our Texas heat.

Fertilizers

Why Use Fertilizers?

There are several reasons why fertilizers may be required for your garden.

- You may not have sufficient quantities of manure or compost on hand.

- Your soil may be working overtime to keep up with your growing expectations.

- Your soil is lacking in particular nutrients, and you want a quick fix to correct the situation.

Before You Fertilize

Before you do anything, take the time to find out whether your soil is acid or alkaline. Most of the soils in the Central Texas area are somewhat alkaline, but we have a surprising number of acid soil pockets as well. The alkalinity or acidity of your soil will be a

Before you do anything, take the time to find out whether your soil is acid or alkaline. Most of the soils in the Austin area are somewhat alkaline, but we have a surprising number of acid soil pockets as well. The alkalinity or acidity of your soil will be a determining factor in the type of plants you decide to grow.

Xeriscape for Central Texas

Table 6.1: Management Practices for Clay & Limestone/Alkaline Soils

Soil Type	How to Work in Amendments	How to Treat Drainage Problems	Best Types of Organic Matter
Clay	Best amended in autumn when enough rain has softened it, but not so much that it is soaked. Leave surface rough and uneven during the winter to allow it to break into smaller clods. Work organic material into upper levels.	Add coarse grit into soil at approximately 1-2 bucketfuls every square meter/yard. To improve drainage, raise a section of the soil above its immediate surroundings. After improving the soil, do not walk on it at times when it is wet, as this could reverse all of the work you've done. Walk on boards laid down across the soil first.	Add bulky organic matter to hold the tightly-packed particles apart. Organic materials, which can be added, include: • Leaf mold. • Sawdust. • Straw. • Manure.
Limestone/Alkaline	Dig in shallowly in spring a few weeks before sowing or planting. For small areas, add a layer of topsoil to the surface.	Drainage is not a problem in this type soil. The biggest need is to hold the water in to help retain soil nutrients.	Try to keep the soil covered to keep it from blowing away. Mulch or spread organic material on top of soil surface during growing season. When possible, use acid materials to counteract soil alkalinity.

determining factor in the type of plants you decide to grow. It is much easier to choose appropriate plants than it is to change the pH level of the soil.

There are many types of kits available for testing soil pH. These all work on the same principal and are simple and accurate enough for home use. The local County Extension Service provides an even more in-depth soil analysis (which includes a pH analysis) for a small fee.

How to Raise the pH (How to Make it More Alkaline)

If you've got acidic soil and want to make it more basic (or alkaline), try adding lime. The changes won't be especially dramatic or quick. To avoid scorching plants, apply small dressings on a regular basis.

The best time to apply lime is a few weeks before planting. In the best case scenario, manure is added to the soil in the fall, and lime is added in the spring. Avoid adding lime to soil recently

6—Maintenance: Fertilizers

treated with manure. These two combine to form ammonia gas, which releases nitrogen into the air.

Note: There is seldom any reason to add lime to our soils. Central Texas soils are, for the most part, very alkaline. Do *not* use lime unless you are absolutely positive that you have acid conditions warranting the addition of this amendment. If your soils are slightly acidic, try using plants which appreciate this type of soil rather than trying to change the soil.

Lowering the Soil's pH (Making the Soil More Acidic)

Most of you can expect your water to increase the alkalinity of your soil over time, so you will be faced with trying to lower your soil's pH. Usually, pH can be lowered by adding sufficient amounts of compost and manure. However, if your soil is exceptionally alkaline, using raised beds for plants may be a good solution. Raising beds will allow a slight buffer between the bed and alkaline water drainage. Also, raised beds treated with manure and compost will have the added advantage of a more acidic soil composition.

The major nutrient involved in the way plants grow is nitrogen.

Plant Nutrients and Soil Maintenance

All plants need water, air, and sunlight to supply their hydrogen, oxygen, and carbon needs. They also need a wide range of chemical elements that are found in the soil. These elements are divided into two categories: *essential elements* and *trace elements*. When any one of these elements is missing in the soil, the results show up as symptoms in the plant.

Table 6.2: Primary Nutrient Needs

Vegetables	High
Herbs	Medium to Low
Lawns	Medium to High
Fruits	Medium
Annual Flowers	Medium
Perennial Flowers	Medium to Low
Deciduous Shrubs	Medium to Low
Evergreen Shrubs	Low
Shade Trees	Medium to Low

Why Are Nutrients Important?

To a gardener, nutrient management (in the form of fertilizing) helps control the way a plant grows and the character of that growth. The major nutrient involved in the way plants grow is nitrogen. Different plants require different amounts of primary nutrients such as nitrogen.

What Are the Different Ways to Fertilize?

There are many ways to fertilize depending upon the formula type and the plant requirement.

BROADCASTING

Fertilizer is spread over a wide area at a recommended rate. It should be incorporated into the soil by a light watering.

BANDING

Narrow bands of fertilizer are placed in furrows which are 2" to 3" away from garden seeds and 1" to 2" deeper than the seeds or new plants. Banding placement varies depending on the plant type and spacing requirement.

STARTER SOLUTION

These liquid fertilizers are applied to plants requiring phosphorous for root growth. Follow the manufacturer's directions.

SIDE DRESSINGS

This is dry fertilizer scattered on both sides of a plant, 6" to 8" from the plant, then raked into the soil and watered thoroughly.

FOLIAR FEEDING

This is used as a supplement to regular soil fertilization. Spray is applied to foliage. Absorption is complete within 1 to 2 days for most nutrients, which is good when a quick response is needed.

What the Numbers on the Fertilizer Bags Mean

There are three main elements listed in a fertilizer analysis: *nitrogen*, *phosphorous*, and *potassium*. They are labeled with a corresponding number that indicates the percentage by weight of each of these elements. If a fertilizer has all of these elements in it, then it is termed a complete fertilizer. If not, then it is termed an incomplete fertilizer. (*Note: This is an example only.*)

	Nitrogen	Phosphorus	Potassium
Complete Fertilizer	10	10	10
Incomplete Fertilizer	18	46	0

In addition to the main elements included in a bag of fertilizer, manufacturers add filler and trace elements. Because a manufacturer may not want to guarantee the exact amounts of these trace elements, they may not necessarily be listed on the bag.

When and How Often to Apply Fertilizers

Normally, fertilizer management is determined by the soil type. For instance, sandy soils, with their fast draining tendencies, require more frequent applications of fertilizer than do small-parti-

6—Maintenance: Fertilizers

cled clay soils. Two main rules should be remembered when applying fertilizers:

- Avoid over-applications of nitrogen fertilizers.

- To avoid burning plants, make sure to water-in your fertilizer after applying it. The old idea of fertilizing right before a rain is no longer recommended. Always water-in your fertilizer application to get it in contact with the soil. Otherwise, the first deluge of rain will wash the granules away. The run-off degrades our creeks and rivers by causing excess algae growth.

Note: Fertilizer recommendations on specific types of plants (trees, shrubs, etc.) are located in the maintenance section under the corresponding heading.

Organic vs. Non-Organic Fertilizers

Because there have been few studies in this area, there is little evidence to suggest that one type of fertilizer is better than another. We urge you to think about the environment before using any type of fertilizer. If run-off will cause ultimate damage to water sources or if it contains residual chemicals that will damage the soil and its microorganisms, perhaps a different approach might be in order.

Organic fertilizer—derived from the remains or by-products of once-living organisms.

Chemical fertilizer—a petroleum-based product containing specific quantities of essential and trace elements.

Organic Fertilizers: Advantages and Disadvantages

Organic fertilizer is derived from the remains or by-products of once-living organisms. Plants do not necessarily take in the chemicals derived from these compounds any differently than they do chemical-based fertilizers.

ADVANTAGES OF ORGANIC FERTILIZERS

- Nutrients are normally released over long periods, so fewer applications are necessary.

- Not harmful to the soil and its microorganisms.

- Will benefit the soil by increasing its organic content.

- Low burn potential.

- Improves the soil structure.

- Increases bacterial and fungal activity, which makes nutrients more readily available to plants.

DISADVANTAGES OF ORGANIC FERTILIZERS

- Usually dependent on soil organisms to break them down to release nutrients, so usually most effective in warm conditions with moist soil.

- They may not release enough of their main nutrient at a time when the plant needs it the most.

- Availability may be limited, and cost may be higher per unit.

Chemical Fertilizers: Advantages and Disadvantages

Chemical fertilizer is non-organic. It is a petroleum-based product containing specific quantities of essential and trace elements.

ADVANTAGES OF CHEMICAL FERTILIZERS

- Fast acting.

- Easily accessible.

- Prices are frequently discounted.

DISADVANTAGES OF CHEMICAL FERTILIZERS

- Can leave salt accumulations in the soil.

- Can damage water sources during rain run-off.

- Reinforces our dependence on petroleum products.

Disease Control

What to Look for When Buying a Plant

Make sure to check plants carefully before buying them. Ornamental trees, shrubs, herbaceous perennials, and annuals should be inspected for the slightest sign of disease, pest attacks, or physical damage. Remember, you will normally be fighting an uphill battle when buying inferior quality plants. While they may survive, plants with viruses, fungal disease, pest damage, or physical damage may not flourish.

Daily Vigilance Pays Off

Want to keep your plants as healthy as possible? Here are some rules designed to keep plants vigorous and disease free.

- Use good cultivation practices. Feed the soil instead of the plant.

- Keep the garden clean. Avoid leaving waste lying around. Piles of pulled weeds attract insect pests.

- Quickly treat plants when they develop a disease. Destroy or remove plants that do not respond to treatment.

- Use only pots that are cleaned and sterilized by boiling.

- Try to take a daily walk around the main areas of the garden with hoe in hand. Remove unwanted weeds. Keep an eye out for the first signs of attack from pests and disease.

What to Do if You Think You Have a Diseased Plant

If you have a plant that is declining and appears sickly, there are a couple of resources to use when getting a diagnosis and treatment. One possibility is to take a sample of the diseased plant

Ornamental trees, shrubs, herbaceous perennials, and annuals should be inspected for the slightest sign of disease, pest attacks, or physical damage.

6—Maintenance: Disease Control

(make sure it is more than one tiny leaf), place that sample in a clear plastic bag that is tightly closed (you don't want to spread the disease), and take it to a reputable nursery with a knowledgeable staff. There, they can advise you on a course of treatment. Another thing you can do is to call the County Extension Service and describe your problem to one of their trained helpers. They are happy to provide help. (Helpful numbers are located in the back of the manual.)

Disease Recognition

There are many books which discuss nothing but plant diseases and their treatments. Due to space limitations, diseases and treatments will not be discussed. However, Tables 6.3 and 6.4 explain disease classifications by symptom and should be of benefit when trying to diagnose and seek treatment for a disease.

Table 6.3: Common Disease Characteristics of Plants

Disease Classification	Description
Anthrancnose	Rust-colored spots on leaves, pods, and seeds. Caused by a certain fungi.
Blotch	Leaves with irregular shapes and sizes.
Blight	Young growing tissues of leaves and twigs affected with this disease often extend downward.
Scorch	Browning and shriveling of leaves. Caused by hot sun rays.
Cankers	Open cracks in woody plants caused by shrinking and dying of tissues.
Wilt	A lack of firmness in leaves and stems. Caused by a deficiency of water.
Damping-off	Seedlings, stems, and roots are attacked by a fungus. It kills near the ground line, causing the plants to fall over.
Rot	Large sections of a plant begin to disintegrate. Caused by bacteria or fungus infestation.
Stunts	Plants grow to an abnormally small size. Many causes, including parasites or non-parasitic agents.
Gummosis	Plants secrete heavy amounts of sap. Caused by a parasite attack (not necessarily in that portion of the plant).
Oedema	Watery swelling or galls which may be rust colored in appearance. Caused by abnormal water conditions.
Rust	Rusty infestations to ornamentals. Caused by parasites living on the hosts.
Smut	Powdery black pustules found on cereal crops like corn. Caused by fungi.
Mildew	Grayish, powdery appearance on leaves and stems. Caused by fungi.
Galls	Swellings on leaves, flowers, and roots. Caused by infeston of insects, fungi, or bacteria.
Witches Brooms	Abnormal numbers of accessory shoots along a stem. Caused by fungi.
Mosaic	Mottling of leaves with light and dark patterns and curling of leaves. Caused by a virus.
Chlorosis	Plants which normally produce green leaves experience a loss of color. Those with pale leaves may experience an abnormal greening caused by viruses or mineral deficiencies.

Integrated Pest Management is a system used in insect control. IPM practitioners monitor and evaluate each situation and take action only when a pest level is high enough that it will cause unacceptable damage.

Xeriscape for Central Texas

Table 6.4: Disease Characteristics Caused by Environmental Conditions

Environmental Cause	Description
Mineral Deficiency	Unsightly appearance or poor growth. Caused by absence of balanced diet of major or minor elements.
Chemical Injury	Plant injuries caused by improper application of fertilizers, weed killers, and pollutants.
Spray Injury	Tender, new growth is damaged by insecticide or fungicide spray drift.
Gas Injury	Ornamentals, shrub, and tree roots damaged by leaking mains and fumigants.
Lightning Injury	Tree damage cause by lightning strikes.
Electrical Injury	Plants are damaged by electrical wires or improperly placed bulbs on Christmas lights.
Mechanical Injury	Plant damage from hailstones, motor vehicles, lawnmowers, or line trimmers.
Sun Scorch	New growth is damaged by sun's rays.
Winter Injury	Trees and shrubs damaged by frost, excessive temperature fluctuations, and poorly drained soils in windy areas.

Eventually, pesticides become ineffective, and a homeowner is faced with a real problem—a pest infestation with an ineffective pesticide and no natural predators to help out.

Pest Control

The Organic vs. the Chemical Approach—Which Is Better?

We encourage all gardeners to use environmentally safe methods when approaching disease and pest control, and hope that chemicals will be used only as a last resort. Home gardeners are temporary stewards of small sections of land. It is our responsibility to use products that will maintain the health of our friends and neighbors, protect our limited water resources, and preserve the environment. Because of this, we encourage the use of Integrated Pest Management (IPM) within the home landscape.

What Exactly Is Meant by Integrated Pest Management?

Integrated Pest Management is a system used in insect control. IPM practitioners monitor and evaluate each situation and take action only when a pest level is high enough that it will cause unacceptable damage. The old-fashioned rote calendar method of pest control is discouraged in IPM.

The Main Objective of IPM

In this type of program, pests are not completely eradicated. Instead, they are suppressed to an acceptable level. The goal in IPM is to attempt to maintain a biological balance. Why? Well, if a particular pest is completely eradicated, its natural enemies (effective natural predators) will also disappear, thereby causing an inbalance. In addition, when pesticides are used to completely eradicate a pest, there are always a few survivors. These survivors often build-up

116

resistance to a pesticide and pass that trait on to their offspring. Eventually, pesticides become ineffective, and a homeowner is faced with a real problem—a pest infestation with an ineffective pesticide and no natural predators to help out. So, in the long run, it is better to have a few pests that can be monitored rather than risk the consequences of eradication.

The Best Pest Management Strategy

To achieve long-lasting results against pests, the best strategy is to do away with the requirements that allow a particular pest to thrive. This can be done by the following practices:

- Choose appropriate types and mixes of plant species.

- Practice good plant and animal husbandry.

- Make sure to maintain buildings so that they do not become homes for pests.

- Carefully redesign landscapes or structures within the grounds.

- Make sure that landscape sites are contoured to create good drainage.

- Manage organic wastes so they do not pile up and harbor insects.

The Four Steps To IPM

1. Be sure that you properly identify pests in your landscape: a majority of insects are beneficial.

2. Take the time to learn about the pests' biology and its habits: this helps to pick the best control.

3. Decide whether the pest is really doing irreparable harm. Remember, plants have many chemical strategies to fight back—sometime the best thing to do is nothing.

4. If pest control is needed, try to use a method that is the least toxic—one that is specific to that pest and has proven effective.

Major IPM Control Methods

PHYSICAL CONTROLS

Traps. Found at many nurseries or home constructed, these employ lures like baits, colors, hormones, or light to control pests.

Barriers. These can also be found at nurseries and are designed to keep pests at a controllable level.

Hand-picking. Sometimes this is the best method for larger pests like caterpillars, snails, or slugs. Make sure to destroy the pest after removal.

High pressure mists of water. This is a good way to get rid of slow movers.

NATURAL PREDATORS AND BIOCONTROLS

Common and easily obtained, Ladybugs will not necessarily stay in the garden after the problem is eradicated.

Lady Beetles (Ladybugs). Common and easily obtained, they will not necessarily stay in the garden after the problem is eradicated.

Lacewings. Bright green and delicate in appearance with lacy wings, their larvae are voracious eaters of many garden pests. Eggs are available through mail order companies.

Praying Mantis. This predator eats both good and bad insects, and each other at times. They must be hatched from a chrysalis and should be spread around to prevent them from eating one another.

Trichogramma Wasps. These tiny wasps are parasites that attack the eggs of over 200 types of pests, preventing those eggs from hatching. Plant wasp eggs in the garden in the springtime.

Other Types of Natural Predators. Birds, lizards, toads, spiders, paper wasps, ground beetles…and many, many more.

BIOLOGICAL CONTROLS

Bacillus thuringiensis (Bt). This is a naturally-occurring bacteria. There are several varieties available, each of which is geared toward a specific use (make sure to find out the correct variety to purchase for your problem). It works by releasing a protein which causes a crystalline formation inside the pest's gut. This destroys the gut lining, the pest stops feeding, and eventually dies. It is not harmful to animals or other beneficial insects.

Avermectins. These antibiotics are formed by bacteria which occur naturally in the environment. A downside of this control is that it can harm mammals and aquatic life, so use with care.

Beneficial Nematodes. These look like worms through the lens of a microscope, and that is what you'll need to see them. They attack pests that dwell in the soil by boring into the pest's body and releasing a toxic bacteria. This type of nematode is a completely different critter than the nematodes that do so much damage in the garden. They are purchased as pastes or powders.

SAFE ALTERNATIVES

Pyrethrum. Made from dried blooms of the chrysanthemum plant, the synthetic form is called pyrethroids, and it controls many pests. Watch out for the additives in pyrethrum products, as some may not be environmentally-friendly.

Neem. This is a compound that is formed from the neem tree of Africa and India. It works as a repellent, a growth regulator, and insect poison. It is a great product that doesn't harm beneficial insects.

6—Maintenance: How to Clear Uncultivated Ground

Retenone. This natural insecticide comes from several plants native to South America. It should be used with care as it is toxic to fish, and run-off water containing retenone could cause environmental damage.

Diatomaceous Earth (DE). Looking like a whitish powder, DE is composed of the pulverized and fossilized remains of ancient sea algae. It works by sticking to pests and destroying their outer skeleton, causing them to dry up. DE needs to be kept dry to work effectively.

Horticultural Oil. This works by blocking an insects' breathing, smothering them. It also damages insect egg development and can be used in warm or cool weather. It may damage plants and harm beneficial insects as well, so use carefully.

Insecticidal Soaps. These specially formulated soaps contain Potassium Salt of Fatty Acids, which penetrate insect bodies and cause the collapse of cell walls.

How to Clear Uncultivated Ground

This can be done in a number of ways. However, remember that this is not an easy process, and it is best to do in small incremental stages, rather than trying to tackle a huge expanse (with the exception of lawn installation) at once. Some of the ways this can be accomplished follow.

Weed Control

Weeds are the scourge of all gardens. They are true survivalists and are designed specifically to conquer new territories, including the blank spaces in your landscape. While weeding is an ongoing battle, the amount of weeds in a garden can be significantly lessened by following three main principles listed below.

Weeds are true survivalists and are designed specifically to conquer new territories, including the blank spaces in your landscape.

Ways to Limit Weeds in the Home Landscape

- Limiting light to bare ground also limits weeds. In lawns, this means mowing a little higher than normal. In beds, this means mulch, mulch, mulch.

- Stay on top of weed control. When you see one, reach down and remove it. Try to prevent weeds from getting established. Regular hoeing also prevents weed establishment.

- Prevent weeds from flowering and seeding. Cut them down. Dig them up. Treat them. Keep those multitudes of seedlings from dispersing into nearby areas on windy days.

Xeriscape for Central Texas

Table 6.5: IPM Control Table

Pest	Physical Controls	Natural Predators/ Biocontrols	Alternatives
Aphids	• Pressure Spray	• Lady Beetle & their larvae • Lacewings • Syrphid Fly larvae • Parasitic wasps	• Insecticidal Soaps • Neem • Retenone • Pyrethrum • Diatomaceous Earth • Horticultural Oil
Caterpillars	• Hand-pick • Barriers	• Bt • Birds • Spined soldier or pirate bugs • Trichogramma or paper wasps	• Insecticidal Soaps • Neem • Diatomaceous Earth
Chinch Bugs	• Traps - drag flannel cloth over infested area.	• Pirate bugs • Lady Beetles • Lacewings • Birds	• Insecticidal Soaps • Neem • Diatomaceous Earth
Cucumber Beetles	• Hand-pick • Barriers	• Beneficial nematodes • Tachnid fly	• Neem • Rotenone • Pyrethrum
Fall Webworms	• Prune affected branches to destroy nests.	• Bt • Paper Wasps • Birds • Predatory Stinkbugs • Tiny parasitic wasps	• Insecticidal Soaps • Horticultural Oil
Fleas	• Flood affected areas to drown larvae.	• Nematodes • Ants	• Insecticidal Soaps • Pyrethrum • Diatomaceous Earth • Growth-regulating products like Methoprene
Fire Ants	• One gallon of near-boiling water poured over mound just after sunrise.	• Nematodes • Native Ants	• Rotenone • Pyrethrum • Boric Acid • Avermactins • Diatomaceous Earth • Citrus-based drench
Leaf Cutter Ants	• Barrier of teflon-coated tape around vulnerable vegetation.	• Other types of ants. • Toads • Lizards	• Bait products with hydramethylmon
Mosquitoes	• Screens • Mosquito netting • Protective clothing • Citronella candles	• Bt • Mosquito fish (Gambusia) • Purple Martins & Bats • Spiders • Water-striders & Dragonflies • Frogs & Toads	• Wearing insect repellents. • Surface oils applied to standing water. • Treat breeding sites with growth regulator such as Methoprene.
Snails/Slugs	• Hand-pick • Snail & slug traps with stale beer bait.	• Bt • Decollate beetles • Ground beetles • Raccoons • Ducks & chickens	• Diatomaceous Earth • Poison baits in protected containers.
Ticks	• Hand-pick • Trap—white flannel cloth dragged over affected area.	• Fire Ants • Beneficial Nematodes	• Diatomaceous Earth • Pyrethrum
White Grubs	• Hand-pick • Spike soil with aerator sandals.	• Beneficial Nematodes • Milky spore disease	• Pyrethrum
Whiteflies	• Trap—handheld vacuum can be used to remove adults from plants.	• Parasitic wasps • Predatory beetles	• Insecticidal Soaps • Horticultural Oil • Growth inhibitors like Kinoprene.
Yellowjackets	• Traps	• Skunks & raccoons will dig out nests that have honey poured around the entrance (do this at night).	• Pyrethrum • Baits with slow acting poisons or growth regulators.

6—Maintenance: How to Clear Uncultivated Ground

Table 6.6: Ground Clearing Methods

Clearing Method	Remarks
Organic sprays (Example: pickling vinegar at a 10% solution)	Works within 1 - 4 days. Does not stay in the soil
Chemical sprays (Glycosate, sold as Roundup or Finale)	Works within 1 - 4 weeks.
Physical digging	Time consuming and hard work.
Mechanical digging	Fast, but may compact lower soil areas.
Clear Plastic	Somewhat slow. Unsightly. Wet ground is covered with a sturdy clear plastic using soil to seal the edges. Leave in place for 6 weeks during the growing season. This supposedly cooks the weeds and ungerminated weed seeds. However, it destroys many beneficial soil microbes as well.

The Importance of Mulch

One of the best ways to prevent weeds after clearing a section of land is to use mulch. This is a great organic way to prevent weeds, keep the soil moist, and provide nutrients to the soil as the mulch breaks down. In addition, mulch provides a cooling effect to the soil in the summer and keeps plants warmer in the winter. In short, mulch is a must.

Mulch is a great organic way to prevent weeds, keep the soil moist, and provide nutrients to the soil. In addition, mulch provides a cooling effect to the soil in the summer and keeps plants warmer in the winter.

How Much Mulch Should Be Used?

Generally speaking, it is best to keep mulch depths to 4" and under. Too much mulch can inhibit water and oxygen penetration, and too little mulch can encourage weed growth.

Good Weeds—Is There Such a Thing?

While a yard tangled full of weeds can be neighborhood nightmare, weeds can be beneficial in certain conditions. How? Well, consider the following jobs that weeds perform. They can:

- Shade and cool the ground.
- Prevent erosion.
- Balance soil minerals.
- Serve as pioneer plants.
- Build soil through nitrogen fixing.
- Serve as indicators of soil deficiencies.
- Act as companion plants.
- Repel insects.
- Act as wicks, transporting water from deeper to shallower soils, and making it available to other plants.

Xeriscape for Central Texas

Generally speaking, it is best to keep mulch depths to 4" and under. Too much mulch can inhibit water and oxygen penetration, and too little mulch can encourage weed growth.

Table 6.7: Organic Mulch Chart

Type of Organic Mulch	How to Use	Pros & Cons
Shredded leaves (Avoid using unshredded Live Oak leaves. They are slow to break down and do not allow adequate water penetration.)	• 4" layers	• Easily blows or washes away. • Thin layers will not inhibit seedlings.
Straw	• 2" - 4" layers. Use in berry or vegetable beds. Can be used as winter mulch around fruit trees.	• Weed seeds often abound in straw.
Compost	• 3" - 4" layer in ornamental or vegetable beds.	• Seed germination possible if used in thin layers. May blow away with the wind.
Pine Needles	• Use around bushes and trees.	• Adds acid to our alkaline soils. • Not readily accessible in our area. • Will float or blow away.
Bark Chips	• Use around shrubs and trees. • Use a 2" - 4" layer in perennial flower beds.	• Inhibits seedling emergence. • Won't easily blow away, but certain types may float away in heavy rains.
Bark Mulch	• 2" - 4" layer used in ornamental beds.	• Slowly breaks down so must be reapplied seasonally.
Coarse Shredded Bark (Example: Cypress which does not float and lasts a long time.)	• 2" - 4" layer used in flower and vegetable gardens. The only mulch which works well on slopes.	• Seeds can still germinate if applied in a thin layer. • Will not smother bulbs.
Grass Clippings	• 4" - 6" layer in flower or vegetable beds.	• Good source of nitrogen. • May introduce weed seeds. • Can be blown away by wind. • Bermuda clippings may root in the beds if conditions are good.
Newspaper (Black print only, as colored ink contains heavy metals which are poisonous.)	• Overlapping sheets (approx. 10 to 15 sheets thick) around plants.	• Slow to break down. • Ugly. • Requires some sort of covering to keep it from blowing away. • Inhibits seedling emergence.

6—Maintenance: How to Clear Uncultivated Ground

Table 6.8: Inorganic Mulch Chart

Type of Inorganic Mulch	How to Use	Pros & Cons
Black Polyethylene Plastic	• Temporary weed prevention used under rock or bark. • Seen used around warm weather crops, e.g., melons, tomatoes, squash.	• Forms an unhealthy barrier to water and air. • Seedlings cannot germinate. • Warms the soil, which increases warm weather crop yield.
Perforated Black Poly-ethylene Plastic	• Temporary weed prevention used under rock or bark. • Seen used around warm weather crops, e.g., melons, tomatoes, squash.	• Water and air penetration possible. • Warms the soil, which increases warm weather crop yield.
White Plastic	• Used around certain fruits and vegetables which like cool roots.	• Cools the soil. • Forms an air and water barrier. • Will prevent seedling emergence.
Aluminum Foil	• Used around members of the cabbage family.	• Helps keep roots cooler. • To allow water penetration, poke holes in the foil. • Will blow away. Must be weighted down. • Inhibits aphid infestation. • Will prevent seedling emergence.
Black Weed Barrier Fabrics	• Used around warm weather crops. • Can be used under rock or bark chips.	• Warms the soil. • Breaks down quickly. • Air and water penetration possible. • Will prevent seedling emergence. • When mulches on top of fabric decay, a new layer of growing media is created on top of the barrier.
Decomposing Barrier	• Used as a cover to seeded areas or to cover young seedlings.	• Discourages weed growth until roots and seeds are most established. Can later be incorporated into the soil.
Remay (non-woven lightweight white fabric)	• Used to cover seeded areas and young seedlings. May also be used to protect delicate crops such as lettuce as they mature.	• Keeps the soil temperature moderate. • Evaporation reduction. • When mulches on top of fabric decay, a new layer of growing media is created on top of the barrier.
Rock	• Good around pathways and patios. • Lines stream beds or drainage ways. • Used in rock garden and around heat loving plants. • Provides accent.	• Collects and re-radiates heat. • Finer-type gravels stay in place. • Water and air can penetrate. • Tough to weed.

- Attract beneficial insects.

- Provide seeds and nesting places for birds.

Granted, weeds should not be grown in conditions where they compete with ornamental and cultivated plants. But, in certain settings, they are appropriate. Think before trying to completely eradicate all of the weeds in your landscape.

How Can You Tell a Bad Weed from a Good Weed?

This is difficult to do. Probably, the best thing to do is to determine how easy the weed can gain a foothold in the garden by the way it grows. Some of the following growth habits could indicate an invasive type of weed.

- Underground creepers and above ground creepers.

- Plants with long tap roots.

- Plants with storage roots that break off in the soil.

Avoid weed-and-feed products. When applied anywhere near the root zones of trees (and remember tree roots wander far and wide), weed-and-feed products can cause irreparable damage to those trees.

Lawns

Maintenance of Newly-Planted Seed Lawns

FEEDING NEWLY-SEEDED LAWNS

Newly-planted lawns don't need fertilizing until they have been mowed at least five times. The reason for this has to do with leaf versus root growth. Fertilizers encourage the lush growth of leaves. Leaves grow at the expense of roots and, in new lawns, establishing a strong root growth is the most important goal. Slow release fertilizers are recommended. Look for those with ratios such as 3-1-2, 12-4-8, or 15-5-10. Avoid weed-and-feed products. When applied anywhere near the root zones of trees (and remember tree roots wander far and wide), weed-and-feed products can cause irreparable damage to those trees. Before doing any type of feeding, however, take a few minutes to calculate the square footage of your lawn, since most fertilizer applications are calculated this way.

WATERING

New lawns haven't yet established a good root system. The best thing to remember is to keep the lawn lightly watered at regular intervals during the initial germination and growth period. The seed needs to be kept moist, but not saturated during this initial growth time. During hot, windy days, this may necessitate watering 4 to 5 times per day. Remember that if young plants are allowed to dry out, they will die. After about two weeks, a good root system should be established, and then the water frequency can be reduced to once every five days for about one month. Then, treat the lawn like an established turf area.

MOWING

Begin mowing lawns when the grass is about 3" (7 cm.) high. Mow at recommended heights. If the new lawn is Buffalo grass, remember that mowing is optional.

Maintenance of Newly-Sodded Lawns

FEEDING NEWLY-SODDED LAWNS

Use the same feeding practices for turf-type lawns as with seeded lawns (see above).

WATERING

Newly-planted turf should not be deprived of water. Drying causes shrinking between sod squares, creating unsightly gaps. Until such time as a corner of a section of sod can no longer be easily lifted, the soil beneath the sod needs to be kept moist. It is imperative to use the sprinkler lightly and often during this period. As soon as the grass begins to look green and begins to stand up, it has rooted. After the sod roots, cut back on the watering to every three days (except when it rains), and continue the three day routine for two weeks. Thereafter, begin to water on a five-day schedule.

MOWING

When the grass reaches a height of about 3" (7 cm.) high, recommended mowing practices can begin.

Maintaining Established Lawns

FEEDING ESTABLISHED LAWNS

Established lawns can be fed with a variety of materials. Some of these are:

- Slow-release organic fertilizers.
- Slow-release chemical fertilizers.
- Compost.
- Slow-release blood, fish, and bone meal in early spring.
- 'Dillo Dirt.

HOW CAN I TELL WHEN MY GRASS NEEDS TO BE WATERED?

You will do yourself and your grass a big favor by waiting until it shows signs of drought stress before watering. These signs are:

- A dull, purplish cast to the lawn.
- Tracks show up in the lawn as someone walks across it.
- Leaf blades begin to roll or fold together.

When lawns are allowed to stress somewhat between waterings, grasses do exactly as they are designed. They send their roots deeper into the soil in search of water. If grasses are spoiled with

When lawns are allowed to stress somewhat between waterings, grasses do exactly as they are designed. They send their roots deeper into the soil in search of water.

Xeriscape for Central Texas

The very best time to water is before 10:00 A.M. This is because winds are normally quiet, and sprays won't be carried off into the atmosphere. Also, at this time of the day, the temperature is low and little water is lost due to evaporation.

frequent waterings, the roots have no reason whatsoever to go in search of water, and they stay close to the surface. And if they stay close to the surface and a stressful condition occurs where they need extra reserves provided by the roots, they won't have anything extra to give.

HOW MUCH SHOULD I WATER?

This is determined by factors such as soil type, slope, fertilizer, management factors, and water quality. During the summer, an average lawn requires an application of 1" of water every 7 to 14 days. Remember, big droplets go into the ground and fine droplets simply float away. Make sure to adjust your sprinkler to emit large droplets.

WHEN IS THE BEST TIME TO WATER?

The very best time to water is before 10:00 A.M. This is because winds are normally quiet, and sprays won't be carried off into the atmosphere. Also, at this time of the day, the temperature is low and little water is lost due to evaporation. The next best time to water is after 7:00 P.M. Some grasses are more susceptible to disease when staying wet all night, but these instances are uncommon in Central Texas.

WHAT IS AERIFICATION?

After a lawn has been in for awhile, the top 1 to 2 inches of the soil may become compacted through typical traffic. When this happens, less oxygen can enter the soil and less carbon dioxide can escape. This is a bad situation, since the roots of turf grass require oxygen intake as well as a carbon dioxide escape. As the soil becomes increasingly compacted, the turf will look thinner and thinner until it no longer can support turf growth.

This is where a machine called a core aerator comes in. This machine has hollow metal tubes called tines which help relieve compaction by pulling out small plugs as it is pushed across the lawn. The resulting small holes become a way for the oxygen and carbon dioxide to make their way in and out. This encourages root growth around the holes and increases the vigor of the grass.

Some lawns never require aerification. Other highly trafficked areas require it frequently. The best time to do this is when the turf-grass is actively growing.

DRAINAGE

Improve drainage by aerating the soil. Heavy soils with poor drainage will have a tendency to become waterlogged. To improve this condition, aerate the soil and then brush coarse grit (granite sand is a good choice) into the core holes. Light soils will drain too quickly and can cause a brown appearance to the grass. If this is the case, compost can be added in the core holes.

WEEDING

If the grass is grown at an appropriate height and not cut too low to the ground, weeds will have little chance to become established (see Table 6.9). Weeds which do make an appearance can be spot treated (organically or with chemicals) or dug out.

PRE-EMERGENTS & WEEDS

Pre-emergents are great when annual weeds are a problem. This type of product eliminates certain types of weed *seeds* before they can germinate. If this type of product is used, make sure to use one which is listed for your variety of grass. Areas with longer growing seasons may require pre-emergents in the spring and fall.

THATCH BUILD-UP AND HOW IT CAN BE CONTROLLED

Thatch is a build-up of decomposing organic material produced in the natural life span of the grass. While a certain amount of thatch is good in that it protects the lawn from traffic, too much thatch (over 1/2 inch) is detrimental because it reduces water and air movement into the soil. It can also harbor insects and disease and slow the release of fertilizers and insecticides into the soil. To check for thatch, probe deeply into the soil and remove a small plug of turf. Measure the amount of thatch and if it is deeper than 1/2 inch, take steps to dethatch the turf.

Thatch is a build-up of decomposing organic material produced in the natural life span of the grass. While a certain amount of thatch is good in that it protects the lawn from traffic, too much thatch (over 1/2 inch) is detrimental because it reduces water and air movement into the soil.

The best time to dethatch is in early spring, just before the grass turns green again. Specialized dethaching machines are available. If using this type of equipment, make sure the blades penetrate just to the soil surface and no deeper. Dethatching can also be done with a garden rake by raking vigorously across the grass surface and gathering together the resulting piles of built-up materials.

Note: Do not use dethatching blades on your rotary mower. They damage warm season grasses.

TO AVOID THATCH, FOLLOW THESE GUIDELINES:

* Avoid soluble nitrogen fertilizers at rates of more than 1 lb. nitrogen per 1,000 sq. ft. per application.

* Pesticides should be avoided as much as possible.

* When mowing, avoid mowing more than 1/3 of the leaf blade.

* Water thoroughly and only when the grass needs it.

LAWN REPAIRS

Lawns can be repaired by hatching (crisscross scoring the affected areas) and reseeding. Areas needing repair can also undergo replacement with new sod.

Xeriscape for Central Texas

Important Mowing Facts

The 1/3 Rule

How frequently do you mow? The frequency between mowings should not be determined by the day of the week. Rather, it should be determined by factors such as seasonal growth demands. A rule of thumb is that *no more than 1/3 of the existing green foliage should be removed at any one mowing.* Also, try to remember that there are many chemical processes which go on each time the grass receives a wound from the lawnmower blade. So that the wound can heal quickly, inner compounds are needed from the plant. To make these compounds, the plant has to dip into food reserves. Mowing too often requires the grass to frequently dip into these reserves, gradually causing a weakened condition.

No Close Shaves, Please!

When mowing it is important to remember to *never, ever shave the lawn too close.* Contrary to popular belief, this doesn't create less of a maintenance problem, it creates more maintenance. Cutting a lawn too close can encourage bare spots. These bare places encourage weed invasions. It also destroys the food producing leaf blade.

Keep Aware of Grass Height

Conversely, *it isn't wise to let a lawn get too high before mowing.* Leaf blades can be completely sheared when waiting too long in between mowing times. If this happens, you will be left with a dead-looking yard and stressed turf. Remember, lawns need grass blades to collect oxygen and sun so that they can undergo their chemical process and make food. Removing too much of a leaf blade severely reduces the plant's ability to do this job.

Lawn Clippings Are Free Food

Try to *avoid carting away lawn clippings.* These are also a great source of free food. Lawns mowed with mulch type blades have small clippings returned to them. These mulched clippings are an excellent source of instant food. Mulching mowers return the equivalent of one fertilizer application per year.

Sharp Blades Do Make a Difference

Make sure to use a sharp blade when mowing. Not only does this practice make a neater looking lawn, it is also better for the grass. A straight cut takes less energy from the plants' food reserves to heal than does one that is jagged.

A rule of thumb is that no more than 1/3 of the existing green foliage should be removed at any one mowing.

MOWING HEIGHTS

Mowing heights vary depending on the type of grass. Table 6.9 lists suggested mowing heights and intervals.

Table 6.9: Recommended Mowing Heights For Turf

Type	Mowing Height	Mow Again When
Common Bermuda	3"	4"
Hybrid Bermuda	1" - 2"	2" - 3"
St. Augustine	3-1/2"	4-1/2"
Zoysia	1-1/2" - 2"	2-1/2" - 3"
Buffalo (mowing is optional)	4"+	5"

Trees

What we often call a tree is, in fact, a treelike shrub. So, this a good time to give a definition of a tree. *Trees* are perennial plants that bear a single woody stem at ground level. Trees can range in heights from 2' to 100' or more, depending on the species.

Feeding Trees

If an ornamental tree is planted in nutrient-rich, well drained soil, it doesn't necessarily need annual fertilization. However, if a tree appears to have difficulty in growing, fertilizing may help. Whatever the type of fertilizer used, it should be applied around the drip line of the tree. This is the area that is directly below the outermost branches of the tree. The tree's feeder roots are located below this area. In the past, homeowners were encouraged to place fertilizer in small holes dug in the soil along the drip line. However, current studies show that this is not necessary. Fertilizer that is broadcast across the surface is just as effective.

How can you tell if a tree needs fertilizing? Look for the following signs:

- Annual twig growth is short.

- Leaves are light green or yellow.

- Leaves appear smaller than normal.

- Branch tips appear to be dying back.

- Foliage appears wilted.

- Leaves have an abnormal amount of dead spots.

- Production of leaves and/or flowers is less than normal.

Once they are established, native and adapted species of trees become fairly drought tolerant and can go for long periods without significant irrigation.

Watering Trees

Newly-planted trees should receive deep, regular watering for their first year in the ground. Once they are established, native and adapted species of trees become fairly drought tolerant and can go for long periods without significant irrigation. This is especially true for native trees like our oaks. The reason they do so well in this area is because they are specifically designed to withstand seasonal drought conditions. They do not need to be pampered unless they are new to the landscape.

When watering a tree, remember that the water should be directed toward the drip line—the area beneath the outermost branches. This is where the feeder roots of the tree are located. The feeder roots are doing most of the work of seeking out water and nutrients to supply to the tree. Try to make sure the entire perimeter of the tree receives water. The best way to do this is to lay a bubbler or some other slow moving water source at different drip line spots, and let it slowly percolate into the soil.

Pruning and Supporting Newly-Planted Trees

Gardeners should remember that pruning is not a must-do type of maintenance issue. Just because you have a tree does not necessarily mean that the tree needs to undergo pruning. Try to limit pruning activities to those times that the plant really needs it.

After a tree is planted, pruning is sometimes necessary; however, only damaged and broken branches should be pruned. Recent studies have shown that the long-held practice of removing part of the top growth is not effective, and that this practice can even slow the growth of newly-planted trees.

Contrary to popular belief, supporting a tree is not always necessary either. A certain amount of swaying is required to create a vigorous tree able to withstand blasts of wind as it attains its mature size. Generally speaking, support should be provided for all bare-root trees that exceed 8 feet in height. In addition, trees that have a trunk that is 6 inches or more in diameter should also be supported. If a support system is used for a tree, it should be removed one year after planting.

The following are three ways to support a newly-planted trees:

1. *Single support* (only used with bare root trees).

   At a distance of 2 to 4 inches away from the center of where the tree is to be planted, drive a single stake (which measures about 3/4 the height of the bare root tree) into the southwest side of the tree trunk. After that, plant the tree. Then, fasten the tree to the stake with a material which will not cut into the tree using a loose loop. This method of staking does away with guy wires extending outside the planting hole.

2. *Double support*.

   At opposite sides of the tree and embedded into the firm soil beyond the planting hole, drive two parallel stakes 18 inches into the ground. After being driven in the ground, the top of the stakes should reach about two-thirds the height of the tree.

After that, the tree is supported by wires with protected loose loops wrapped around the tree trunk.

3. *Triple support.*

   Firmly fix three stakes into the soil around the edge of the planting hole, making them equal distances from each other and the hole (a triangular configuration). Stakes should be driven in at 45 degree angles and at a depth of about 18 to 24 inches. Make sure the tops of the stakes have deep notches in them to hold wire. About 2/3 of the way up the trunk, place three loose loops around the tree. Avoid using unprotected wire or rope. Using equal tightness, connect the three loops to wires fastened to the three stakes. Do not put a strain on the trunk, but rather allow for movement.

Figure 6.1: Supporting Newly-Planted Trees

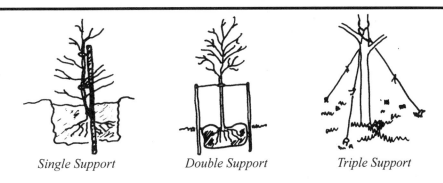

Single Support *Double Support* *Triple Support*

Pruning Established Trees

The four main reasons to prune an established tree are:

1. To train the plant into a more desirable shape.
2. To help keep the plant healthy.
3. To improve the vigor of foliage, stems, flower, and fruit.
4. To keep growth in bounds.

Gardeners should remember that pruning is not a must-do type of maintenance issue. Just because you have a tree does not necessarily mean that the tree needs to undergo pruning. Try to limit pruning activities to those times that the plant really needs it.

The Best Time to Prune Established Trees in Central Texas

The best time to prune most trees is during their dormant season. Because of the rampant oak wilt problem in Central Texas, Red Oaks and Live Oaks should not be pruned between February 15 and July 1. For these types of oaks, the optimum time of pruning is between July 1 and August 15 and also between November 1 and February 15. Prune spring flowering trees just after they finish their flowering. Fruit trees should be pruned in late fall or early winter.

The best time to prune most trees is during their dormant season. Because of the rampant oak wilt problem in the Austin area, Red Oaks and Live Oaks should not be pruned between February 15 and July 1.

Pruning Paint—The Appropriate Time to Use It

With the exception of oaks, the use of pruning paint is not advised for normal pruning jobs. Most trees have natural healing agents already in place which help to seal and heal wounds. Because oaks are currently subject to disease and insects, they should be painted within 30 minutes of cutting. Make sure to treat tools with a disinfectant like Lysol between each cut when pruning oaks.

Pruning Large, Heavy Branches

When removing large branches on trees, remember that they should be pruned back to the collar of the tree rather than flush to the trunk. The reason for this is because the collar contains a zone of protective chemicals. These chemicals are designed to help a tree heal quickly when it undergoes natural branch drop. Going beyond this collar to the trunk can remove this protective area and allow a type of fungi, which causes wood-decay, to invade the main portion of the tree trunk. If this happens, the tree can be seriously damaged.

- If you are going to cut a branch that is more than 1-1/2 inches around, try to use the three-part pruning method as explained below and shown in Figure 6.2:.

Figure 6.2: Pruning Established Trees

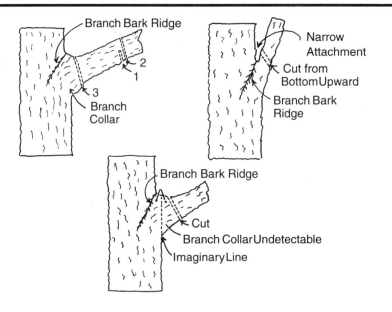

When removing large branches on trees, remember that they should be pruned back to the collar of the tree rather than flush to the trunk.

- First, look to see if the branch is going to damage surrounding limbs when it falls. If it might, rope it or support it so that it can be slowly lowered to the ground after it is cut.

- Then, going out about 6 to 8 inches away from the trunk, saw an undercut from the branch bottom, going in about one-third into the branch.

- Next, go about 3 inches out farther than you did with the undercut and make a second cut from the top, sawing until the branch falls away.
- Finally, cut the leftover stub back to the collar of the branch.

Pruning Smaller Twigs and Branches

Smaller twigs and branches also benefit from careful pruning because it promotes quicker healing. Here are some tips:

- Cut the branch back to a point where you can see a healthy looking bud or intersecting branch.
- If you cut back to a bud, take a quick look at it before pruning. The direction in which the bud points is the direction in which the new growth will head. If that isn't the effect you are aiming for, pick another bud.
- Avoid cutting too close to a bud or leaving a length of empty stub over it.
- If you want to cut back to an intersecting branch, try to choose a branch with an angle that is less than 45 degrees with the branch that you want to remove.
- Also, before cutting to an intersecting branch, make sure that the intersecting branch has a diameter that is at least 1/2 of the one you are removing.
- If a branch points upward, try to make the cut at a slanting angle. This helps prevent water from collecting and helps speed the healing process.

Figure 6.3: Pruning Smaller Branches

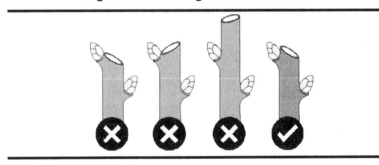

Avoid cutting too close to a bud or leaving a length of empty stub over it.

Safety Issues and Tree Pruning

While pruning make seem like a simple task, many people are injured each year by not taking the time to heed the following safety rules.

- Always, always, *always* use protective eye gear when pruning. Remember, you are normally looking upward, and pieces of bark are scattering in all directions. It is easy for one of those pieces of bark to cause serious eye damage.

Xeriscape for Central Texas

Always, always, always use protective eye gear when pruning.

- Likewise, consider using protective head gear.
- Never climb up into a tree and prune with a power chain saw. This type of saw is best reserved for cutting up firewood or lower portions of a tree.
- Use the proper tool for the job (see Table 6.10).

Table 6.10: Proper Pruning Tools

Branch Size	Proper Tool
Up to 1/2 inch in diameter	Hand pruning shears
1/2 to approx. 2 inches	Lopping shears
2 inches and up	Combination pole saw pruner
Small trees, close-up work	8-point hand saw
Heavy limbs	4-1/2 point hand saw

Shrubs

Shrubs are often mistakenly referred to as trees because of their size and form. A *shrub* is a perennial plant that bears several woody stems at ground level. They range in size from a few inches high up to 20' tall. Many can be trained into treelike forms.

Feeding Shrubs

Native and adapted shrubs go by the same fertilizing rules as do trees. If they appear to be growing well, they do not necessarily need fertilization. If a shrub does appear sickly, fertilization may cause it to green up quickly, but it may not help the underlying cause of the poor growth. Ask yourself these questions before using a fertilizer as a quick fix:

- Have these plants undergone transplant shock within the last year?
- Is the soil drainage adequate?
- Is the appropriate plant being used in the correct location?
- Are you trying to use a species of plant that is better suited to another part of the country?
- Has the plant undergone any hot or cold type of weather injury in recent times?
- Has the plant suffered injury from insect, disease, or pollution?

Physical Signs that a Shrub Needs Fertilizer

Certain physical signs are good indicators of poor nutrition. These include:

- Poor terminal (end) growth on branches.
- Leaves that appear yellow or pale green.

6—Maintenance: Shrubs

- Leaves that have a splotched appearance.

- Branches that are dead or dying back.

- Leaves that are deformed or stunted in appearance.

- Early leaf loss (this can also be attributed to a lack of water).

If a shrub does require extra feeding, the best type of fertilizer is a mulch of well-rotted manure or compost. If using another type of shrub food, try to use a fertilizer that is appropriate to your type of soil.

Watering Shrubs

WATERING *NEWLY-PLANTED* SHRUBS

After a shrub is planted, the most critical time for its success is the first year while its roots become established. It is vital that the plant receive consistent and adequate moisture during this time. This is especially important with container-grown plants. The best way to water shrubs is to water them thoroughly and deeply and then let them dry out some before watering again. A deep watering will wet the soil to a depth of about 6 inches. To do this, 1 to 2 inches of surface water is necessary. Be sure to provide adequate mulch to reduce watering frequency. When the soil is allowed to dry out some between deep waterings, the root system begins to explore for water in the surrounding area. If the plant receives frequent, light watering, roots will have a tendency to grow their roots closer to the soil's surface and wilt in between waterings.

WATERING *ESTABLISHED* SHRUBS

After woody plants become established, they appreciate a drink about every two weeks. Certain plant species that are adapted to drier climates can go even longer without irrigation. To best determine the needs of your plant, learn about its cultural requirements. This can be found in a good reference book or by learning the native habitat of your plant.

Pruning New Bare-Root Shrubs

Sometimes deciduous shrubs are sold and planted in bare-root form. If any of the roots are damaged or appear dead (lightly scratch the root surface and look for moist tissue), light pruning may be needed. Avoid shearing the uppermost branches of bare root plants as it is usually not required. If necessary, the branches can be pruned or thinned.

Pruning New Balled or Container Shrubs

This type of shrub usually requires little to no pruning, with the exception of damaged branches. If any pruning is done, it should be done judiciously to achieve a certain shape or size.

The most critical time for a newly-planted shrub is the first year while its roots become established. It is vital that the plant receive consistent and adequate moisture during this time.

Before Pruning Shrub

After Pruning Shrub

Shrubs can be shaped and kept within healthy bounds by regular pruning. The best time to do this is in late winter.

Pruning Established Shrubs

Shrubs can be shaped and kept within healthy bounds by regular pruning. Most deciduous types of shrubs (those that lose their leaves each year) respond best with a thinning out type of pruning. The best time to do this is in late winter. To thin out a shrub, cut a branch or stem off at the point where it originated. This point can be the parent stem, a branch junction, ground level, or from a lateral side branch. Thinning out older shrubs can improve their looks by opening them up and allowing for side growth. Also the plant's natural appearance can be maintained this way. This type of pruning is best done with pruning shears, beginning with the oldest and tallest stems.

If you have a deciduous shrub that is old and overgrown and want to give it a healthier look, try removing one-third of its oldest and tallest branches. This can be done at a point which is either at ground level or slightly above ground level. The best time to do this type of rejuvenation is before the year's new growth starts.

Pruning Shrubs that Flower

Some shrubs are grown specifically for their flowers. If this is the case of your shrubs, try to prune them at a time which will not disrupt their show. A general timeframe for pruning flowering shrubs is as follows:

- Prune *spring flowering shrubs* soon after they finish blooming.
- Prune *shrubs that bloom after June* in late winter.

Pruning Evergreen Shrubs

The best time to do major pruning chores on evergreen shrubs is in late winter before their new growth spurt begins. After that, light pruning can be done on-and-off throughout the year. Like deciduous shrubs, evergreen shrubs benefit from a thinning-out type of pruning method even if they are grown in a formal, sheared fashion. Avoid severely hacking back evergreens such as sprawling junipers. Once they undergo this type of amputation, they seldom recover their graceful appearance because they are unable to make new needles from the old wood.

Pruning Hedges

A beautiful hedge takes time and care to come into its own. It also takes a great deal of training and maintenance. However, to those who seek a living screen, fence, wall, or edging, a hedge may be the way to go. Hedges are not necessarily long rows of boxlike shrubs. They come in all shapes and sizes, with a rounded or a somewhat pointed shape being conformations that tend to be more successful. Hedges do not just happen and should not be attempted with a shrub that has achieved its final height. The results are usually disappointing.

In addition, a vital pruning key to maintaining attractive hedges is to make sure that the lower branches receive sun. If the lower branches get shaded out, they will have less foliage. If a boxed form of a hedge is your goal, make sure to trim the top narrower than the bottom so the sunlight can reach the lower leaves. Here are some general guidelines for pruning specific types of shrubs.

Proper Pruning Technique

Table 6.11: Pruning Practices for Shrubs

Shrub	Pruning Practice
Slow growing shrubs.	Trim before growth exceeds 6-inches.
Faster growing shrubs.	Trim before growth exceeds 1-foot.
Overgrown, badly shapen, or thin-bottomed deciduous shrubs.	Prune back to 1-foot below desired height before new growth begins in spring. Thereafter, carefully trim for the next few years until plant achieves desired look.
Evergreen hedge rejuvenating.	Do not severely prune. Needles will not come back on bare wood. Replace hedge.

Improper Pruning Technique

A vital pruning key to maintaining attractive hedges is to make sure that the lower branches receive sun. If the lower branches get shaded out, they will have less foliage.

Pests and Diseases

There are a number of pests and diseases which attack shrubs. Check plants regularly, and treat only when necessary.

Ground Covers

Ground covers are low growing plants that are often used as turf replacement or to cover large expanses of bare ground in a landscape.

Weeds and Ground Covers

One of the most important maintenance issues associated with ground covers is weed suppression. Making sure that weeds are kept out of ground covers is key to their looking their best. It is nearly impossible to kill off a vigorous clump of bermuda or nutgrass growing within an established bed of ground cover without the use of chemicals.

TIPS FOR KEEPING WEEDS OUT OF GROUND COVER

- Prepare beds destined for ground covers far in advance of their planting time, taking care to completely eradicate weeds and grasses. Remember, all it takes is one sprig or root of some types of weeds for the weeds to re-establish themselves.

- After ground covers are initially planted, make sure to add a 3" to 5" layer of mulch around the plants to keep annual weeds from sprouting. Do this after the soil has warmed in the spring.

- When the ground covers are first planted, try to work a weekly visit to the ground cover bed into your routine. Pull up any weeds that are making an appearance. Place the weeds in a bag, and get rid of them.
- For weeds that have invaded established ground cover beds, a post-emergent herbicide may be a necessity. Make sure to read the label to see if the herbicide will do any damage to your ground cover when deciding to go this route. Always spray herbicides when winds are still.

Watering Ground Covers

When first planted, young ground cover plants should receive regular watering so that their root systems can become firmly established. This is especially important their first year in the ground. After they become established, ground covers do not need to be watered as frequently. However, when they are watered, follow the practice of irrigating deeply so that the roots receive adequate moisture.

Trimming Ground Covers

There are numerous ways to keep ground covers neat. Line trimmers, mowers, and hand pruning are three of the more common methods. The method of keeping your ground cover bed should depend on the type of plant that is being used. The main thing to remember is that ground covers do require tidying from time-to-time. Ignoring this part of maintenance will result in a scraggly looking appearance.

Ground Cover Pests and Diseases

Depending on the type of plant used, pests and disease may be a factor in ground cover maintenance. If a serious infestation occurs, refer to the pages covering Pests and Disease in this chapter and treat as needed.

Antique Roses

Feeding Antique Roses

Roses are heavy feeders, and that is why soil formulas designed specifically for their needs are often seen in stores. Because they are heavy feeders, their vigor and flowering capabilities are increased with frequent applications of fertilizers. Well-rotted cow manure or compost are great fertilizers to use with roses. If used, spread it around the base of the plant in the winter.

A number of commercial varieties are also available. If using one of these, apply a large tablespoon of the fertilizer to the plant

Roses are heavy feeders, which means their vigor and flowering capabilities are increased with frequent applications of fertilizers.

6—Maintenance: Antique Roses

every four to six weeks. Look for numbers such as 6-10-4 or 8-8-8. Continue this feeding practice until approximately two months before the first frost is expected.

Fertilizing Practices for Antique Roses

Commercial fertilizers should be applied to roses according to the time of flowering:

- Begin feeding *everblooming roses* after the first set of blooms begins to fade.

- Fertilize *one-time bloomers* eight to ten weeks after planting.

Watering Antique Roses

Most modern types of roses require watering on a consistent basis. Antique roses are much more drought tolerant, many even enduring in abandoned sites. Despite this fact, old antique varieties enjoy supplemental watering as well. After their initial establishment, roses need deep watering at 7 day intervals. You can help keep diseases at bay by using a watering practice that keeps the foliage dry.

Pruning Antique Roses

Whether using a modern hybrid or an old variety, all roses require some pruning to keep them vigorous and to keep their flowering profuse. Pruning shears and loppers should be the only tools necessary. Areas on roses which require specific attention are branches which are:

In Austin, the best time to thin out most roses is between February and mid-March. Roses can also be pruned back in mid-August to promote fall flowering.

- Weak and growing toward the center.

- Dead, damaged, or diseased.

- Thin in appearance.

- Crossing one another.

When to Prune Antique Roses

In Central Texas, in general, the best time to thin out most roses is between February and mid-March. Roses with one-time blooms or those which are climbers should not be pruned until after their spring bloom time ends. While it is not necessary, roses can also be pruned back in mid-August to promote fall flowering. Roses which are hybrid teas, floribundas, grandifloras, and miniatures should receive a late winter pruning.

How to Prune Antique Roses

When cutting, try to make your cuts at a 45° angle, and locate the cut above a strong bud which points outward. This pushes the growth toward the outside of the plant. The cut should begin from the inside of the bush and point outward. The following considerations should be observed when pruning:

- Make sure your shears are disinfected beforehand to discourage the spread of disease. Also, make sure your shears are sharp to avoid frayed cuts that are susceptible to attacks from pests and fungus.

- Locate damaged and diseased wood. Then, cut 1-inch below that area.

- Look for weak shoots and remove them.

- Remove any branches that appear to cross or which are on the verge of crossing.

- Hard prune newly planted and older rose bushes. In older bushes, cut out one or two of the oldest canes annually.

- Cut back remaining canes, taking into account the typical growth habit of that type of rose.

- Suckers which arise from rootstock should be removed. They are light green in appearance and often have more thorns than the bush from which they appear. To remove them, dig down and pull or cut them off at the root.

Table 6.12: Antique Rose Pruning Chart

Rose Type	How Much to Prune	Pruning Time
Hybrid Teas	18" - 24" from the ground	Late Winter
Floribundas	18" - 24" from the ground	Late Winter
Grandifloras	18" - 24" from the ground	Late Winter
Miniatures	3" - 4" above ground	Late Winter
Standards or Tree Roses	6" - 10" above crown base	Late Winter
Ramblers	Remove entire length of some of the older canes, and tie new canes to a support.	After flowering ends
Ever-Blooming Climbers	Prune dead and diseased canes, then at ground level, remove 1 or 2 of the oldest canes. (Do this each season.) Finally, shorten side shoots 3"- 6" back from present growth. Keep main canes tied to some sort of support. Allow more canes for more vigorous plants, less with weaker plants.	In Fall before the first freeze

Deadheading flowers as they fade will encourage a longer bloom time.

Additional Maintenance Tips for Roses

Try to remove flowers as they fade. This is known as *dead-heading*, and will encourage a longer bloom time. This practice is especially important with the ever-blooming varieties.

Be sure to keep an eye out for pests and diseases on your plants. Early detection is the best way to prevent the problem's spread.

COMMON DISEASES OF ANTIQUE ROSES

Black Spot — A fungal disease on leaves which looks like black spots surrounded by a yellow circle. Treat with a fungicide.

Powdery Mildew — Looks like a white powder on leaves and shoots. Most often seen in the spring and fall months. Treat with a fungicide.

Herb Gardens

Feeding Herb Gardens

Most herbs benefit from a yearly top dressing of compost or well-rotted manure. A 2-inch layer of compost used as a mulch will benefit your herb garden in a number of ways. As it breaks down, it will slowly feed your herbs, weed growth is inhibited, moisture is better retained, and finally, soils are kept cooler during the warmest growing periods.

Watering Herb Gardens

Herbs should receive deep, regular watering in between rainfall. During the hot summer months, the best time to water your herb garden is between the hours of 7 P.M. and 10 A.M. Certain types of herbs require dry feet, while others require more moisture. Try to avoid indiscriminate watering practices with your herbs. Learn about their moisture requirements when you purchase them, or keep a reference book on hand so that you can make yourself knowledgeable as to their needs.

Weeding Herb Gardens

Making sure that weeds are kept at bay is a vital part of success within the herb garden, since weeds pull needed nutrients away from the herb plants. It is especially important to stay vigilant while plants are becoming established. A thick layer of mulch will help keep weeds to a minimum after seeds sprout and plants become taller.

Pruning Herb Gardens

Careful pruning on a regular basis is important to keeping your herbs in top form. This will help ensure lusher foliage growth. Avoid severe shearing of plants unless the plant has gone rampant within the garden. Many plants become unsightly in appearance and suffer from stress when they are cut back too far. It is usually

Rosemary

Making sure that weeds are kept at bay is a vital part of success within the herb garden, since weeds pull needed nutrients away from the herb plants.

Xeriscape for Central Texas

best to tip prune herbs. Of course, when harvesting a plant for leaves, you may need to harvest more than the tips. However, harvesting doesn't necessarily mean destruction. Even when collecting larger portions of the plant, try to avoid cutting back too much. Avoid pruning or reshaping plants until their bloom time is finished.

Thinning Herb Gardens

Some herbs are prolific in their reseeding tendencies. When this is the case, new seedlings should be removed before they get too much of a foothold in the garden. Examples of these are borage and balm plants.

Perennials

Perennials are any type of plant (trees, shrub, or flower) that continues to live year after year and which has a growing and a dormant season.

Perennials are any type of plant (trees, shrub, or flower) that continues to live year after year and which has a growing and a dormant season. This section discusses *herbaceous flowering perennials*—flowering plants with non-woody stems.

Feeding Perennials

While flowering perennials enjoy regular fertilization, they do not require great quantities of supplemental food to maintain their health. The following granular fertilizer (organic or non-organic) program should keep your herbaceous perennials in top shape. Make sure to water after applying the fertilizer to make it available to the plant.

- In early March, spread fertilizer throughout the beds.
- Repeat application in six-week intervals after the first application.
- Fertilize late blooming plants in late summer.

If you use compost or well-rotted manure as a fertilizer for your perennials, try applying a 2" layer each spring and fall.

Watering Perennials

Perennials require regular deep watering to maintain their best appearance. When purchasing your plants, make sure to ask about their watering requirements. Another way to determine your plants' watering needs is to learn about their background. For example, a perennial that is native to West Texas will have completely different water needs than would a perennial that is native to East Texas. Grouping plants with similar water needs together (hydrozoning) will simplify watering maintenance significantly.

> **Note**: Remember to give dormant plants an occasional drink during the winter months since the roots continue to absorb nutrients during this time.

Supporting Perennials

Some perennials get tall and top-heavy as they mature. These may need some sort of support to keep them looking tidy and to keep their stems from breaking. While there are many types of support available at retail stores, the truth is that anything can be used as a support. Some examples are bamboo canes, branches, and wire mesh netting (set on top of young plants). If stakes are used, try to make them 6 to 12-inches shorter than the height of the mature plant. Place the stake on the back side of the plant, and then loosely tie the plant to the stake using a soft material. When you tie the plant to the stake, make two loops: one around the plant and the other around the stake. If you tie the plant and stake together using a single loop, the tie may dig into the plant should the plant lean to one side or sway in the wind.

Cutting Perennials Back

Longer growing seasons such as we typically have in Central Texas can make for leggy-looking perennials. There are two times each year that perennials should be cut back:

- *Fall*: After the first frost or after foliage has died back, cut off dead leaves, stems, and flowers. Remove them from the area as they may harbor insects or disease. A layer of mulch will keep the plants protected during the colder months.

- *July* (approximately): Many perennials, like salvias, begin to look tall and leggy at this time of year. If this is the case, cut plants back by 1/3 to 1/2 to promote additional lush growth and flowering.

Marigold

Dividing Perennials

After several years, herbaceous perennials may become overgrown and crowded. This weakens their vigor. To revitalize them, divide the clumps. This is a simple process in which the plant is separated into new clumps, each with 3 to 5 healthy shoots. Try to take these from the sides of the parent plant since the middle portion of the plant usually has little to offer in the way of new growth. The best time to divide and replant perennials is during the fall months. This allows their roots to become reestablished before the fall frost sets in.

Try to avoid dividing all of the plants in one particular area at the same time. It usually takes a season for plants to regain their vigor and size. If all of the plants are divided at the same time, your bed may not look its best while it recovers.

Herbaceous Perennials and Disease

Perennials can sometimes be affected by disease, and specific plants tend to be affected by specific diseases. When purchasing a plant, it is a good idea to ask workers about possible diseases associated with that type of plant. Despite our best efforts, plants sometimes do become diseased. If, after diagnosis, the plant does not respond to treatment, pull it out of the garden and baby the surrounding plants a bit to make sure they are not stressed to the point where they can be infected. Throw diseased plants away. Do not compost them.

Another way to keep diseases to a minimum is to use sound growing practices. Making sure that plants are receiving suggested water, sun, soil and light requirements can go a long way toward preventing disease. In addition, keeping plant litter cleared can help prevent diseases or help prevent reinfestation of disease.

Annuals and Biennials

Annuals are plants that grow from seed, flower, and then die back all in one year. *Biennials* grow from seed, produce leaves and stems in the first season, then go on to produce a flower and seed out the second season.

Feeding Annuals

When fertilizer is used for annuals, it is best to apply it at the time of planting so the seeds can benefit from it. After the seeds sprout and foliage begins to make a good showing, add an additional application of a fertilizer that has a high nitrogen content. Make sure to water well after fertilizer is applied.

Watering Annuals

Annual beds need regular watering from the beginning. The key to success is to make sure the bed is thoroughly moistened, but not saturated. Allow the soil surface to dry out between waterings. A layer of mulch applied around plants will help retain the moisture and lessen irrigation frequency. Flowers can become damaged and foliage more prone to disease by use of overhead type sprinkling systems, so if possible, use a watering method (such as a drip system or a soaker hose) that doesn't cause a splashing effect around plants.

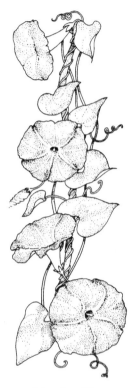

Morning Glory

Deadheading Annuals

To keep plants vigorous and to extend annual bloom time, try to remove old flower heads from plants.

Staking Annuals

If a plant attains a size that causes it to flop over, staking may be necessary. Many materials can be used as stakes. Just make sure that the stake is placed behind the plant, that a double loop is used to secure the plant (to keep the plant from getting girdled), and that the stake is 6 to 10 inches shorter than the mature height of the annual plant.

Annuals—Disease and Insects

Annuals are specifically designed to flower profusely and go to seed. To avoid disease, try to select plants which are considered disease resistant. If your annuals become diseased, carefully apply the recommended pesticide.

While insects can also be a problem, they usually do not cause significant damage. If they begin to spread, however, an insecticide may be necessary. Take care when applying insecticides as they can cause damage to annual flowers and the surrounding foliage.

Bulbs, Corms, Tubers, ...

Bulbs are underground storage organs characterized by overlapping, fleshy, scalelike leaves attached to a stem base.

Corms are enlarged underground stems which grow upright. They do not have fleshy scalelike leaves like bulbs.

Tubers are horizontal underground stems with very enlarged tips. They do not have a covering of dry leaves, nor do they have a bottom plant from which the roots can grow. They reproduce by growing roots from an eye or bud.

Tuberous roots are thick, horizontal underground stems with the stem portion located at one end and true roots located at the other end.

Rhizomes are fleshy, horizontal underground stems that produce roots on the lower surface, and extend leaves and flowering shoots above ground.

Despite the diversity of terminology in the above lists, this section will use the generic term bulb when discussing maintenance.

Annuals *are plants that grow from seed, flower, and then die back all in one year.* *Biennials* *grow from seed, produce leaves and stems in the first season, then go on to produce a flower and seed out the second season.*

> **Note**: When selecting bulbs, corms, tubers, tuberous roots, or rhizomes to use in your garden, make sure they are drought tolerant. Avoid buying the tempting selections offered in out-of-state catalogs. Most of the advertised selections will not withstand our severe climate. Check with a reputable garden center, local garden club, or landscape professional to learn what varieties are best for our area.

Feeding Bulbs

When bulbs are finished with their bloom time, lightly place a balanced fertilizer in the planting area, taking care to keep the fertilizer off of the foliage and away from the roots. Try to use one with the numbers all the same, such as 10-10-10, rather than one with a large first (nitrogen) number. Bonemeal is a good alternative. What you want to do is to make sure that the plant is getting enough phosphorus, which is the element responsible for good root growth. After the foliage has died down, apply a layer of compost to the soil.

Fading Foliage and Bulbs

After the dramatic flower show from bulbs, only the foliage portion of the bulb remains, gradually fading and yellowing. Since there is no longer a showy flower in sight, it is tempting to cut the foliage back or to tie the foliage into knots in order to neaten things up. Do not do this. Leave that foliage alone! It is performing an important job during this time. Wait until the foliage has completely yellowed before removing the leaves, since it is during this post bloom time that the leaves are harvesting the energy needed to make next year's flowers. The leaves left over after the bulbs bloom provide the underground portion of the bulb with a continuous food supply in order to do this job.

Watering Bulbs

During the hot months, bulbs benefit from a weekly drink (an exception to this are naturalizing bulbs). However, for the most part, bulbs survive very well on rainfall. Try to remember to supply water to your bulbs during their off season when they are not blooming.

Lifting and Storing Bulbs

Certain tender types of bulbs need to be stored after their leaves turn yellow. Here is how to do this:

- Take a spading fork and gently lift the bulbs from the ground. With the exception of bulbs that require a layer of dirt around them, wash the bulbs off, removing soil. Discard bulbs that appear diseased or severely damaged.

Hyacinth

After the dramatic flower show from bulbs, only the foliage portion of the bulb remains, gradually fading and yellowing. Wait until the foliage has completely yellowed before removing the leaves, since it is during this post bloom time that the leaves are harvesting the energy needed to make next year's flowers. The leaves left over after the bulbs bloom provide the underground portion of the bulb with a continuous food supply in order to do this job.

- Find a shady spot, and spread the bulbs to dry. Then, store them in a cool, dry place where temperatures range from 60°-65°. Good air circulation is important.
- Bulbs can be stored in layers. However, the layers should not exceed a depth of three layers.
- For bulbs like cannas and dahlias which require some soil to be left, store these in clumps in slightly moistened peat or sawdust in a dark place. They can be rinsed and separated just prior to planting.

Bulb Division

Dividing Bulbs

Bulbs do not necessarily need to be divided often. Many types can be left in the ground for years without suffering any harm. If, however, you notice that your bulbs are not blooming as well as they once did, it may be time to divide the bulbs. To do this, carefully lift the bulbs with a spading fork after they have bloomed and their foliage has died back. Then, separate the clumps into individual bulbs. Make sure each new bulb has a root section at its base. Replant.

Corm Division

Climbing Plants

Climbers are plants that use various parts of their anatomy to cling to a support. They may cling by tendrils, twining, leaf stalks that curl, or adventitious roots (roots growing in unexpected places).

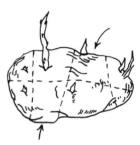

Tuber Division

Feeding Climbers

Good garden soil is usually sufficient for climbers. An occasional feeding or a top dressing of compost will go a long way toward promoting lush and vigorous growth.

Watering Climbers

Most of the climbers recommended for Central Texas will require extra water only in the drier months. During those times, water infrequently, but deeply every 7 to 10 days.

Rhizome Division

Pruning Climbers

Annual pruning will help improve the flowering of perennial climbers. Those which are annual types will not need pruning except to keep them in bounds. Early flowering varieties should be deadheaded and pruned immediately after they finish their bloom time. Those which are late season bloomers should be pruned back early in the following spring.

Training Climbers

Some climbers need support, while others are self supporting. Self-clinging climbers need only be planted at the base of a wall and pointed in the general direction of desired growth. Climbers that twine will need to have some sort of support provided—wires, trellises, and netting are all good choices. Some plants are shrub-like, but with the capability of sending out long shoots. They, too, can be used as climbers. Tie the long shoots to a support as they appear. To increase the flowering of this type of climber, pull the shoots down to where they are nearly horizontal.

Ornamental Grasses

Ornamental grasses are clumping types of grasses used to provide color, texture, and visual interest in a garden. They come in a variety of forms such as tufted, mounding, upright, upright divergent (up and out), upright arching, and arching.

Feeding Ornamental Grasses

Once established, ornamental grasses do not require special feeding regimens. However, many varieties will benefit from an annual top dressing of compost.

Watering Ornamental Grasses

Newly-planted grasses should be watered deeply and regularly until they are established. Avoid letting them dry out during this phase, as this can damage their chances for survival. Applying a thick layer of mulch around the plant will help retain moisture and reduce watering frequency. Once the plants are rooted, water frequency can be adjusted to suit the needs of the different types of grasses. Like turf grasses, different varieties of ornamental grasses require different watering needs. However, as a general rule, once established, grasses will become more drought tolerant if they receive deep watering every 10 to 14 days during the growing season.

Cutting Back Ornamental Grass Foliage

The best time to cut back foliage in most ornamental grass species is in late winter or early spring, before the new foliage begins to appear. At this time, most warm season grasses respond well to a shearing to within a few inches of the ground. Cool-season grasses and *Stipa* spp. may respond better to a less aggressive shearing. Cut them back to 2/3 of their mature size. Depending on the leaf texture and the size of the clump, hedge clippers, lopping shears, or a weed trimmer can be used. Avoid cutting grasses back in fall. Most warm season grasses are fall bloomers, and the plumes bring a great deal

The best time to cut back foliage in most ornamental grass species is in late winter or early spring, before the new foliage begins to appear.

Ornamental Grass Division

of visual interest to the garden during the fall and winter months when little else is growing.

Dividing Ornamental Grasses

Follow these simple steps to divide and transplant ornamental grasses:

1. In late winter or early spring (before new foliage appears), cut the old stems back.

2. Prepare the new beds to receive the divisions by loosening the soil to a depth of 12-inches and adding some sort of organic matter. A small amount of rock phosphate can be added to this soil to promote root growth.

3. Dig around the perimeter of the clump. Pry up the edges as you go. (*Hint*: this operation goes much quicker with two people working around the perimeter.) Once the plant is loose in the ground, lift it onto a tarp or piece of burlap beside the hole. Try to keep as much soil around the roots as you can.

4. Separate the roots of the clump with a sharp knife or by placing two garden forks back to back and prying the mass apart. Divide the old clump into four or five sections that are semi-mature in size. Discard the mid-portion of the parent clump.

5. Replant each division. Make sure that the plants are positioned at the same depth as the parent plant, then space them at least 2 feet apart. Water thoroughly, and mulch well. Continue watering until the clump is established and is well-rooted.

6. Clumps grow quickly. They will usually reach their mature size within three years.

Container Plants

Feeding Container Plants

Since container plants lose their soil's nutrients through watering, it is necessary that they receive regular feeding. Feeding them with a weekly dose of a fertilizer like liquid seaweed or animal manure during the growing season will keep them healthy and vital.

Watering Container Plants

Regular and frequent watering is essential for container plant success. During the hot, dry months of summer, container plants can quickly lose the moisture contained within their soils. In the Austin area, non-desert type container plants usually require watering every day if they are in the sun. Plants in other conditions should be watered as needed. During the winter months, water on a weekly basis when the weather is dry.

Feed container plants with a weekly dose of a fertilizer like liquid seaweed or animal manure during the growing season to keep them healthy and vital.

If you use drip irrigation, or apply just enough water to soak into the planting medium, salts may build up in the soil. Every 30 to 60 days, let water slowly run through the pot for 10 minutes. Don't let the excess water go down the drain. Rather, place the pot in an area of the landscape that needs water.

Deadheading

Make sure to remove spent flower heads to extend the flowering season of your container plants.

Plant Propagation Methods

Listed below are ways to propagate plants:

START INDOORS FROM SEED

Start seeds in one of the following:

- Sterile soil mix.
- Commercial soilless mix.
- Vermiculite (requires weekly fertilizing with an all-purpose fertilizer).
- Perlite (requires weekly fertilizing with an all-purpose fertilizer).

SEEDS SOWED IN THE GROUND

Sow seeds in early spring or early fall (depending on whether the plant is a warm-season or a cool-season type of plant). With adequate moisture, seedlings should emerge within 2 to 3 weeks. When they reach a height of 2" to 3", thin the seedlings to the recommended spacing.

CUTTINGS

Take a 3" to 6" cutting of a plant from the growing end where the newest leaves are located. Remove the leaves from the bottom 1/3 of the cutting. Moisten the bottom end of the stem, and dip the bottom end into rooting powder. Have a container with a moist (not saturated) rooting medium prepared. Poke a hole in the medium with a stick or your finger. Carefully insert the stem, and firm the medium around the stem. Place the container in a small clear plastic bag, and secure the bag with a tie. Place the cutting on a windowsill (direct sun is not necessary), and do not open it or water it for several weeks. After 2 to 3 weeks, the plant should have developed at least 1/2" roots. It can then be planted in the garden or transplanted to a container with regular potting soil.

CROWN DIVISION

This is done when the plant is not actively growing (usually in winter). Lift a growing plant from the soil. Shake off excess soil and divide into pieces, with each piece having a good supply of

Take a three to six inch cutting of a plant from the growing end where the newest leaves are located.

roots. Prune any damaged roots and replant the plant divisions. Water the replanted division, and cut back the foliage by 1/3. Avoid feeding for 2 to 3 weeks (the time it takes the plant to begin to establish its roots again).

STOLEN DIVISION

This is associated with plants which grow outward via creeping rootstock (called *stolens*). Stolen portions growing somewhat apart from the parent plant are cut away. Foliage on the newly-cut portions are trimmed back to 5" to 6". The new pieces are replanted and consistently watered until they reestablish themselves.

ROOT CUTTINGS

Roots are cut into 1" to 2" sections. The sections are then placed horizontally into a good soil and covered with soil. Make sure roots receive adequate moisture until root piece begins to reestablish itself and new leaves begin to form (usually between 2 to 3 weeks).

ROOTING IN WATER

Plant cuttings are placed in water where they form roots. Once a good supply of roots have formed, transplant the cuttings into the soil, taking care not to damage the very fragile roots.

AERIAL ROOTING

Cut just below the little knobs of tiny roots (adventitious roots) that form along the stem of certain plants. Place stem portion into a container of good soil. Place the containers in a partially shaded area to avoid sun damage. Avoid too much watering, but do carefully tend the plants for 1 to 4 weeks until they seem to be well rooted.

Tools

The Right Tool for the Right Job

Gardeners have a bewildering array of tools available for purchase at garden centers. Each performs a specific function, and it is tempting to spend a large amount of cash for the privilege of owning one of each. Equally tempting are tools that are sold at cheap prices that seem too good to be true. And those prices *are* too good to be true since cheap tools are not built to last.

So, here are three bits of sound advice for garden tool buyers:

1. If your budget is limited, buy one quality tool at a time. You will never regret it, because that well-made tool will serve you well and should last you for life.

2. Watch out for wonder tools—you know, the ones that seem to be too good to be true. They usually are.

Xeriscape for Central Texas

3. Buy a tool that fits your physical size. Avoid buying a tool that is too big or too small for your body. Tools are meant to work *with* you, not against you.

Table 6.13: Useful Large Gardening Tools

Tool		Description
Digging Fork		Good for loosening soil. Can substitute for a spade in many digging jobs. Inverted, it can serve as a rake. Buy one that is made of forged steel with a wooden or metal handle. Other types of steel can bend easier.
Spade		Stainless steel types are the best. Next best are the forged steel types. Make sure to keep it cleaned off after each use.
Lawn Rake		
Flat Rake		Buy forged steel types. The *lawn rake* is good for raking leaves, removing lawn thatch, and raking in grass seeds. The *flat rake* is invaluable for raking soil, smaller rocks, and bulky debris.
Dutch Hoe		
Swan-necked Hoe		*Dutch hoes* are pushed back and forth while you walk backward so you don't step on weeds you've already removed. *Swan-necked hoes* are used for larger weeds, digging up vegetables, and for helping to seed. An *onion hoe* is a small hoe that is used to work between closely spaced plantings. For the larger hoes, make sure you purchase one with a long enough handle. When using these, you should be able to work in a near upright position.
Onion Hoe		
Rounded Shovel		
Flat Shovel		Shovels are invaluable for transferring soil, mixing compost, or mixing cement (if ever used this way, get off every bit of concrete before it dries). *Rounded shovels* work best for digging, and *flat shovels* are better at scooping up material from a flat surface.

152

6—Maintenance: Tools

Table 6.14: Hand & Cutting Garden Tools

Tool	Description
Hand Tools	
Hand Fork	Used for weeding and mixing small amounts of soil together, stainless steel hand forks are best.
Trowel	Trowels are used for planting seeds or small plants as well as for mixing small amounts of soil. Stainless steel types are best.
File	The file is used for sharpening shovels and hoes. Professional landscapers carry one with them to quickly sharpen frequently-used tools several times a day.
Cutting Tools	
Pocket Knife	Look for a pocket knife that easily slips in and out of your pocket. This is a handy tool with uses ranging from taking quick cuttings to cutting string. Make sure your knife is kept sharp.
Pruning Saw	This tool is useful when you are faced with cutting a branch that is too large for pruners. The blade is curved and narrow, allowing easy access to tight places.
Pruners	This tool is a workhorse in the garden, but should only be used for branches that are small in diameter. There are several types of pruners available, and there is no rule that says one type of pruner is better than another. The choice is purely personal.
Loppers	Loppers are long-handled pruners used for cutting smaller branches that are too large for pruners.
Shears	This tool is used to cut hedges. Blades are long to cut a larger expanse at one time, and longer handles facilitate better leverage. Buy an expensive pair that will hold their edge longer. This will save sharpening time.

153

Cultivation Methods

Digging Heavy Soils

The best time of the year to dig heavy soils is during the fall months at a time when they are neither too wet or too dry. Dig backward and leave large clods in your wake. Avoid stepping on the newly-dug soil. During the colder months, exposure to the elements will help break the large clumps of soil down to a more workable texture.

Digging Light Soils

Light soils have a tendency to blow away and to leach nutrients. The best time to dig light soils is just before planting. Until that time, keep them covered with a mulch or a green manure crop.

Weed Removal When Digging

Take a large bucket with you when you dig. Weeds can be collected in the bucket and thrown away. Leaving them in the area may promote reseeding or an infestation from insects that enjoy living in debris.

The Five Basic Rules to Digging

1. Never, never, ever dig wet soil. If it can stick to the soles of your shoes, it is too wet.

2. Make sure to use the right sized digging tool for your body. You'll only be working at a fraction of your ability if you try to dig with a tool that is too large or too small.

3. Be kind to your back. It is healthier to dig small spadefuls of dirt rather than to try to move large, unwieldy amounts at one time.

4. Working at an easy, rhythmic pace will make the digging job much easier. Large jobs should not be done all at once. Remember, there is nothing wrong with working in stages. Stop digging when you begin to tire, since pushing your body beyond its comfort zone is dangerous.

5. Keep all your digging tools clean and sharp. When you are finished for the day, take the time to clean off your tools and dry them thoroughly to prevent rust. A light swipe with an oily rag will also help to keep rust from accumulating.

Seasonal Maintenance Guide

6—Maintenance: Seasonal Maintenance Guide

SPRING
February 1 - April 1*

Lawn Care

- Rake lawn to remove thatch build-up (if it is a problem) before grass begins to green up.
- Sow grass seeds in new lawns. Reseed bare spots as needed.
- Lay turf lawns.
- Feed lawns with a complete type of lawn food after they begin to green up.
- Apply pre-emergent weed killer (kills weed seeds) in early spring.
- Check out underground irrigation systems.
- Water as needed.

Borders

- Feed with layers of compost or all purpose fertilizer. Wait to mulch borders until April 1.
- Divide and transplant overly crowded summer and fall flowering perennials.
- Plant fall blooming bulbs.
- Plant spring annuals.
- Sow summer flower seeds.
- Plant perennials.
- Deadhead winter annuals to extend their bloom time.
- Plant ground covers.
- Cut back ornamental grasses before they begin to green up.
- Cut back frost damaged foliage (after March 1).
- Prune back ground covers.
- Water as needed.

Trees and Shrubs

- Plant trees, shrubs, and roses. Discontinue planting bare-root types after March 15. Use only container types thereafter.
- Prune trees, summer flowering shrubs, and fall flowering shrubs. (Last chance to prune area oaks is February 15).
- Prune established roses which are bush types. Wait to prune climbers and antique roses until after their spring bloom time finishes.
- Feed established roses.
- Water as needed.

*Note: This seasonal maintenance guide is for the Austin area. Other Central Texas areas may differ slightly.

155

Xeriscape for Central Texas

SPRING
April 1 - June 1*

Lawn Care

- Mow lawns as needed. Cut at recommended heights, but do not remove clippings.
- Sow grass seeds in new lawns. Reseed bare spots as needed.
- Lay turf lawns.
- Water as needed.

Borders

- Plant summer flowering bulbs (April).
- Fertilize annuals.
- Keep spring annuals lightly pruned to encourage lush growth.
- When they begin to wear out, clear cool season annual beds and replace with summer flowers.
- Plant summer or fall flowering perennials.
- Mulch annuals and perennials with 3" to 4" of compost to keep weed growth under control.
- Plant herbs in prepared beds.
- Plant ground covers.
- Water as needed

Trees and Shrubs

- Plant container shrubs, trees, and roses.
- Mulch shrubs.
- Prune climbing roses and spring flowering antique roses after bloom time is completed.
- Watch for *Black Spot* on roses.
- Prune hedges. Make sure top is narrower than bottom to encourage lush bottom growth.
- Prune spring flowering shrubs just after their bloom time ends.
- Water as needed.

*Note: This seasonal maintenance guide is for the Austin area. Other Central Texas areas may differ slightly.

6—Maintenance: Seasonal Maintenance Guide

SUMMER
June 1 - August 1*

Lawn Care

- Mow lawns as needed. Cut at recommended heights, but do not remove clippings. (*Note: Do not mow Buffalo grass after June.*)

- Check lawns for soil-borne pests or disease, and treat as needed.

- Sow grass seeds in new lawns. Reseed bare spots as needed.

- Lay turf lawns.

- Water as needed.

Borders

- Avoid planting warm season annuals or perennials after July 1.

- Fertilize flowering plants.

- Deadhead spent blossoms and prune plant tips to encourage lush growth.

- Plant summer bulbs (up until July 1).

- Mulch beds where needed.

- Keep weeds under control.

- Cut back tall, leggy flowering perennials by 1/3 to 1/2 (in July) to encourage lush growth and continued flowering.

- Water as needed.

Trees and Shrubs

- Plant container shrubs and trees (until July 1).

- Fertilize shrubs with preferred all-purpose fertilizer.

- Check shrubs for disease or deficiency symptoms, and treat as needed.

- Remove damaged wood from shrubs when necessary.

*Note: This seasonal maintenance guide is for the Austin area. Other Central Texas areas may differ slightly.

Xeriscape for Central Texas

SUMMER
August 1 - October 1*

Lawn Care

- Mow lawns as needed. Cut at recommended heights, but do not remove clippings. (*Note: Do not mow Buffalo grass after June*).

- Check lawns for soil-borne pests or disease, and treat as needed.

- Sow grass seeds in new lawns. Reseed bare spots as needed (finish by September 15).

- Lay turf lawns (finish by September 15).

- Water as needed.

- Fertilize lawns (beginning mid-September).

Borders

- Sow cool season annual seeds.

- Prepare flower beds for spring bulbs and winter annuals (September).

- Plant all types of perennials for color next year (begin mid-September).

- Transplant and divide over-crowded spring flowering perennials (begin mid-September).

- Mulch beds where needed.

- Keep weeds under control.

- Plant fall flowering bulbs (mid-August to September).

- Fertilize mums with bonemeal (September).

- Transplant and divide spring flowering bulbs.

- Water as needed.

Trees and Shrubs

- Plant container shrubs and trees (begin mid-September).

- Fertilize shrubs with preferred all-purpose fertilizer (late August).

Wildscapes

- Begin planting spring flowering wildflower seeds (September 15). (*Note: Our fall rainy season is usually Sepember 15 - October 15. If rain isn't making an appearance at this time, be sure seeds receive supplemental irrigation so they can germinate.*)

*Note: This seasonal maintenance guide is for the Austin area. Other Central Texas areas may differ slightly.

6—Maintenance: Seasonal Maintenance Guide

AUTUMN
October 1 - December 15*

Lawn Care

- Mow lawns as needed. Cut at recommended heights, but do not remove clippings.
- Check lawns for soil-borne pests or disease, and treat as needed.
- Fertilize lawns (until November 1).
- Plant cool season grasses.
- Water as needed.

Borders

- Plant cool season annuals.
- Plant spring and summer perennials for color next year (finish by December 1).
- Transplant and divide over-crowded spring flowering perennials (finish by December 1).
- Dig up and store caladium tubers (end of October).
- Plant (or divide) spring flowering bulbs (finish by mid-November).
- Fertilize bulbs, annuals, and perennials.
- Mulch beds where needed.
- Keep weeds under control.
- Water as needed.

Trees and Shrubs

- Plant container shrubs and trees.
- Cut back overly long shoots in shrubs. Avoid doing major shrub pruning jobs.
- Do not fertilize shrubs or roses at this time.
- Tree pruning can begin at this time.

Wildscapes

- Plant spring flowering wildflower seeds. (until November 1). (*Note: If rain isn't making an appearance at this time, be sure seeds receive supplemental irrigation so they can germinate.*)

*****Note:** This seasonal maintenance guide is for the Austin area. Other Central Texas areas may differ slightly.

WINTER
December 15 - February 1*

Lawn Care

- Warm season grasses will be dormant during this period.

Borders

- Keep borders well-mulched.

- Cut back the top portion of dormant perennials to neaten their appearance.

- Finish spring bulb planting.

- Plant for fall color.

- Fertilize fall blooming annuals.

- Prune finished blooms on perennials.

- Water dry areas to prevent winter damage.

Trees and Shrubs

- Prune damaged wood on dormant trees and shrubs as needed.

- Plant containerized, bare-root and balled-and-burlapped trees, shrubs, and vines (avoid planting at times that ice storms or prolonged severe freezes are imminent).

- Lightly prune evergreens to neaten their appearance. Avoid severe pruning.

- Transplant dormant trees and shrubs.

- Perform pruning on Red Oaks and Live Oaks at this time.

- Remember to give plants a drink during prolonged dry times.

*Note: This seasonal maintenance guide is for the Austin area. Other Central Texas areas may differ slightly.

Bibliography

Dimond, Don and Michael MacCaskey. *All About Ground Covers.* San Francisco, California: Ortho Books, 1982.

Hamilton, Geoff. *The Organic Garden Book.* London, England: Dorling Kindersley Limited, 1987.

Hessayon, Dr. D. G. *The Tree & Shrub Expert.* Herts, England: pbi Publications, 1983.

Hill, Madalene, Gwen Barclay, and Jean Hardy. *Southern Herb Growing.* Fredericksburg, Texas: Shearer Publishing, 1987.

IPM Plans (City of Austin packet).

Meltzer, Sol. *Herb Gardening in Texas.* Houston, Texas: Lone Star Books, 1987.

Odenwald, Neil G. and James R. Turner. *Southern Plants.* Baton Rouge, Louisiana: Claitor's Publishing Division, 1996.

Olkowski, William, Helga Olkowski, and Shelia Daar. *What Is IPM?* Michigan State University Cooperative Extension. Common Sense Pest Control IV(3), 1988. (Article)

Reiley, H. Edward and Carroll L. Shry, Jr. *Introductory Horticulture.* Albany, New York: Delmar Publishing, 1991.

Salisbury, Frank B. and Cleon W. Ross. *Plant Physiology.* Belmont, California: Wadsworth Publishing Company, 1992.

Shirey, Trisha. *Culinary Herbs For The Xeriscape,* 1997 (Handout given at a past XGC meeting).

The Antique Rose Emporium, Brenham, Texas, 1996 Reference Guide (Mail-order Catalog).

Tree Growing Guide For Austin and The Hill Country. TreeFolks (Brochure).

Welch, William C. *Perennial Garden Color.* Dallas, Texas: Taylor Publishing Company, 1989.

Welsh, Douglas F., Everett E. Janne, and Calvin Finch. *Fertilizing Woody Ornamentals.* Bulletin L-1097. Texas Agricultural Extension Service (A&M handout).

What's Bugging You? A Guide For Managing Lawn & Garden Pests (City of Austin brochure).

Woody Plants (Chapter 14 out of *The Master Gardener's Reference Book.* Provided by Texas A&M University).

Xeriscape for Central Texas

Notes & Ideas...

Chapter 7

Efficient Irrigation

In This Chapter...

Water in Central Texas

Planning for Efficient Water Use
- Maximizing Rainwater Retention
- Hydrozones
- Water Budgeting

Irrigation Equipment
- Hoses and Portable Sprinklers
- Manual and Automated Irrigation Systems
- Irrigation System Maintenance and Repair

Irrigation Management
- Water, Soil, and Plant Associations
- Scheduling Irrigation

Bibliography

Watering to supplement rainfall—irrigation—is an important part of keeping your Xeriscape looking its best. Whether your landscape is simple and casual or manicured and formal, you should irrigate it as efficiently as possible. Efficient irrigation means providing proper amounts of water at the right time. It means watering no sooner than the plants need it, but when the time is right, saturating the soil area as deeply as is necessary. This chapter will provide you with some basic information which should enable you to match your watering equipment and techniques to your landscape objectives.

Xeriscape for Central Texas

Watering to supplement rainfall—irrigation—is an important part of keeping your Xeriscape looking its best. Irrigation is especially important if you are trying to establish new plants in your landscape, and absolutely *critical* if you are doing this during the warm season. Even drought-tolerant plants may need irrigation for a few growing seasons to get them well established. Once they reach that level, plants adapted to our climate will need irrigation only during a severe drought. Less-adapted plants, however, need regular and frequent watering to maintain their health and beauty. While all seven Xeriscape principles are important in an effort to conserve water, effective and efficient irrigation is usually *the critical factor* in determining the size of your water bill.

When people think of irrigation, they often automatically think "irrigation system" (or sprinkler system). But for the well-informed Xeriscape gardener, this shouldn't be the first or only choice. Your irrigation equipment may be as straightforward as a hand-held hose, or as sophisticated as an automatic sprinkler system. Becoming familiar with various irrigation options will help you choose the right equipment for your landscape. Your goal should be to match your watering equipment and techniques to your landscape objectives.

Whether your landscape is simple and casual or manicured and formal, you should irrigate it as efficiently as possible. Yet, what do we mean by *efficient* irrigation? With efficient irrigation as your goal, your strategy should be to implement the following approach:

1. *Plan* your landscape for efficient water use.
2. *Equip* your landscape with appropriate and efficient irrigation components.
3. *Manage* your irrigation for efficiency and effectiveness.

This chapter will provide you with some basic information on each of these topics. First, however, we delve into the critical role of water in Central Texas. Becoming more aware of this issue will demonstrate *why* it is important to conserve water.

Water in Central Texas

Water is many things to many people. The drought of 1996, the worst in Texas since the 1950s, proved that water can never be taken for granted. The drought cost the state's economy $5 billion, with farmers and ranchers feeling much of that pain (*Austin American-Statesman*, 1997). Many cities and industrial plants came close to running dry. Central Texas sweated it out, like most parts of the state. Some local agencies put in place mandatory water rationing. Xeriscapers believe that the time to conserve water should not be restricted to times of drought, but should be part of our ever day lives. Dramatic population growth in many Central Texas cities strains limited supplies and requires the construction and operation of expensive water and wastewater facilities.

The drought of 1996, the worst in Texas since the 1950s, proved that water can never be taken for granted. The drought cost the state's economy $5 billion, with farmers and ranchers feeling much of that pain

7—Efficient Irrigation: Water in Central Texas

Not only is net consumption of water rising in Central Texas, but the impact of water pollution will continue to deteriorate the quality of our water supply. Non-point pollution, in particular, will continue to degrade local creeks and rivers. *Non-point pollution* is water pollution that does not come from "point" sources (such as pipes), but from parking lots, fertilized lawns, and many other aspects of urban development in general. More efficient use of water is essential if Texans are to have adequate, clean, and affordable water in the future.

Texas' conventional fresh water supplies are already almost fully developed. It is anticipated that, in our children's lifetime, many local communities will need to use more creative ways to meet the growing demand for clean water. Techniques such as water reuse, and especially water conservation, will become more critical to our future.

The State of Texas estimates that the potential total annual water savings from conservation could increase threefold between the years 2000 and 2040, saving Texans billions of dollars (TWDB, 1990). Thus, irrigating your landscape as efficiently as possible will not only lower your water bill, it will benefit the entire community. Many local water utilities now recognize the importance of water conservation and have responded by implementing rate structures that encourage responsible use.

Local Water Rate Structures

Many local municipalities use an "increasing block" rate structure for water charges. This type of rate structure tends to encourage water conservation by charging customers higher rates when greater amounts are used. At high levels of water use, rates are twice as much or more than the rates charged for low water usage. Refer to Figure 7.1 for examples of increasing block water rates (in effect during Spring 1998) used by the City of Austin and an adjacent area MUD. By limiting your use of potable water through efficient irrigation, your rates remain low. Thus, knowing how and when to water not only promotes healthy plants, but keeps money in your pocket as well.

Figure 7.1: Examples of Local Water Rate Structures

Shady Hollow Municipal Utility District Water Rates	City of Austin Water Rates
$6.60/1,000 gallons over 70,000 gallons	$4.00/1,000 gallons over 14,900 gallons
$4.50/1,000 gallons over 50,000 gallons	$2.75/1,000 gallons over 6,900 gallons
$3.00/1,000 gallons over 2,000 gallons	$2.00/1,000 gallons over 2,900 gallons
$10 Base Charge for the first 2,000 gallons	$3.90 Base Charge + $1.25/1,000 gallons for the first 2,000 gallons

Source: Austin Water and Wastewater Utility Department

Not only is net consumption of water rising in Central Texas, but the impact of water pollution will continue to deteriorate the quality of our water supply. Non-point pollution—water pollution that comes from parking lots, fertilized lawns, and many other aspects of urban development in general—will continue to degrade local creeks and rivers.

Planning for Efficient Water Use

Efficient irrigation begins with planning your landscape for efficient water use. An important aspect of this planning is determining your watering "policy." You may decide that you wish to do little or no watering after your Xeriscape has become established. Or, perhaps you consider seasonal irrigation on a modest scale to be just fine. You may even desire that a certain portion of your landscape be an "oasis," where frequent irrigation is required. (These areas are typically the highly-visible, highly-used, and/or drought-sensitive areas of your landscape.) This is appropriate in a Xeriscape as long as the "oasis" is limited in size and is irrigated efficiently. If well-planned and properly executed, all these schemes fit with the Xeriscape concept.

When planning your Xeriscape for efficient water use, consider the following water conservation techniques:

- Maximize your landscape's ability to retain rainwater.

- Use the concept of "hydrozones" in your landscape design and management.

- Create a water "budget" for your landscape to guide your overall water consumption.

Water Conservation Techniques

- *Maximize rainwater.*
- *Use hydrozones.*
- *Create water budget.*

Maximizing Rainwater Retention

Water absorption into the ground—infiltration—can be enhanced through mulching and soil conditioning. It is a good idea to amend your garden soil with organic matter, such as compost, wherever appropriate. The organic matter will bring nutrients to plant roots, and can absorb and hold more water than soils lacking it. You can also capture rainwater by incorporating drainage elements such as swales, berms, and basins into your landscape design. Elements such as these can be used in your landscape to catch and use rainwater. You might also consider using them as a subtle way to "harvest" the run-off from impervious covers such as your roof. (For more about rainwater harvesting, see Appendix G.)

Swales are long level or gently sloping landscape depressions. They can vary greatly in width and treatment, and can channel run-off or capture and temporarily store run-off. Together with *berms* (mounds), they can hold water for a few hours or even for days and let it slowly infiltrate (Mollison, 1991). Consider the following ways to slow down, capture, and retain run-off in your landscape.

- Use slightly depressed landscape areas (swales or shallow basins) in landscape areas between driveways, streets, walks, and patios to capture run-off.

- If you are building a new driveway or walkway, design the surfaces to slope into turf grass areas, planting beds, or water storage basins.

- On slopes, use swales, terraces, low retaining walls, and berms "on the contour" to channel and slow down run-off and encourage infiltration in collection basins (see Figure 7.2).

- Extend your roof gutter downspouts into the ground with slotted flexible pipe. The slotted openings in the pipe will allow the water to seep underground. The pipe should eventually open up to daylight at some point.

- Allow the run-off from downspouts to flow into a swale of cobblestone or "river-rock." The rock should be big enough to stay in place during heavy rains.

- Use collection basins, ponds, or cisterns (storage tanks) to catch run-off from impervious cover. The cisterns could even be small, such as a 55 gallon drum, and could have either a solid or open bottom (depending on intent).

Figure 7.2: Cross-Section Showing Drainage Features

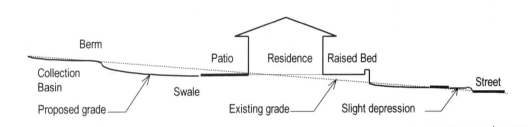

You can capture rainwater by incorporating drainage elements such as swales, berms, and basins into your landscape design. Elements such as these can be used in your landscape to catch and use rainwater. You might also consider using them as a subtle way to "harvest" the run-off from impervious covers such as your roof.

Adequate provisions for overflow should be included in any collection system to prevent possible damage from flooding. While these ideas are easier to incorporate into a new landscape, retrofitting is usually possible. Not only will your landscape plants benefit from the additional water, but there could be additional benefits to the whole neighborhood. Landscape elements such as these help to offset the impact of all the impervious surfaces (roofs, pavement, etc.) created when development occurs. Impervious cover greatly increases the amount of run-off compared with pre-development conditions. Collectively, if these were used on a more widespread scale, these design elements would tend to reduce erosion and enhance water quality for downstream inhabitants. And, as the saying goes, "we all live downstream."

Some government agencies, such as the City of Austin Watershed Protection Department, require that certain drainage facilities be built on all new developments. (Requirements, however, are highly dependent upon the location and other factors of the development.) Depending upon their function, they may be called detention ponds, filtration ponds, or something similar. While some of them are unattractive, they don't have to be and, with some forethought, can easily be made to blend into the landscape. Gradually, developers, planners, and engineers, as well as homeowners, are being educated on these issues.

Xeriscape for Central Texas

Hydrozones

A hydrozone is a landscape area with a distinct moisture regime. The reason for this moisture regime could be due to plant type, micro-climate, or other natural or cultural factors.

Becoming aware of existing or potential hydrozones in your landscape involves raising your level of consciousness. A *hydrozone* is a landscape area with a distinct moisture regime. A regime is a system of management. The reason for this moisture regime could be due to plant type, micro-climate, or other natural or cultural factors. Awareness of hydrozones will help you accurately establish the overall "water demand" for your yard.

Xeriscapes that employ the use of hydrozones take a different approach than that of traditional landscapes. In traditional landscapes, shrubs, ground covers, trees, and lawns are arranged in order to achieve a desired "look." In many cases, the results are a mix of high, medium, and low water use plant material. This kind of mixture is difficult to irrigate efficiently, especially if the mix is highly varied. Usually, to make up for any uncertainty regarding your plants' irrigation requirements, landscape caretakers will over-water a landscape. When water conservation is important, as in a Xeriscape, this approach is just too "sloppy." Although many plants are quite content with the amount of water they receive, stress, disease, and death of plants can often be attributed to over- or under-irrigation.

HYDROZONE CATEGORIES

Using a hydrozone approach, a designer or homeowner will carefully try to coordinate the moisture requirements of a specific species with soil moisture "supply." Hydrozoning is a simple landscaping principle, but highly useful to Central Texas gardeners. Since plants with similar water requirements are situated in one location, it's easier to provide them with the amount of water they need—no more, no less. Hydrozoning also:

• Allows you to budget landscape water use more accurately.

• Provides guidance and discipline to your overall landscape design and implementation.

Some commonly used hydrozone categories are described as follows.

Very Low Water Use Zones. These lowest water use zones in a Xeriscape provide the greatest savings of water when compared with the way landscaping has been traditionally undertaken. Plants in these zones are very drought-tolerant and will thrive even during typical summer drought conditions.

Low Water Use Zones. Once the planting in these zones has been established, natural rainfall should be sufficient to maintain the plants. During very dry conditions, some plants in the low water use zone may require supplemental watering from time to time. When employing the use of an automatic irrigation system, this zone should not be irrigated.

168

7—Efficient Irrigation: Planning for Efficient Water Use

Figure 7.3: Example of a Landscape Hydrozone Plan

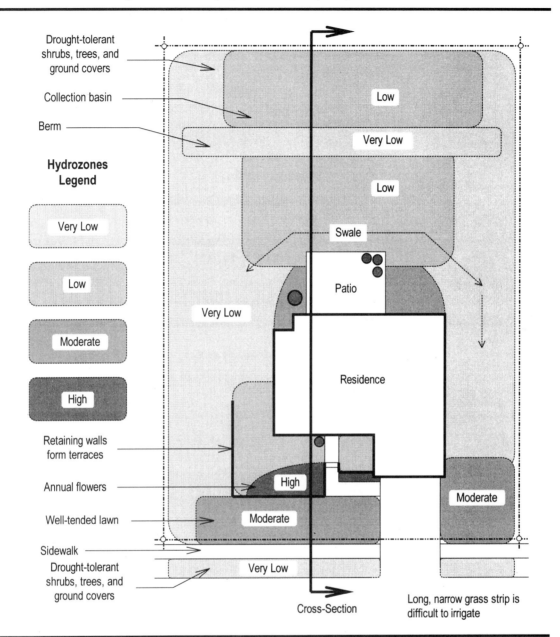

Moderate Water Use Zone. Plants that will require occasional supplemental watering, once established, should be planted in this zone. Supplemental watering of plants should be done only to the extent necessary to maintain plants in a healthy, flourishing condition. Plants watered in this fashion will be able to survive short-term drought conditions. When a significant rainfall does occur, irrigation may be postponed until the next scheduled watering time.

High Water Use Zone. Even though this zone requires regular watering, it still uses less water than a typical landscape that has not been designed to be a Xeriscape. The amount of area devoted to this zone should be minimized for maximum water conservation. During dry conditions, it will be necessary to water the plants in this zone regularly. Therefore, this zone is most appropriately located in a high-visibility area that is easily irrigated.

One simple way to approach hydrozones in your landscape is to consider plant bedding areas as a separate hydrozone from your lawn. The irrigation needs of each of these two types of landscape areas are likely to be quite different. If you are planning to irrigate your landscape with an automatic sprinkler system, take care to plan the system so that lawn watering zones are separate from non-turf zones. Slopes, shade, and other factors can also be important (see Figure 7.3). When determining the hydrozones that exist in your own landscape, consult the following information:

- Chapter 4 on Plant Selection will assist you in classifying individual plant species into hydrozones.

- Appendix F will provide additional information on hydrozone classifications and their use.

- Review the factors described in the "Water, Soil, and Plant Associations" section of this chapter.

- Refer to Table 7.1, Hydrozones for a Water Budget.

Water Budgeting

Consider preparing a water budget for your landscape. If you truly want to lower your water bill during our long, hot summers, it will be time well-spent. Apportion your landscape, as best you can, into the hydrozone categories mentioned in the previous section. Then, establish an approximation of your current landscape water demand. If your existing landscape is overly water-demanding, go one step further and set goals for a more modest water budget. This approach will allow you to be specific and focused if you are planning to convert high and moderate hydrozones into low and very low hydrozones.

Table 7.1: Hydrozones for a Water Budget in Central Texas

Hydrozone	Water Demand*	Lawn/Soil/Management Type**	Landscape/Plant Examples
High	> 50"	St Augustine in sun (in typical urban soils)	Annual bed, hybrid roses
Moderate	40"	St. Aug./Bermuda mix (some Zoysia species)	Flowering perennials, ground covers
Low	30"	Bermuda or Buffalo (constantly green)	Adapted shrubs and perennials
Very Low	< 20"	Bermuda or Buffalo (allowing dormancy)	Existing native vegetation

*In Inches/year, based on evapotranspiration (ET) rates.
**Beside variation in water use between species, there is a large diversity in rates of ET on a cultivar level (Balogh, 1992).

7—Efficient Irrigation: Planning for Efficient Water Use

WATER CONSUMPTION LEVELS

How does your water consumption compare with your neighbors (see Table 7.2)? For example, the average *interior* per capita use in Austin is about 77 gallons per day (the average household size is 2.68 persons per single family dwelling). The average *exterior* use per dwelling is about 118 gallons per day (Montgomery Watson, 1992). When considering both interior and exterior water use, the national average is estimated to be 100 to 150 gallons of water per capita (person) per day (gpcd). Per capita use of customers of the City of Austin Water and Wastewater Department averages roughly 121 gallons per day. Some homeowners on large estates in the United States use 600 or more gpcd (Ellefson et al., 1992). Unfortunately, it's likely that much of this excessive water use is wasted through poor irrigation practices.

Table 7.2: Water Consumption Levels

Indoor and Outdoor Use*			Conservation Rating Based on Consumption Levels	Outdoor Use Only** Per residential landscape in Central Texas
Gallons per Capita per Day	Family of Three	Family of Five		
100	300	500	*Very Heavy Use*, little or no conservation evident	30,000 gal/month and over
75	225	375	*Heavy Use*, including lawn & garden use	20,000 to 29,999 gal/month
60	180	300	*Moderate Use*, with some outside lawn & garden watering	10,000 to 19,999 gal/month
45	135	225	*Conservative Use*, with little or no lawn watering	Under 10,000 gal/month
30	90	150	*Very Conservative* household use, no outside watering	Under 5,000 gal/month

* Adapted from Campbell, 1983.
** Adapted from Browning, 1983.

DETERMINING YOUR LANDSCAPE WATER DEMAND

To calculate a rough approximation of your landscape's water demand for an average year, you will need to have some numbers ready. You need the square footage of your landscape hydrozones and their demand in inches (from Table 7.1). Use these figures in the following exercise to determine your outdoor water demand in gallons. Does your current water demand fit your budget? However, it's best to view your calculations as a long-range budget or guide for your homestead, since we rarely experience an average year. Actual water use will vary from the average depending on whether rainfall is above or below average.

1. Multiply the water demand (inches per year) times your landscape area per hydrozone (square feet) and divide by 12. This will give you the cubic feet of water demand per year. _____ cu. ft.

2. Multiply the number of cubic feet of water demand per year (line 1) times a conversion factor of 7.48. This gives you the number of required gallons of water per year. _____ gal.

3. Multiply the inches of natural rainfall (32") times your landscape area per hydrozone (sq. ft.) and divide by 12. This gives you the cubic feet of water supplied by natural rainfall. _____ cu. ft.

4. Multiply the cubic feet of natural rainfall times a conversion factor of 7.48. This gives you the gallons of natural rainfall per year. _____ gal.

5. Subtract the gallons of natural rainfall (line 4) from the required water demand for your landscape area per hydrozone (line 2). This gives you the gallons required (TWDB, 1997).

For example, 3,000 sq. ft. of lawn managed as a high water use zone needs about 33,660 irrigated gallons during the growing season. By incorporating Xeriscape principles into your landscape and properly accounting for summer rainfall, it could be managed as a moderate water use zone and still look great. In so doing, less than half as much water would be needed (about 15,000 gallons). Over several years, the difference between the water management levels would amount to hundreds of dollars.

Whether you are installing a new system or managing an existing one, it helps to become familiar with the various system components. Table 7.3 and Figure 7.4 describe a typical system, starting from the point where the water is discharged and working back to the point of connection with the water supply.

Table 7.3: Irrigation Component Descriptions

#	Component	Symbol	Comments
1.	Nozzle	●	Sprinkler part from which water is directed to the plants.
2.	Head	●	Holds the nozzle and is usually buried with the top flush with the soil surface.
3.	Driplines		Drip system component from which water is directed to the plants.
4.	Lateral lines	_____	Connects all the heads/driplines in one zone to the mainline.
5.	Turf bubblers	○	Low flow component w/short tube for "flood" irrigating lawns
6.	Zone valve	⊕	Controls the operation of a zone of heads.
7.	Controller	▨	Electronic "brains" control when the system operates and for how long each zone waters.
8.	Rain shut-off	▭	Prevents a system from turning on during rainfall or immediately after rainfall.
9.	Mainline	▬▬	Major waterline that services all the zones.
10.	Main shut-off valve (gate valve)	⋈	Separates the irrigation system from the other water service (Figure 7.6 shows typical alignment for a residential system).
11.	Check valve/ back-flow preventer	▢	Required by most building codes to prevent irrigation system water from flowing back into the water supply.
12.	Hose bibb	⊣	Outdoor water faucet for hoses and portable sprinklers.
13.	Meter	⊙	Measures the amount of water flowing from the supplier to the user, for billing.
14.	Water main	_____	Water supply for the household water service.

Figure 7.4: Components of an Irrigation System

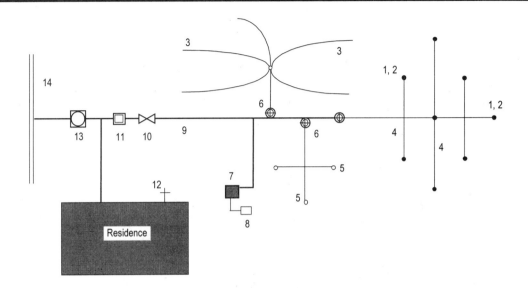

Irrigation Equipment

The equipment you use is an important factor in efficient watering. Whether you have a hand-held hose, drip irrigation, or sprinkler system, the intent is the same: you want to apply water to the plant's root zone. (The soil where the roots of plants are growing is called the root zone.) You may want to use several techniques to water your landscape efficiently. For best results, the type of watering system should be selected based on the landscape arrangement, type of plants, and the hydrozones. In most landscapes, there is not just one irrigation method appropriate for watering every plant in the landscape. Hose-end sprinkler systems are best for those homeowners with a fairly simple, small, or drought-tolerant landscape. A well-designed automatic irrigation system is usually a combination of several different methods that may include various types of sprinkler heads and drip and/or other low-flow irrigation.

Efficient watering equipment does not spray water high in the air; nor does it create "mist" that is blown away or evaporated. It does not water sidewalks, buildings, streets, or other non-living surfaces. To avoid excessive evaporation, use a sprinkler that produces large drops of water, rather than a fine mist. In addition, large drops of water are not easily moved by wind, so the water falls where you want it. Sprinklers that send droplets out on a low trajectory also help control evaporation. Low-volume irrigation avoids these problems by applying the water slowly near the soil surface.

Irrigation System Components

Whether you are installing a new system or managing an existing one, it helps to become familiar with the various system components. Table 7.3 and Figure 7.4 describe a typical system, starting from the point where the water is discharged and working back to the point of connection with the water supply.

Hoses and Portable Sprinklers

The most common type of irrigation system is the sprinkler attached to the end of a garden hose. Hose-end sprinklers may be less convenient than automatic sprinklers, yet they are inexpensive and are all that is needed for many landscapes. This type of equipment is best used on Xeriscapes that limit the extent of high and moderate water use zones. For homeowners who use hose-end sprinklers, the use of hydrozones will minimize the need to "spot-irrigate," which means less "hose-dragging." Choose an efficient hose-end sprinkler. A revolving-head, non-pulsating type of sprinkler, such as an impact or traveling sprinkler, tends to be more efficient than the oscillating, back-and-forth type. Oscillating sprinklers tend to throw the water too high and distribute it unevenly (Peavy, 1979).

When purchasing a hose, look for the highest quality available. These days, most hoses are rated according to durability. Lower quality hoses quickly develop kinks and become unusable. Hoses are commonly available in 1/2", 5/8", and 3/4" inside diameters.

The threads are the same on each, so you can use the same nozzle with any size hose. The larger the hose, the larger the volume of water it delivers. Using a nozzle or sprinkler minimizes the differences because these devices tend to equalize the amount of water coming out of the hose. Any hose will serve you longer if you store it in winter, keep it out of the hot sun when not in use, and avoid running over it with your car.

Manual and Automated Sprinkler Systems

Manual and automated sprinkler systems are quite convenient and can be a real time saver. This convenience, however, also makes it very easy to spread vast amounts of water with no effort. Therefore, the question of whether the system will conserve or *waste* water totally depends on the person turning the system on and off (or scheduling the electronic controller). Manual sprinkler systems depend on a person to turn them on and off. With an automatic system, that job is delegated to an electronic controller. The caretaker of the irrigation system simply has to schedule when the water will start flowing and when it should stop. The controller directs the watering cycles by activating valves at various stations throughout the system. Within a home landscape, there are typically four or five stations. A variety of controllers are available ranging from $100 to $500 or more, depending on the features included.

Because most sprinkler systems are connected to potable water supplies and potential contamination of drinking water exists, the design, installation, and maintenance of such systems are regulated by state law. While a homeowner is allowed to install a system on their own property, an irrigator's license is necessary if the system is not for such personal use. If you want a contractor-installed irri-

7—Efficient Irrigation: Irrigation Equipment

gation system, ensure that they have an irrigator's license. This license, obtained by passing the Texas Board of Irrigator's exam, is required by law to sell, design, install, maintain, alter, repair, or service landscape irrigation systems. Whether you do-it-yourself or you use a contractor, your system will be more efficient if it is capable of the following:

1. Adjustable flow controls on remote control valves.

2. Pressure regulation (this is required if the water pressure at your house is greater than the manufacturer's recommendation.

3. Matched precipitation rates within each control valve circuit.

4. Turf area valve circuits separated from non-turf valve circuits (see hydrozones).

5. Check valves at low-head drainage areas.

6. Head-to-head coverage, with minimum run-off and overspray.

7. Controller capability for:

    a. Dual or multiple programming.

    b. Multiple start capacity.

    c. Five-day schedule capability.

    d. Rain sensor shut-off.

    e. Water budget.

    f. Emergency shut-off valve.

Keep in mind that the proper layout of a system is just as important as quality components. Be sure to coordinate your sprinkler system with your landscape hydrozones. One irrigation valve, or a set of valves with the same schedule, should serve each unique hydrozone.

There is a relatively inexpensive device which should be used on all irrigation systems. This component, called a *rain shut-off*, prevents the irrigation system from turning on during, or immediately after, rainfall. This is a wonderful public relations tool, as well as a water and money saver. It is capable of adjustment so that a brief shower does not interrupt the schedule. Another useful device is a soil-moisture sensor that can be integrated into your system. It will take readings of soil moisture at the plant root zone and only allow the system to operate at a preset moisture level. This keeps the system from operating too frequently, including following sufficient rainfall (Welsh, 1990).

Some cities, such as the City of Austin, offer residents a water bill credit (CoA) or rebate (MUD) for upgrading your *existing* automatic sprinkler system with water conserving features. Check with your local water department to see if they offer any type of water conservation program. Appendix H offers an explanation of the City of Austin program.

*There is a relatively inexpensive device which should be used on all irrigation systems. This component, called a **rain shut-off**, prevents the irrigation system from turning on during, or immediately after, rainfall.*

Low-Volume Irrigation

Low-volume irrigation, also called micro-irrigation, allows you to distribute water slowly and directly to the roots of a plant. This type of system emits water at lower precipitation rates than sprinklers, which is ideal for our typically heavy soils. Low-volume irrigation components include drip tubing, perforated pipe, microsprays, and bubblers. These systems are generally quite water-efficient since they:

- Minimize or eliminate run-off.

- Reduce the amount of water lost through evaporation and over-spray.

Drip irrigation is most appropriate for watering vegetable gardens, shrubs, and trees. For flower and vegetable beds, you may want to use perforated pipe (sometimes called soaker hose). Perforated pipe is best used for temporary applications since the holes tend to clog eventually. Good filters and regular maintenance are critical for any kind of a low-volume system.

Micro-sprays are ideal for watering small, detailed areas such as containers. Bubblers are often used for trees, shrubs, and ground cover. Recently, turf bubblers have become available. Turf bubbler irrigation is a method of irrigating lawns in a way that combines some of the finest attributes of both drip and sprinkler systems. A matrix of plastic tubing is buried underground, with vertical emitter tubes whose openings are barely above the soil surface. Water is discharged at about 20 gallons per hour (gph) and slowly "floods" the surrounding area. Water distribution is accomplished through the wicking action of the turf thatch and by progressively exceeding the infiltration rate (rate of absorption) of the soil. Turf bubbler irrigation is new and relatively unknown at this time (1998), but seems quite promising.

If drip lines are placed carefully, they may indirectly help suppress weeds in your garden. Drip systems apply water slowly enough for plants to absorb most of it soon after it reaches the roots, so little moisture is left over to support weeds. By contrast, overhead irrigation systems apply water indiscriminately over the soil surface, watering both garden plants and weeds.

Irrigation System Maintenance and Repair

As much as one-half of the water used on traditional landscapes for irrigation during the summer watering period is estimated to be wasted (TWDB, 1990). One reason water is wasted is that homeowners do not schedule irrigation properly. Another reason is that homeowners do not maintain their system adequately. Automatic irrigation systems allow an inattentive homeowner to simply forget about the issue of watering, sometimes for months or even years. However, periodic evaluations of the irrigation system are abso-

Low-volume irrigation, also called micro-irrigation, allows you to distribute water slowly and directly to the roots of a plant. This type of system emits water at lower precipitation rates than sprinklers, which is ideal for our typically heavy soils.

7—Efficient Irrigation: Irrigation Management

lutely necessary. Identify any problems affecting irrigation performance and efficiency. Observe the sprinklers while in use to ensure that the spray is properly directed, components are working well, and that the amount of water seems to be evenly distributed. A system that operates properly won't waste water, even as it helps your garden thrive. Check the system at least a few times a year, or more frequently if the system is being heavily used.

When monitoring your system, look for problems with run-off. When slopes are a problem, or when you put out too much water too quickly, run-off results. This run-off is a primary cause of water waste. Check each spray head to make sure that it isn't broken or leaking, and that the spray isn't being blocked by plants. Look at the sprinkler patterns. Is the water falling where it belongs? Uneven spray patterns may be due to clogged heads. Clear any debris that may be in the openings. With drip systems, inspect emitters and tubing to ensure that all are attached to the main lines and that water flows through. Open the end caps on the tubing and flush the lines occasionally, especially during winter. You may want to perform simple repairs by yourself, while more complicated problems will require calling in a specialist.

Irrigation Management

Using appropriate irrigation equipment in an efficient manner is key to proper irrigation management. Landscape irrigation should be used to supplement rainfall only when necessary to promote plant health and vigor. Be aware that your experience and management skills *play the most important role* in conserving water in your landscape. A critical aspect of gaining the necessary skills is learning about the interaction between water, soil, and plants. As you put this knowledge to work and your gardening experience increases, you will learn to recognize when irrigation is needed, as well as how much and how long to water. Proper irrigation management is critical to achieving a water-efficient landscape, regardless of the plant materials used. Unfortunately, many supposed Xeriscapes are simply over-watered.

Proper irrigation management is critical to achieving a water-efficient landscape, regardless of the plant materials used. Unfortunately, many supposed Xeriscapes are simply over-watered.

Water, Soil, and Plant Associations

We often think of plants in human terms and want to water them whenever *we* are hot. However, the best time to water plants is when *they* need it. Learn how both natural and (horti-) cultural factors affect a plant's need for irrigation.

When determining moisture requirements of a landscape area or plant, some of the factors which should be taken into account are:

177

Xeriscape for Central Texas

Table 7.4: Moisture Requirement Factors

Natural Factors	Cultural Factors
Climate, Weather, and Drought	Shallow Watering
Plant Species Type, Location	Fertilizing and Mulching
Root System Size	Container Plants
Soil, Slope, and Drainage	Turf Management

Natural Factors

Climate, Weather, and Drought. Texas lies at the convergence of several different climate zones within North America. For this reason, and because it is such a large state, Texas has an incredible amount of climate variety. In the United States, the moisture-surplus wet climates lie to the east, and include east Texas. The moisture-deficient arid climates actually begin right here in Central Texas and extend westward (see Figure 7.5). The Austin area averages about 32" of rainfall a year and is considered "semi-arid." Texas is also a transition area for temperature zones. To the north lie the middle-latitudes with their distinct cold winters, while the winterless tropics are about the same distance toward the equator. Much of the state, including South Central Texas, is considered subtropical (Norwine, 1995).

The moisture-deficient arid climates actually begin right here in Central Texas and extend westward. The Austin area averages about 32" of rainfall a year and is considered "semi-arid."

Figure 7.5: Texas Rainfall Patterns

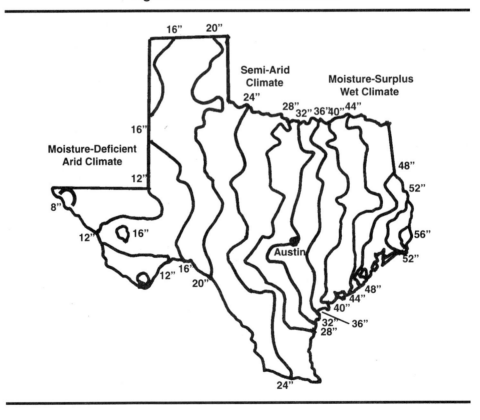

178

7—Efficient Irrigation: Irrigation Management

Typical summers are long and hot in Central Texas. Average daytime temperatures in July and August hover in the high 90s, and rainfall is sporadic. In the heat of the summer, your body can quickly lose fluids, as can your landscape. The term which describes this natural water loss in your landscape is *evapotranspiration*, or ET for short. ET is a term that explains the combined effect of evaporation and transpiration. *Evaporation* is the natural loss of water to the air from the soil, water surfaces, and other non-living materials. *Transpiration* is water loss by plants themselves during their natural life and growth processes. In fact, most of the moisture taken up by plants is lost to the atmosphere through transpiration. Summer temperatures cause a great difference between the average rates of evapotranspiration and rainfall (see Figure 7.6).

Dry conditions and high temperatures increase the transpiration in plants. This kind of weather puts stress on plants, and some respond by slipping into a type of "dormancy." Species that lack this or other types of drought-survival mechanisms will not thrive unless they are planted near a source of water or irrigated.

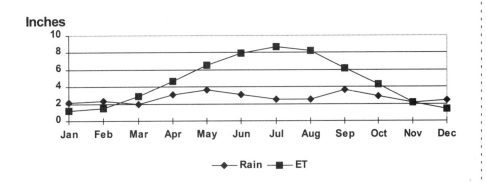

Figure 7.6: Rainfall/ET Data for Austin

*The term which describes this natural water loss in your landscape is **evapotranspiration**, or **ET** for short. ET is a term that explains the combined effect of evaporation and transpiration. Evaporation is the natural loss of water to the air from the soil, water surfaces, and other nonliving materials. Transpiration is water loss by plants themselves during their natural life and growth processes.*

High humidity curtails a plant's need for water; so do calm, cloudy days. Short day length, as in spring and fall, also slows down their water use. The timing of the availability of moisture is also important. Dry weather during our region's normally wet spring will affect most plants for the entire growing season. Adequate moisture during the last half of the growth period will not compensate for an inadequate supply during the first half. Stunted growth with little foliage will be the result.

Plant Species Type and Location. Plant species vary greatly in their water needs and ability to tolerate drought. This is evident when one looks at the huge diversity of their habitats. However, the location or position of the plant in the landscape may be as important in determining water requirements as the choice of plant species or variety. For example, a plant in an area with full sunlight all day may use twice as much water as that same plant in a shaded location. Some plants are not adapted to shade, of course, and their growth will be hampered from lack of sunlight. Recent research has determined that, in some cases, small plants within the root zone of certain tree species benefit from the trees' ability to extract soil moisture at deeper levels. During the day, moisture moves up from tree roots toward branches and leaves. At night, the moisture will flow back down into the shallow roots of the tree and be released into nearby topsoil. Although there is some competition for water under a tree canopy, occasionally plants growing near trees are more vigorous due to this phenomenon.

Root System Size. Plants with small root systems, such as turf and annuals, need more frequent water applications than plants with larger root systems, such as trees and shrubs. Also, newly-installed plants have much smaller root systems than established plants. Deep rooting, high-root density, and extensive development of root hairs contribute to water stress avoidance (Beard, 1989).

Soil, Slope, and Drainage. The quality and depth of soil greatly affects a plants ability to tolerate drought. Rich, deep soil provides a larger reservoir for moisture absorption and encourages plants to develop extensive root systems. (Keep in mind that, although most plants prefer good garden soil, some do not. Many plants native to Central Texas either do not need, or will not do well in, deep, rich soil since they did not evolve with those soil conditions.) Sandy soil allows water to pass through quickly, and thus will dry out sooner than most other soils. Clay soil does not absorb water quickly, but when it does become moist, it dries out slowly. Generally, typical soils in Central Texas have a high clay content. In fact, all the rock and clay soil in Central Texas tend to reduce the *effectiveness* of the amount of rainfall that we receive. In addition, our typical thunderstorms quickly outpace the absorption capacity of our soils.

Cultural Factors

Shallow Watering. How much or how often you water has a pronounced effect on root system development. Most plants, including lawns, develop deeper root systems and tolerate drought better if watered deeply. Generally, plant roots will grow where the moisture is, so shallow watering will create shallow root systems. These roots are not deep enough to reach soil moisture at deeper levels and are more sensitive to drought. Instead of light daily watering, you should give plants a weekly soaking. *When you water, allow the soil to become wet to a depth of five or six inches. This will place water into the root zone where plants can readily absorb it.*

Fertilizing and Mulching. A reasonable amount of fertilizing is necessary to develop the root system and keep the plant healthy. Plants with a healthy, vigorous root system make better use of less water and are more drought tolerant. However, excessive growth

When you water, allow the soil to become wet to a depth of five or six inches. This will place water into the root zone where plants can readily absorb it.

due to over-fertilization will increase the water demand of the plants. The best times to fertilize are when adequate moisture is available, such as spring and fall. Keep in mind that to protect water resources downstream, do not fertilize just before a rainstorm. You may think this is a good way to "water it in," yet a heavy thunderstorm could easily send those nutrients into a nearby creek. Nitrogen and phosphorus can hurt aquatic wildlife. Besides, you paid for the fertilizer, you might as well get some good use out of it! If grass clippings are left on your lawn, little additional fertilizer will be needed.

Mulching the soil surface around plants reduces water evaporation from the soil by sun and wind, thereby providing a larger reservoir of moisture for the plants to utilize. Mulches also moderate soil temperatures, prevent soil compaction and erosion, and reduce weed populations.

Container Plants. Container plants dry out quickly, especially in warm weather, because of lightweight soils, evaporation through the pots' porous walls, and heat buildup. In general, water container plants until water flows out of the bottom of the plant. Consider using soil polymers to increase the soil's moisture-holding capacity. *Soil polymers* are sponge-like granules that absorb water. They can be mixed into the soil near the root zone of plants and will swell up to many times their original size when provided moisture. The roots then access the liquid, which reduces the need to irrigate. There are many available on the market, and some work better than others.

Turf Management. For lawns, the height of mowing affects the water use and the root development of the grass. Drought resistance of most plants is, to a large degree, in proportion to root development, number of roots, and depth of development. Also, plants can be weakened by prolonged droughts or by continuous close mowing. Either will prevent individual plants from completing their normal growth cycle and developing normal root systems. A closely mowed lawn with shallow roots will undergo acute water stress in the summer. Even with sufficient soil moisture, acute moisture stress occurs if the rate of transpiration exceeds the ability of grass root systems to supply sufficient moisture (Beard, 1985). Grass should be cut fairly often, so that only 1/2- to 3/4-inch is trimmed off. A better looking lawn will result.

Grass roots need oxygen along with water and nutrients; compacted or heavy soils restrict water absorption and the effective exchange and replenishing of oxygen from the atmosphere. Aerating the lawn helps eliminate this problem. Lawn aeration involves the creation of many small holes or tears in the turf through the use of an aerating machine, a pitchfork, or any other appropriate tool. Aeration improves not only the soil's gas exchange, but also improves water infiltration, promotes root growth, and reduces sur-

Container plants dry out quickly, especially in warm weather, because of lightweight soils, evaporation through the pots' porous walls, and heat buildup. In general, water container plants until water flows out of the bottom of the plant.

Xeriscape for Central Texas

face compaction and thatch accumulation. All these benefits are essential to producing a healthy lawn.

Scheduling Irrigation

"When" and "how much" are the kind of questions many gardeners ask about watering plants. While the natural and cultural factors described previously affect the amount of water used in your landscape, the factor that most determines the answers to watering questions is *you*. Your experience with the plants in your landscape is the best guideline to follow. Knowing when to water can be a big water-saver. Your approach to irrigation scheduling should be to:

- Recognize when to water.

- Water in response to rainfall, not necessarily on a set schedule.

- Allow little or no run-off.

Here are some other guidelines to follow that will help you determine the "when" of irrigation:

- Try to water plants just before they begin to show signs of stress. Look for slightly wilted foliage, or a loss in luster or color change that is darker, grayer, or bluer than normal. Other signs are curling or falling leaves. Be aware though, that water-logged plants often have the same symptoms as plants that are too dry.

- Lawns under drought stress show evidence of tracks after someone walks on it. Grass tends to lie flat after being walked on and is a dull color if moisture is low.

- If leaf edges turn dry or leaves are yellow, this indicates a more advanced state of drought. Many plants lose their gloss and start to droop before wilting. Others will drop leaves, buds, or flowers.

Observation and experience are the best ways to learn which of your plants are sensitive and which are more hardy.

As a general guideline, plants need approximately one inch of water per week in the active growing season. How deep does an inch of water wet the soil? A little water goes down a long way in sandy soil. One inch of water will wet sandy loam down to about 16 inches. But the same amount of water, if it all goes into the soil, wets a clay soil down to only about 5 inches. Not only will the water reach different depths, but the rate at which the soil absorbs the water (the infiltration rate or permeability) will be different per soil type (see Figure 7.7).

The rate at which your irrigation system applies water is called its *precipitation rate*. To determine the precipitation rate of your sprinkler, do the following:

1. Place three to five empty containers (for example, tuna cans) at different distances around the sprinkler.

As a general guideline, plants need approximately one inch of water per week in the active growing season. One inch of water will wet sandy loam down to about 16 inches. The same amount of water, if it all goes into the soil, wets a clay soil down to only about five inches.

Figure 7.7: Water Infiltration in Soil

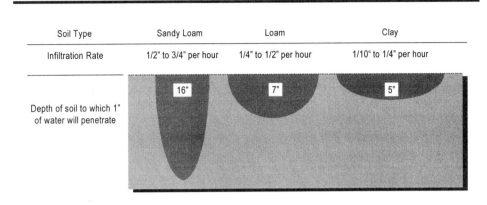

2. Turn the sprinkler on for 1/2 hour.
3. Measure the amount of water (in inches) in each can. Add the amounts, and divide by the number of cans to obtain an average. This is the amount your sprinkler puts out in 1/2 hour.
4. Multiply the average by two to determine a precipitation rate in inches per hour. Use this rate to gauge how long to irrigate to achieve a specific amount of water in your landscape.

Deep, periodic waterings are usually best for plants in any region, but they are especially useful in arid lands because of the high percentage of soil salts. Long, slow irrigation will wash salts from the root zone. Try to wet the soil to a depth of 4" to 6", if that depth is available. When soaking the soil, avoid run-off by matching the precipitation rate to the soil's infiltration rate. If your landscape has clay soil or slopes (both are prevalent in Central Texas), it may be especially difficult to irrigate efficiently. For you, it is extremely important to apply water in several short repeated cycles, instead of once single long irrigation. This type of irrigation is sometimes called "cycle and soak." This means irrigating a landscape area until just before run-off, stopping the irrigation in that spot, and irrigating another area. Then, come back to the first area and irrigate again after an hour or so to allow the previous watering to soak down into the soil. Keep cycling until one inch is applied. This multi-cycling of irrigation can be performed whether you use an automatic system or hose-end sprinklers.

Allow the soil to dry somewhat between waterings from either irrigation or rainfall. This allows air—necessary for all plant life—to get to the roots. To maintain plant health and vigor, however, do not allow the soil to become bone-dry between irrigation in high or moderate water use zones. Generally, for lawn irrigation, a 50% depletion of soil moisture is suggested. Below this level, it is extremely difficult for plant roots to extract water from the soil. Established plants in the low water use zones should tolerate short periods of little soil moisture. Established plants in the very low water use zones should tolerate long periods of little soil moisture.

Allow the soil to dry somewhat between waterings from either irrigation or rainfall. This allows air—necessary for all plant life—to get to the roots.

Xeriscape for Central Texas

You should check the soil moisture before each irrigation. How do you know how much moisture is in the soil, or how deep the moisture is? One simple way is to stick your finger down into the soil to the second knuckle and feel it. While this method is somewhat effective, it is subjective, and you may not want to get your finger dirty. Consider obtaining and using a soil moisture meter. These devices are more objective and are inexpensive. These meters have a long slender probe about 8" long. Near the tip of the probe is a plastic band insulator. This bottom half-inch is the sensor that detects the moisture content. When inserted into the soil, moisture allows electrical current to flow through the sensor, which is hooked up to a needle and a calibrated dial. The more soil moisture that is present, the higher the reading.

If you own an automatic sprinkler system, it is recommended that, whenever possible, you manually start the system based on the apparent need of your plants. As we've said, "read" your plants to determine appropriate watering times. If you go on vacation or if Central Texas is experiencing an extended dry period, then you may want to rely on a the "automatic" setting of your controller. However, please take the time to understand how to program your controller properly. A vast quantity of potable water is wasted every year by way of improperly used and scheduled controllers.

Your controller should be set according to the specific conditions in your yard. An irrigation system controller that is capable of multiple programs will allow different zones to operate on varying days of the week. Up to three cycles per program are sometimes desired during one operation. Whether you irrigate your landscape with a manual or automatic system, changes in the frequency and amount of irrigation should be made at least *monthly!* As a guide, refer to the sample irrigation schedules in Table 7.5. Your schedule will vary from these since the GPM (gallons per minute for the zone) and other factors are unlikely to be the same as the example.

Table 7.5: Sample Irrigation Schedules

#	Station or Zone Description	Irrigation Components	GPM* x Minutes =	Schedule Gallons/ Zone	Irrigation Frequency
1.	St. Augustine in full sun	Spray heads	15 x 10 =	150	Every 5 days, 3 start times @ 12, 2, & 4 A.M.
2.	St. Augustine in part shade	Spray heads	15 x 8 =	120	
3.	St. Augustine in part shade	Spray heads	15 x 6 =	90	
4.	Bermuda grass in full sun	Rotors	20 x 15 =	300	Every 14 days, 2 start times @ 2 & 4 A.M.
5.	Buffalo grass in full sun	Rotors	18 x 15 =	270	
6.	Xeric shrubs in full sun	Spray heads	16 x 8 =	128	
7.	Ground cover in shade	Spray heads	14 x 7 =	98	Every 5 days, 2 start times @ 1 & 3 A.M.
8.	Vegetable garden in sun	Spray heads	6 x 10 =	60	
9.	Azaleas in part shade	Bubblers	8 x 20 =	160	

If you need help with scheduling, consult an appropriate irrigation or landscape professional. Some cities, such as the City of Austin for example, may offer irrigation audits (see Appendix H.) Be sure to water at the best time of day to decrease evaporative water loss. The hours just before and after dawn are the best for water-

184

ing. This is the coolest time of the day, and as the sun rises, it will quickly dry the water from plant leaves so that you don't create an environment for diseases and pests.

Eliminating water waste is quite possible, but will require some effort. Remember, though, plants don't waste water, people do. Thus, even a well designed Xeriscape will only be water-efficient if it is managed that way. By using these ideas in your landscape, you can take the heat off your plants, yourself, and your water bill.

Bibliography

The information presented in this document is necessarily a composite of many people's knowledge, opinions, and experience. Every effort has been made to transcribe this information accurately; please report inaccuracies or alternative opinions to the Xeriscape Garden Club. Information for this chapter was obtained from the following sources:

Balogh, James C., and William J. Walker. *Golf Course Management & Construction: Environmental Issues.* Chelsea, Michigan: Lewis Publishers, 1992.

Banks, Suzy, and Richard Heinichen. *Rainwater Collection for the Mechanically-Challenged,* 1997.

Beard, J. B. "An assessment of water use by turfgrass." In Gibeault, V. A. and Cockerham, S. T. (Eds.). *Turfgrass Water Conservation.* University of California, Riverside, Division of Agriculture and Natural Resources, 1985.

Beard, J. B. *Turfgrass Water Stress: Drought Resistance Components, Physiological Mechanisms, and Species Genotype Diversity.* In Sixth International Turf. Res. Conference, Tokyo, 1989.

Browning, Waldi F. *Landscape Style, Irrigation Patterns, and Water Use: An Exploratory Study.* Prepared for the City of Austin. Austin, Texas: Browning & Associates, 1986.

Campbell, Stu. *The Home Water Supply: How to Find, Filter, Store, and Conserve It.* Pownal, Vermont: Garden Way Publishing, 1983.

Ellefson, Connie Lockhart, Thomas L. Stephens, and Douglas Welsh. *Xeriscape Gardening: Water Conservation for the American Landscape.* New York: Macmillan Publishing Company, 1992.

Mollison, Bill. *Introduction to Permaculture.* Tyalgum, Australia: Tagari Publications, 1991.

Montgomery Watson. *Water Conservation Plan for the City of Austin,* 1992.

Norwine, Jim, John R. Giardino, Gerald R. North, and Juan B. Valdes. *The Changing Climate of Texas: Predictability and Implications for the Future.* College Station, Texas: Texas A&M University, 1995.

Peavy, Dr. William S. *Southern Gardener's Soil Handbook.* Houston: Gulf Publishing Company, 1979.

Rahn, James J. *Making the Weather Work for You: A Practical Guide for Gardener and Farmer.* Garden Way Associates, Inc., 1979.

Plants don't waste water, people do. Even a well designed Xeriscape will only be water-efficient if it is managed that way. By using these ideas in your landscape, you can take the heat off your plants, yourself, and your water bill.

Reed, Porter B. *National List of Plant Species That Occur in Wetlands: South Plains, Region 6*. St. Petersburg, Florida: U.S. Fish and Wildlife Service, National Wetlands Inventory Center, 1997.

Texas Water Development Board (in cooperation with the Center for Maximum Potential Building Systems). *Texas Guide to Rainwater Harvesting*, Second Edition. Austin, Texas: Conservation, Texas Water Development Board, 1997.

Texas Water Development Board. *Water for Texas: Today and Tomorrow*. Austin, Texas: Texas Water Development Board, 1990.

Welsh, Douglas F. *TALC Certified Landscape Professional: Certification Manual*, College Station, Texas: Texas Agricultural Extension Service, The Texas A&M University System, 1990.

Chapter 8

Texas Wildscapes

In This Chapter...

Texas Wildscapes: Backyard Wildlife Habitat
Attracting Wildlife
Food Sources
Providing Shelter
Water Sources
Wildlife Problems
Co-existing With Deer
The Hummingbird Garden
Butterfly Gardening
The Texas Wildscapes Program
Acknowledgments
Bibliography

Texas wildscapes are small habitats that provide food, water, and shelter for wildlife. A careful combination of these basic resources can make your property more attractive to butterflies, reptiles, song birds, and other wildlife. Most of the information in this chapter was written by staff biologists at the Texas Parks & Wildlife Nongame and Urban Program and is reprinted with permission. By inviting wildlife to your backyard, you help offset the loss of natural habitat due to urbanization or pollution.

Texas Wildscapes: Backyard Wildlife Habitat

Source: TX Parks & Wildlife Dept.

Urban sprawl affects more and more natural habitats every year. In recognition of this growth and the fact that, according to census data, 82% of Texans now live in nine metropolitan areas, the Texas Parks and Wildlife Department (TPWD) started a habitat restoration program called *Texas Wildscapes*. *Texas wildscapes are small habitats that provide food, water, and shelter for wildlife.* A careful combination of these basic resources can make your property more attractive to butterflies, reptiles, song birds, and small mammals. The *Texas Wildscapes* program recognizes individuals through a certification process whereby each wildscape is registered with the TPWD's Nongame and Urban Program.

To help get the word out, TPWD is partnering with gardening clubs like the Xeriscape Garden Club of the Austin Area. The information in this chapter was extracted from several of the excellent booklets included in the *Texas Wildscapes* information packet. More information about this beneficial program, plus phone numbers and an address for requesting more information, is included in the last section of this chapter.

By inviting wildlife to your backyard, you help offset the loss of natural habitat due to urbanization or pollution. Establishing a wildlife sanctuary or a naturalist's garden in your backyard helps to put back a little of what has been taken away.

Attracting Wildlife

The secret to attracting wildlife consists of supplying them with four basic requirements for survival:

- Food.
- Cover to provide shelter from the elements and from predators.
- Reproductive sites to provide an area to nest and rear their young.
- Water.

Birds and Butterflies

Of the different types of animals you will attract to your yard, birds will be the most abundant. You can attract a large variety of bird species depending on the vegetation available to them. Of all the birds attracted to backyards, hummingbirds are among the most spectacular. Butterflies flitting about are also a favorite sight in a backyard. You can attract both butterflies and hummingbirds by using plants such as lantana, phlox, morning glories, and butterfly weed to perform double duty in attracting both types of wildlife. The following sections describe hummingbird and butterfly gardening in more detail.

Small Mammals

Many small mammals will also be attracted to your backyard habitat. Squirrels will often inhabit a yard with mature trees (oaks, cedar elms, pecans, etc.) which provide nesting and food sources. When tree cavities are lacking, squirrels will sometimes use the bird boxes, unless special squirrel boxes are also provided. If you notice moss protruding from what once was a Bluebird or Chickadee house, you may have a squirrel in residence. If your property is located near a pond or stream, putting up a bat house will help attract the fly-by-night creatures which will help control insect populations in the area.

Amphibians and Reptiles

To encourage amphibians and reptiles to take up residence in your backyard, allow leaf litter to accumulate in an area of the yard. Tree stumps, rotting logs, and stones should also be left in an area of the yard not frequently used. Building a wall of stones, brush, or a woodpile at least three feet wide by three feet high provides shelter and basking sites for these small visitors. In addition, salamanders, frogs, and lizards will be attracted to these sites for the food provided by insects and spiders. Some people would prefer not to have snakes included in their backyard, but snakes can prevent rodent problems. Knowing how to identify a snake, and being aware of the poisonous ones in the area, can help you to become a little more at ease with including them in your backyard sanctuary. Box turtles may also be part of your backyard habitat. They will eat insects, worms, fruits, vegetables, and a variety of low-growing plants. They use leaf litter and underbrush to escape summer heat or the winder cold.

To encourage amphibians and reptiles to take up residence in your backyard, allow leaf litter to accumulate in an area of the yard.

Food Sources

Naturally-Occurring Food Sources

Naturally-occurring vegetation or native species of plants can provide food to wildlife species in your area. A variety of trees, shrubs, grasses, and flowers provide food sources such as acorns, nuts, berries, buds, fruit, nectar, and seeds which can be used by a variety of wildlife. Nectar-bearing flowers feed butterflies, hummingbirds, and bees. Any red or orange flower with a long tubular shape will attract hummingbirds. Plants with acorns and nuts feed squirrels. Plants that produce berries, seeds, or nuts provide birds with food. Many birds feed on insects as a large part of their diet which, in turn, provides natural pest control in your garden. For a year-round supply of food, choose different plantings that produce food throughout each of the four seasons.

Deciduous plantings generally bear the most fruit, nuts, and seeds for wildlife. In addition, they offer shady, leafy nest sites.

Xeriscape for Central Texas

However, they shed their leaves in autumn. Evergreens, which hold their leaves throughout the year, offer a good source of berries and seed-filled cones. They also offer year-round shelter, protection, and some breeding sites.

Of the different types of animals you will attract to your yard, birds will be the most abundant. You can attract a large variety of bird species depending on the vegetation available to them.

Type Bird	Attractive Plantings
American Goldfinch	Bachelor's Buttons, Cosmos, Elm, Sunflowers, Zinnias
American Robins	Barberry, American Beautyberry, Cotoneaster, Elderberry, Honeysuckle, Juniper (a.k.a. Cedars), Mulberry, Sumac, Virginia Creeper
Black-Capped Chickadee	Elms, Oak Trees, Virginia Creeper
Blue Jays	Elms, Grape Vines, Junipers (a.k.a. Cedars), Mulberry Trees, Oak Trees, Plum Trees
Brown-Headed Cowbird	Lawns
Cardinals	Thicket-forming bushes, American Beautyberry, Blackberry, Cotoneaster, Elms, Greenbrier vines, Hackberry, Mulberry, Roses, Sumacs, Virginia Creepers
Cedar Waxwings	Cotoneaster, Honeysuckle, Junipers (a.k.a. cedars), Persimmon, American Beautyberry
Chipping Sparrow	Rose thickets, Vines of all types, Zinnias
Common Flicker	Blackberry, Grape Vines, Greenbrier vines, Hackberry, Honeysuckle, Mulberry, Virginia Creeper
Eastern Bluebird	Elderberry, Hollies, Honeysuckle, Persimmon, Sumacs
European Starling	Lawns
House Finch	Cotoneaster, Elderberry, Elm, Honeysuckle, Marigolds, Willow, Zinnias
House Sparrow	Zinnias, Dandelions
House Wren	Trees: Both dead and mature types
Mockingbirds	Thicket-forming bushes, American Beautyberry, Blackberry, Cotoneaster, Crabapples, Elderberry, Firethorns, Grape vines, Greenbrier vines, Hollies, Honeysuckle, Lantana, Mulberry, Junipers, Virginia Creeper
Morning Doves	Sunflowers
Purple Martin	Lawns
Scrub Jay	Juniper (a.k.a. Cedars)
Song Sparrow	Amaranth, Bachelor's Buttons, Blackberry, Cosmos, Mulberry, Poppy, Zinnias
Tufted Titmouse	Elderberry, Hackberry, Mulberry, Oak, Wax Myrtle
White-Crowned Sparrow	Amaranth, Poppy, Zinnia

Artificial Food Sources

When vegetation cannot supply enough food, supplemental food can be provided with one or all of three different types of feeders.

• Hanging feeders.

• Ground feeders.

• Suet feeders.

HANGING FEEDERS

When providing a *hanging feeder*, it may be best to use sunflower seeds only. If a feeder is filled with mixed seeds, birds will often toss aside unwanted seeds to get to their favorites, which can create a mess under the feeder. Sunflower seeds are the number one choice of most songbirds, especially black-oil sunflower seeds, which are easier for birds to open. Squirrels love sunflower seeds also, so you may have to protect your hanging feeder with a baffle—a dome-shaped plastic cover that is placed above the feeder. This deters squirrels from jumping onto your feeder and eating the seeds *and* destroying your feeder!

GROUND FEEDERS

Ground feed varies from seeds placed on an elevated feeding tray, to seeds just tossed on the ground. When used along with hanging feeders, a *ground feeder* will often distract squirrels from the other feeders. Cracked corn provides an inexpensive source of starch for large ground feeding birds. You can also supply the feeder with mixed seeds such as millet and peanut kernels, which will keep squirrels and most ground feeding birds busy and happy.

Sunflower seeds are the number one choice of most songbirds, especially black-oil sunflower seeds, which are easier for birds to open.

Birds Attracted	Sunflower Seeds	Cracked Corn	Peanut Kernels	Millet
American Goldfinch	X			
Blackbird species		X		X
Blue Jay	X	X	X	
Caroline Chickadee	X			
Dark-eyed Junco		X		X
Evening Grosbeak	X			
House Finch	X			
Mourning Dove		X		X
Native sparrows		X	X	X
Northern Cardinal	X			
Red-winged Blackbird				X
Rufous-sided Towhee				X
Tufted Titmouse	X		X	
White-winged Dove		X		X

Source: TPWD Nongame & Urban Program

SUET FEEDERS

Another type of feeder many birds enjoy is a *suet feeder*. Suet is a hard beef fat, from the kidneys and loins, which provides high energy during winter months. You will attract a variety of birds to your suet feeder especially woodpeckers such as the Downy, Ladder-backed, Red-bellied, and Golden-fronted woodpeckers as well as Yellow-bellied sapsuckers to your yard. This type of feeder can be as simple as hard fat placed in an old onion bag and hung outside on a tree limb. Some people like to melt the suet and add a variety of well-loved seeds and raisins to make a special treat for birds. Vegetable shortening can also be used. Pine cones can be dipped in the warm mixture and serve as a decorative suet feeder once the fat mixture is allowed to cool and set. Suet feeders are ideal during cold weather, but suet becomes rancid very quickly during warm weather. In Texas, suet feeders should be watched closely for spoilage.

FEEDER MAINTENANCE

Regardless of what type of feeder is placed outdoors, regular maintenance and cleaning is important to keep the feeder disease-free and to keep the seeds or suet from spoiling. Usually, no more than a two-day supply of food should be placed in the feeders at a time.

Providing Shelter

Protective Cover

The goal is to provide varying degrees of shape, heights, and density to meet the needs of various species of wildlife.

Planting different types of vegetation not only provides a variety of food, but also has the added benefit of providing different places for wildlife to protect themselves from weather and predators. If you have mature trees with an open lawn, create some understory by planting small shrubs or trees and native wildflowers. If your yard has too many trees which create a heavy canopy, thinning the poorer ones will allow sunlight to reach any understory vegetation. If your yard is open, add some quick-growing native vines, tall shrubs, and trees. The goal is to provide varying degrees of shape, heights, and density to meet the needs of various species of wildlife. Maintain an open clearing (i.e., your lawn) in the center of your backyard and create an irregular border around it consisting of low vegetation. Gradually increase the vegetation height to the level of nearby trees to make an ideal wildlife sanctuary. It is best to avoid planting in rows or lines; the irregular borders or islands of various vegetation help to create an "edge effect." This provides a diverse habitat which can accommodate a variety of wildlife.

Reproductive Sites

Reproductive sites can be created with shrubs and mature trees. These provide branches and cavities for nesting birds and den-dwelling squirrels and birds.

NESTING BOXES

Nest boxes can serve as a substitute where trees or cavities are lacking. If a dead or dying tree exists on your property and doesn't create a human hazard, leave it for Downy, Ladder-backed, or Red-bellied woodpeckers which will excavate nest cavities in these dead trees. When they abandon their cavities after their young have fledged, other birds such as Chickadees, Titmice, Nuthatches, Screech Owls, Bluebirds, and some species of Flycatchers may take up residence within the cavity. These same birds, and others, will also gladly accept nest boxes, provided they are of specific dimensions and placed in a suitable area for the particular bird you want to attract. Nest boxes can also be used to provide housing for squirrels.

Wrens are not particularly picky about where they nest and will accept a nest box quite close to your house if it is hung on a partly sunlit tree limb. Woodpeckers can be attracted to your yard with suet feeders; however, only two species will utilize a nest box. The Northern Flicker and Red-bellied Woodpecker prefer their box hung high on a tree trunk exposed to direct sunlight. Cover the interior with a two-inch layer of wood chips or coarse sawdust. Eastern Screech Owls will readily use a box located near an edge of a field and lined with one to two inches of wood shavings. If cleaned out in the late spring after the fledglings have left the nest, you may be able to attract an American Kestrel. Putting up a bat roosting box could help rid your yard of numerous pests, including mosquitoes, since one bat can eat thousands of insects in a night.

NESTING SHELVES AND PLATFORMS

American Robins will accept a nesting platform, 6 feet or more up a shaded tree trunk or under an overhang of a shed or porch. Though most Robins migrate further north to nest, a few do remain in Texas to raise their young. If a mud puddle is provided nearby, this will further entice them since they line their nests with mud. Barn Swallows may nest where you would rather they did not, such as on the ledges of your house. Provide nesting shelves nearby where you would prefer to have the birds nesting.

Water Sources

Water is a requirement for wildlife that should be provided year-round. People often think animals can find water with ease during winter months. However, if you are creating a habitat in your backyard in an urban or suburban area, most likely you will not have a pond or lake nearby, and puddles of water won't sustain the animals throughout the winter months.

Ways to Create a Water Source

Creating a water source can be as simple as filling an inverted aluminum trash can lid with a few rocks placed in the center or as elaborate as building your own pond with overflow pipes, drains, and a small waterfall. Wildlife is especially attracted to moving water, which can be provided by a dripping hose or a mini-waterfall. A simple means of creating a "drip" is to drill small holes in the bottom of a bucket and then plug the holes with a cotton wick. Then fill the bucket with water and place it on a strong tree branch or some type of support to allow the water to slowly drip into a shallow receptacle placed beneath the bucket. A garden hose can even be hung over a limb and allowed to drip into your small pond or birdbath below.

Creating a water source can be as simple as filling an inverted aluminum trash can lid with a few rocks placed in the center or as elaborate as building your own pond with overflow pipes, drains, and a small waterfall.

Important Points when Providing a Water Source

- Always keep it full, clean, and chemical-free. A regularly cleaned birdbath, especially critical during the summer months, helps to prevent the spread of disease.

- Avoid creating a mosquito breeding area by including live fish, larvae control devices (available at garden centers), or by changing the water frequently.

- In winter, frozen water needs to be removed and replaced with fresh water. There are commercial outdoor water heaters available to prevent water from freezing which will not harm any visitors to the water sources. In many of the warmer parts of Texas, however, this won't be necessary.

- Most songbirds prefer water that is no more than three inches deep. Rough edges around the water source will help keep birds and other wildlife from slipping.

- The water source should be positioned in an area where there is an overhanging limb or nearby cover where wildlife, especially birds, can escape from predators. However, the cover should not be so close as to hide a hungry cat lying in wait for an easy meal.

- Elevate the water source at least three feet. This will also help keep cats away.

Wildlife Problems

Wildlife such as deer, armadillos, raccoons, and other larger mammals can quickly wear out their welcome when they dig up planting beds and devour the landscaping.

Although living with nature has its charms, it also has some drawbacks. There are a few animals that can cause problems in urban environments. Wildlife such as deer, armadillos, raccoons, and other larger mammals can quickly wear out their welcome when they dig up planting beds and devour the landscaping. Unfortunately, these species often visit our yards without an invitation. While an occasional wildlife visitor may be welcome for awhile, long-term guests can cause problems. Fortunately, there are steps which can be taken to minimize the potential damage.

Skunks, which eat insects, rodents, and fruit, can also damage gardens. It is not a pleasant experience having one take up residence under the porch or patio. Mothballs placed in the dens may help to evict them.

Cottontail rabbits, although very cute, can also cause problems in the garden. Look for droppings and tracks to make sure it is a rabbit eating your produce. A tight-wired three-foot-high fence buried one foot deep, can help keep rabbits out of your garden. Planting clover, alfalfa, or other succulent forage on the opposite side of your yard may also help to distract them from your garden.

Raccoons and *opossums* are cute when small, but they can become aggressive and sometimes destructive in an effort to get to pet food. An electric fence with one or two wires placed at least six inches from the ground can be an effective deterrent. In addition, keep all pet food stored inside.

Non-native introduced species, such as the House Sparrow and the European Starling, compete very aggressively with our native species for food and housing. Their nests may be removed since neither bird is protected by state or federal law. They are very determined nest builders, so nests may need to be removed quite frequently. Make sure you are destroying the House Sparrow's nest and not a nest belonging to one of our native species of songbird!

Co-Existing With Deer

Central Texas has an exploding urban deer population. When rainfall is scarce and natural food supply limited, deer will invade the tempting smorgasbord homeowners provide. Even during good years, homeowners will belatedly discover they have planted vegetation that is especially loved by deer. A heavy population of deer also increases competition for food, with the result that plants relatively unpalatable in an area where deer are not numerous will be readily browsed in an area where deer abound.

Nothing is truly deer proof. However, by learning a bit more about deer habits, their likes and dislikes, and by accepting a certain amount of deer damage as inevitable, you can co-exist with deer *and* achieve a pleasing landscape.

Nothing is truly deer proof. However, by learning a bit more about deer habits, their likes and dislikes, and by accepting a certain amount of deer damage as inevitable, you can co-exist with deer and achieve a pleasing landscape.

Deer Traits

Deer are not denizens of the forest, but rather are creatures of its edge. While the forest provides cover and sleeping quarters, it is rangeland, abandoned farmland, and recently cleared land that provide them with the weeds and shrubs they relish. White-tailed deer prefer new growth on shrubs to almost any other food. All the new subdivisions in the Austin area have provided a banquet for native deer, who also find the city a welcome refuge during the hunting season. Don't fall into the trap of thinking that setting up a feeder will keep deer from eating your other plants—you will be sending them an engraved invitation to your yard.

Deer are browsers. They tend to move along a set route during their feeding periods for several days, but will then change their route. What they eat is determined by what they happen to find in their path. For this reason, people sometimes think they've discovered a "sure fire" deer preventative technique, when all that has happened is that the deer just weren't in the area during a critical time in a plant's life. For plants, there is safety in numbers—unless unusually stressed, deer will seldom eat all the plants in a bed, just the most convenient ones. If you make your yard less attractive to deer by using a combination of physical barriers, harassment, and less *tasty* plants, you might discourage them from making your yard a stop on their nightly routes. Be prepared, however, for a certain amount of loss, and include the cost of replacement plants in your budget.

Plant Characteristics which Lead to Deer Damage

- *New, tender growth is irresistible to deer.* Established plants can withstand deer nibbling, but plants set out in the spring from one-gallon pots lack the root structrue to survive a severe "pruning." Try to obtain more mature plants, or cage your plants when they're young.

- *Tender buds and blossoms are deer "candy"*—yuccas and liriope are among their favorites. Although this is the most exasperating type of deer damage for homeowners who have been eagerly anticipating a lovely show of flowers, plants will generally survive this type of raid.

- *Plants with brittle wood can be easily damaged.* Deer may look dainty, but they aren't fastidious about where they put their feet. They will step on plants or brush against them and damage more brittle ones such as *Salvia greggii* or Mexican oregano, even if they don't eat them.

- *Smooth-surfaced tree trunks and tender new bark are deer attractors.* Deer will rub their antlers on trunks of shrubs and trees, and they like to nibble on tender bark in the spring. If they girdle the plant, i.e., strip the bark in a complete circle, they will kill it. Crepe myrtles are especially susceptible. A tree wrap will help prevent this type of damage.

Plant Characteristics Deer Don't Like

There are some plant characteristics which deer really don't like. Remember, however, that environmental stress, such as a drought, can make the most hated plant edible.

Table 8.1: Plant Characteristics and Examples

Characteristic	Plant Examples
Strong herbal smell and taste.	Rosemary, santolina, rue, salvias, wormwood, curry plants, yarrow, lamb's ear, and cenizo.
Tough (wiry, woody, and mature growth).	Nolina (sacahuista, bear grass, devil's shoestring), yucca, various palms, agarito, *dalea greggii*, and nandina.
Poisonous plants.	Oleander, mountain laurel, cherry laurel, snakeweed, pleurisy root, and *datura wrightii* (Jimsonweed).
Some thorny plants.	Fragrant mimosa, cholla, and prickly pear. Not roses, however—deer love them!

If you make your yard less attractive to deer by using a combination of physical barriers, harassment, and less tasty plants, you might discourage them from making your yard a stop on their nightly routes. Be prepared, however, for a certain amount of loss.

8—Texas Wildscapes: Co-Existing With Deer

Physical Deterrents

Physical barriers can deter deer. Therefore, you might want to consider some temporary barriers that will protect specific plants until they are mature enough to withstand deer browsing.

- *Cages made of chicken wire* are excellent temporary barriers.

- *Tree wraps* can serve both as a barrier and as protection against windburn and sunburn for young trees.

- *Electric fencing* can protect an entire yard or individual plants.

- A *wood privacy fence* can protect a back yard if it is at least six feet high.

- If you use *wire fencing* in a rural area, it should be at least eight feet high.

- *Two fences built three to four feet apart* will keep deer out. This method, however, is probably best reserved for professional nurseries.

ADDITIONAL DETERRENTS

- *Dogs*—depending on how diligent they are about keeping intruders out.

- *People*—deer will usually run if you shout or move toward them. Be careful though, they can also attack and have been known to kill.

- *Certain scents*—sometimes, this repels deer, but they have to be re-applied often. Don't bother hanging bars of soap on plants as the deer will eat them for dessert.

- *Cloud Cover* and *Hinder*—both available at garden centers. Cloud Cover has other primary uses such as protecting new transplants from drying out and helping to prevent powdery mildew.

Deer Resistant Plants

Table 8.2 lists some of the plants in Central Texas that are generally successful at co-existing with deer. This should only be used as a general guide. Keep in mind that the resistance of the plant is sometimes related to the availability of other food. If there is adequate supply of natural food in the deer's usual feeding ground, the gardener's ornamental plantings may go largely untouched. If, however, the natural food supply is low, there will be increased browsing in domestic gardens. *If there is an extreme shortage of natural food, then few, if any, plants will prove to be totally resistant to deer.*

Keep in mind that the resistance of the plant is sometimes related to the availability of other food. If there is adequate supply of natural food in the deer's usual feeding ground, the gardener's ornamental plantings may go largely untouched.

Xeriscape for Central Texas

Table 8.2: Deer Resistant Plants

Low to Medium Height Ground Covers		Taller Plants that can be Massed as Ground Cover	
Achillea millefolium	Yarrow	Artemesia ludoviciana	Silver King Artemesia
Ajuga reptans	Ajuga	Artemesia x 'Powis Castle'	Powis Castle Artemesia
Chrysactina mexicana	Damianita	Capsicum annuum*	Chili Pequin
Dalea greggii	Gregg's Silver Dalea	Caryopteris x clandonensis	'Longwood Blue' Blue Mist Spiraea
Melampodium leaucanthemum*	Blackfoot Daisy	Chasmanthium latifolium	Inland Sea Oats
Nepeta fasssenii	'Six Hills Giant' Catmint	Dalea frutescens*	Black Dalea
Origanum spp.	Oregano	Eupatorium coelestinum	Blue Mist Flower
Rivina humilis	Pigeonberry	Eupatorium greggi	Gregg's Mist Flower
Salvia engelmanii	Engelmann Sage	Eupatorium spp.	Joe Pye Weed
Salvia lyrata	Lyre-Leaf Sage	Gaura lindheimerii	Whirling Butterflies
Salvia nemerosa	Blue Bedder Salvia	Hypericum calycinum	St. John's Wort
Salvia roemeriana	Cedar Sage	Lantana spp.*	Lantana
Salvia sinaloensis	Bicolor Sage	Malvaviscus arboreus 'drummondii'	Turk's Cap
Salvia x superba	Blue Queen Sage	Monarda citriodora	Lemon Mint
Santolina	Santolina chamaecyparissus and S. virens	Monarda fistulosa	Bee Balm
Stachys byzantina	Lamb's Ears	Pavonia lasiopetala*	Rock Rose
Stachys coccinea*	Texas Betony	Penstemon tenuis	Brazos Penstemon
Southernwood	Artemesia abrotanum	Perilla frutescens 'atropurpurea'	Perilla
Teucrium chamaedrys	Dwarf Hedging Germander	Perovskia atriplicifolia	Russian Sage
Thelypteris kunthii	River Fern	Salvia azurea var. pitcherii	Pitcher Sage
Thymus spp.	Thyme	Salvia coccinea	Tropical Sage
Tulbaghia violacea	Society Garlic	Salvia farinacea	Mealy Blue Sage
Verbena bipinnatifida	Native Verbena	Salvia farinacea 'Victoria'	'Victoria' Mealy Blue Sage
Verbena tenuisectum	Moss Verbena	Salvia greggii	Cherry Sage
		Salvia guaranitica	Majestic Sage
		Salvia leucantha	Mexican Bush Sage
		Salvia longispicata x farinacea	'Indigo Spires' Salvia
		Salvia penstemenoides	Big Red Sage
		Tagetes lemonii	Copper Canyon Daisy
		Tagetes lucida	Mexican Mint Marigold
		Viguiera dentata	Plateau Golden Eye
		Viguiera stenoloba	Skeleton Leaf Golden Eye
*Deer may browse.		Zexmenia hispida (Wedelia texana)	Orange Zexmenia

Small Trees		Shrubs	
Acacia wrightii	Wright's Acacia	Anisacanthus wrightii	Flame Acanthus
Bauhinia congesta	Anacacho Orchid Tree	Berberis swayseyi	Texas Barberry
Caesalpinia gillesii	Bird of Paradise	Berberis trifoliata	Agarita
Cercis texensis	Redbud	Berberis thunbergii	Crimson Pygmy Barberry
Chilopsis linearis	Desert Willow	Buddleia davidii	Butterfly Bush
Cornus drummondii	Rough Leaf Dogwood	Buxus spp.	Boxwood
Diospyros texana	Mexican Persimmon	Caesalpinia pulcherrima	Pride of Barbados
Eysenhardtia texana	Texas Kidneywood	Cassia lindheimeri	Lindheimer's Cassia
Ilex vomitoria	Yaupon	Caryopteris x clandonensis	'Longwood Blue' Blue Mist Spiraea

198

8—Texas Wildscapes: The Hummingbird Garden

Table 8.2: Deer Resistant Plants (Continued)

Small Trees (cont'd)		Shrubs (cont'd)	
Pistacia texensis	Texas Pistache	Datura meteloides	Datura
Prunus caroliniana	Cherry Laurel	Eupatorium havanense	Fragrant Mist Flower
Rhus lanceolata	Prairie Flameleaf Sumac	Ilex vomitoira 'Nana'	Dwarf Yaupon
Sophora secundiflora	Texas Mountain Laurel	Jasminum mesneyi	Primrose Jasmine
Sophora affinis	Eve's Necklace	Leucophyllum spp.	Cenizo
Viburnum rudifilum	Rusty Blackhaw Viburnum	Lonicera albiflora	Fragrant White Bush Honeysuckle
Vitex agnus-castus	Vitex, Chaste Tree	Myrica cerifera	Wax Myrtle
Large Trees		Myrica pusilla	Dwarf Wax Myrtle
Cupressus arizonica	Arizona Cypress	Nandina spp.	Nandina
Juniperus ashei	Ash Juniper	Poliometha longiflora	Mexican Oregano
Juniperis virginiana	Eastern Red Cedar	Rhus aromatica	Fragrant Sumac
Cupressus x leylandii	Leyland Cypress	Rhus virens	Evergreen Sumac
Pinus eldarica	Afghan Pine	Rosmarinus officinalis	Rosemary
Pinus pinea	Italian Stone Pine	Salvia regla	Mountain Sage
Quercus spp.	Oaks	Tecoma stans	Yellow Bells
Prosopis glandulosa	Mesquite	Teucrium fruticans	Bush Germander
Anacua ehretia	Sandpaper Tree	Vitex rotundifolia	Beach Vitex
Accent Plants		**Grasses**	
Liatris mucronata	Gayfeather	Carex planostachys	Cedar Sedge
Salvia officinalis	Culinary Sage	Carex tumuicola	Berkely Sedge
Thapsus (Verbascum) spp.	Mulleins	Carex texensis	Texas Sedge
Vernonia lindheimerii	Wooly Ironweed	Miscanthus sinensis 'Gracillimus'	Maiden Grass
Agaves, Cacti, Sotols, & Yuccas		M. sinensis 'Gracillimus Nana'	Dwarf Maiden Grass
Agave lechuguilla	Lechuguilla	Muhlenbergia rigens	Deer Muhly
Agave stricta	Agave stricta	Muhlenbergia dubia	Pine Muhly
Dasylirion longissimum	Narrowleaf Sotol	Muhlenbergia dubiodes	Weeping Muhly
Dasylirion wheelerii	Wheeler's Blue Sotol	Muhlenbergia lindheimeri	Big Muhly
Nolina texana	Basket Grass	Muhlenbergia reverchonnii	Seep Muhly
Nolina nelsonii	Nelson's Basket Grass	Muhlenbergia capillaris	Gulf Muhly
Opuntia ficus-indica	Spineless Prickly Pear	Pennisetum alopecuroides	Fountain Grass
Yucca aloifolia	Spanish Bayonet	Pennisetum alopecuroides 'Moudry'	Black Fountain Grass
Yucca pendula (syn. Y. recurvifolia)	Soft-Leaf Yucca	Pennisetum villosum	Feathertop
Yucca rupicola	Twisted Leaf Yucca	Stipa tenuissima	Mexican Wire Grass
Vines		**Annuals**	
Gelsemium sempervirens	Carolina Jasmine	Catharanthus roseus	Periwinkles

The Hummingbird Garden

Feisty hummingbirds zipping about from flower to flower like so many glittering dive-bombers can be yours to behold, right in your own backyard. Their shining, jewel-like colors and fascinating behavior make hummingbirds a welcome visitor to the wildflower garden. Happily, they are easy to attract. Curious to the extreme, and ever on the lookout for new sources of food, hummers will boldly explore your garden for suitable nectar sources.

Attracting Hummingbirds

In the wild, hummingbirds frequent meadows, lowland forest edges, and woodland openings. The key to creating an attractive habitat for these small creatures is to provide them with conditions that most closely approach those found in the wild. Floral variety, rich nectar sources, overlapping bloom times, running water, and adequate cover are prime ingredients.

FOOD SOURCES

Hummingbirds utilize two major sources of food: flower nectar and the tiny insects and spiders that are attracted to it. The sweet tree sap that seeps from the holes made by sapsuckers is another favorite food source. Hummers will also frequent special feeders—placed within easy viewing—which contain sugar water of the proper consistency.[1]

WATER SOURCES

While hummingbirds do most of their drinking at flowers when they sip nectar, it is also good to provide an additional source of running water for them to drink. Bathing on a daily basis is important to hummingbird feather maintenance and health. Even though hummers can be observed using beads of water on a leaf or even the spray from a sprinkler, putting up a birdbath is perhaps the most effective method. Make sure the birdbath has areas of very shallow water so the birds are able to stand in the water if they choose to do so. Placing a few flat rocks in the water is a good way to create various depths. Watching hummers absorbed in their daily bathing routine can be lots of fun for the whole family.

The Makings of a Great Hummingbird Garden

Gardens designed to attract hummingbirds are easy to create. They can be as simple as a flower box or several containerized hummingbird plants arranged on a balcony or patio, or as elaborate as an expansive formalized habitat garden.

- Native trees, shrubs, and vines, along with native wildflowers, should be included.

- Flowering shrubs are very effective hummingbird lures, as are trellises and fences covered with flowering vines.

- Rather than scattering flowers about, plant them in clusters. Incorporate areas of shade, partial shade, and full sun.

"Hummingbirds and how to attract them to your garden"

Source: TX Parks & Wildlife Dept

[1.] Hummingbirds can be easily attracted with a 1-part sugar, 4-parts water solution placed in a feeder. This solution has to be boiled, and unused portions can be refrigerated for up to a week. It is recommended that feeders contain no more than a 2 to 3 day supply of solution, or else the solution begins to ferment especially in hot weather, and could cause illness and even death to the birds. To keep the solution from spoiling, it should be placed in the shade. You must be dedicated to cleaning the feeders every few days (with hot water and vinegar).

- Include tall trees, short, thick shrubbery, and low grassy areas to create a multi-tiered effect. The multi-layered arrangement not only affords a wide choice of suitable foraging, perching, and resting areas, it also provides easy access to all the flowers. Hummers will make use of this extra space around the blooms to hover and forage comfortably.

Plants that Attract Hummingbirds

One of the most important steps in creating a hummingbird garden is selecting and planting appropriate flowers. While hummingbirds will visit nectar-bearing flowers of all colors, *they are particularly drawn to bright red, orange, and pink tubular flowers.* A garden rich in scarlet penstemons, red sages, and bright orange trumpet vine will catch the eye of any hummingbird passing nearby. While hummingbirds will be attracted to red flowers no matter what country of origin, native wildflowers and flowering shrubs are recommended. You do not need to plant an "all red" garden to attract them, however. Once the birds discover suitable-shaped flowers with abundant nectar in yellow, pink, orange, or even white, they will return to them.

THE CLASSIC HUMMINGBIRD FLOWER

Before selecting particular native plants, it is good to review some of the structural principles of the classic hummingbird flower. Many "hummingbird" flowers hang down in pendent fashion or are held horizontally in widely spaced clusters of flowers. This configuration gives the bird plenty of room to feed easily and lessens the possibility of entanglement. Most hummingbird flowers have tubular or trumpet-shaped blossoms with thick petal walls and flexible stalks. Thick petal walls protect the delicate ovary at the base of the floral tube from injury and also discourage cheaters, like carpenter bees, from nipping the base and stealing the nectar. Other blossoms have grooves that guide the cylindrical hummingbird bill away from the fragile flower parts. Because hummingbirds have a very poor sense of smell, many hummingbird flowers save energy by not producing a fragrance. Odorless flowers are not attractive to insects, so non-pollinators are not encouraged to feed from them.

Many "hummingbird" flowers hang down in pendent fashion or are held horizontally in widely spaced clusters of flowers.

Hummingbirds require a great deal of energy to maintain body temperature and sustain flight. For this reason, hummingbird flowers produce large amounts of nectar at frequent intervals to attract the birds. Unlike insects, hummingbirds do not require special floral appendages or platforms on which to land while feeding, as the birds hover in the air in front of the flowers.

NATIVE PLANTS

Hummingbirds feed from a variety of different native plants. Ruby-throated hummingbirds whose range includes eastern U.S. and Canada, westward to Alberta, and south across the Great Plains to East Texas, are especially attracted to red columbine, scarlet

Xeriscape for Central Texas

sage, coral honeysuckle, phlox, trumpet creeper, cross vine, standing cypress, and various species of red, pink, and magenta penstemons.

The Black-chinned hummingbird, which summers throughout most of the western U.S. from Central Texas to British Columbia, is attracted to ocotillo, tree tobacco, chuparosa, lantana, palo verde, butterfly bush, scarlet delphinium, paintbrushes, red columbine, agaves, scarlet gilia, various penstemons, yuccas, and red-flowering currents, to name a few.

One of the most important steps in creating a hummingbird garden is selecting and planting appropriate flowers. While hummingbirds will visit nectar-bearing flowers of all colors, they are particularly drawn to bright red, orange, and pink tubular flowers. Table 8.3 lists some of the many attractive hummingbird plants found in Central Texas.

Table 8.3: Central Texas Plants That Attract Hummingbirds

Common Name	Botanical Name
Anacacho orchid tree	Bauhinia congesta
Autumn sage	Salvia greggii
Big reg sage	Salvia penstemonoides
Buckeye	Aesculus glabra v. arguta
Cardinal flower	Lobelia cardinalis
Cedar sage	Salvia roemeriana
Cenizo	Leucophyllum frutescens
Coral honeysuckle	Lonicera sempervirens
Drummond's phlox	Phlox drummondii
Eastern coral bean	Erythrina herbacea
False indigo	Amorpha fruticosa
Flame acanthus	Anisacanthus wrightii
Globe mallow	Sphaeralcea angustifolia
Heart-leaf hibiscus	Hibiscus cardiophyllus
Hedgehog cactus	Echinocereus triglochidiatus
Indian paintbrush	Castilleja indivisa
Lantana	Lantana horrida
Lead plant amorpha	Amorpha canescens
Mexican buckeye	Ungnadia speciosa
Mountain sage	Salvia regla
Pink-root	Spigelia marilandica
Prairie brazoria	Brazoria scutellarioides
Purple horsemint	Monarda citriodora
Rattlebush	Sesbania drummondii
Red buckeye	Aesculus pavia
Red yucca	Hesperaloe parviflora
Scarlet muskflower	Nyctaginia capitata
Scarlet runner bean	Phaseolus coccineus
Shrubby tobacco	Nicotiana glauca
Snapdragon vine	Maurandya antirrhiniflora
Standing cypress	Ipomopsis rubra
Texas clematis	Clematis texensis
Tropical sage	Salvia coccinia
Trumpet creeper	Campsis radicans
Turk's cap	Malvaviscus arboreus
Wild bergamot	Monarda fistulosa
Wild columbine	Aquilegia canadensis

Many species of hummingbirds occur in the southwestern portion of the state, including the Blue-throated, Broad-tailed, Magnificent, Lucifer, the occasional Anna's, Broad-billed, Calliope, Rufous, Violet-crowned, and White-eared hummingbirds. Native wildflowers and shrubs of the southwest including paintbrush, penstemons, columbines, sky-rocket, agaves, lupines, red salvias, ocotillo, lobelia, and monkey-flowers are highly attractive to these species. Table 8.3 lists some of the many attractive hummingbird plants found in Central Texas.

Hosting hummingbirds in your backyard will require work and planning, but once your habitat is established and the birds have discovered it, they will repay you tenfold with hours of enjoyment. Their beauty more than makes up for the labor involved.

Butterfly Gardening

The image of butterfly wings flitting gingerly from flower to flower like so many bits of confetti bobbing in the sun can bring a smile to any gardener's face. Butterflies add an ethereal beauty to flower gardens and meadows and are second in importance only to bees as plant pollinators. Together with the moths, butterflies make up the second largest order of insects, the Lepidoptera (from the Greek combining forms *Lepido* meaning scale and *ptera* meaning wing). More than 17,500 species of butterflies have been identified worldwide. While the greatest numbers are found in the tropical regions of the globe, approximately 700 species of butterflies occur in North America.

"Butterflies and how to attract them to your garden"

Source: TX Parks & Wildlife Dept.

Why Butterflies Are Endangered

Like many other species of animals, butterflies are suffering from a significant loss of habitat. The loss of native plant communities is a primary cause of species extinction, and butterflies have not escaped this pressure. Urban development transforms "waste" places where butterflies feed and reproduce, and plowing under prairies for cropland removes critical breeding and foraging areas. Widespread use of pesticides targeting insect pests, like the Gypsy Moth and mosquitoes, has resulted in fewer butterflies today than in the past. Rare butterflies, such as the federally-listed Mission blue, Bay checkerspot, Schaus swallowtail, or the Lange's metalmark, are not the only ones affected. Overall numbers of some species once considered plentiful are also significantly down.

This is where the home gardener comes in. By protecting, restoring, and managing natural habitats in our own backyards, we can help protect these beautiful creatures by creating the conditions that promote their abundance and diversity, instead of destroying them. The reintroduction of natural landscape elements into urban and suburban neighborhoods may be one of the greatest contributions to ecosystem conservation that we can make.

Xeriscape for Central Texas

A Natural Synergy: Butterflies and Native Plants

Butterflies and native plant species depend on one another and help each other survive. While butterflies pollinate the flowers, the plants provide butterflies with food, housing, and sometimes, chemical protection. Eggs are laid on appropriate host plants whose leaves provide ample food for the larvae. Nectar plants provide fuel for adults in their quest to find a mate and reproduce.

Planting local native plant species in a rich, well-planned butterfly garden will provide essential corridors between remaining patches of habitat and help repair the patchwork of healthy ecosystems that still exist. Every square meter devoted to a butterfly garden will also provide habitat for many other species of beneficial insects. Besides the conservation benefit, there is the added benefit and delight of watching butterflies flutter about the garden from the first warm days of spring to the last warm days of fall. As Robert Pyle, noted butterfly conservationist, expresses it, "the beauty of a swallowtail-studded patch of phlox confers a deep sense of pleasure that flowers alone are unable to match."

Butterflies add an ethereal beauty to flower gardens and meadows and are second in importance only to bees as plant pollinators. By protecting, restoring, and managing natural habitats in our own backyards, we can help protect these beautiful creatures by creating the conditions that promote their abundance and diversity.

Butterflies and Plants

Butterflies, along with other insects, pollinate more than 65% of the world's flowering plants. Adults of most species of butterflies feed on nectar, while nearly all larvae are plant feeders. *Butterflies generally frequent day-blooming flowers, whereas most moths visit evening or night-blooming varieties.* White flowers that emit their fragrance at night are highly attractive to moths.

CHARACTERISTICS OF BUTTERFLY PLANTS

- The best butterfly nectar plants have tubular flowers of just the right length—no longer that the butterfly's proboscis.

- Florets tend to be arranged either in clusters or around a central flowerhead. These arrangements provide adequate space for landing and allow convenient perching for feeding. Butterflies may spend several seconds to as long as a minute sipping nectar from a given flower.

- Butterflies tend to feed on flowers that produce nectar having a 20% to 25% sugar concentration.

- Butterflies are very keen-sighted, and purple, red, pink, orange, yellow, and white are especially attractive to them. Some flowers have nectar guides that reflect UV light to help butterflies find nectar sources more easily. Unlike most other insects, some species of butterflies are attracted to red flowers.

HOW A BUTTERFLY FEEDS

Butterflies use their proboscis as a feeding tool, plunging it into the floral tube and sipping up the nectar as from a double-barreled straw. Both sweet and unpleasant-smelling flowers attract butterflies. The club-like tips of the butterfly's long antennae are probably the most important odor detectors and are useful in the recognition of food. Smelling and tasting are also done by the tip of the proboscis and especially by the feet (*tarsi*). Contact with sweet liquids, such as floral nectar, causes the proboscis to automatically uncoil. Female butterflies often use their feet to detect appropriate larval host plants. By scratching or tapping the leaves of plants with their hind tarsi, females sense the chemicals contained in the plant and instinctively know whether that plant is suitable for egg-laying and for her larvae to eat.

How to Build a Great Butterfly Garden

Building a butterfly garden sanctuary around your home is not difficult. Whether you have a large house with extensive gardens and fields or a small garden apartment with a modest plot of yard space, anyone can attract and play host to butterflies. Much will depend on how enthusiastic you are and how strongly you can keep your need for neatness and order under control. Remember, though, that the design possibilities are limitless and need not conform to any particular model. You are completely free to create your own special vision. Experiment and have fun.

Make the most of your natural setting. Butterflies like edges. Planting low flowers at the edge of a lawn and high flowers at the edges of trees or along a fence is a way to enhance edge habitat.

Locate a major part of the garden in a sunny, protected area. Butterflies are cold-blooded and need sun to warm their body temperature. They also use the sun for orientation. Analyze your garden's orientation with respect to the sun to determine whether it receives an adequate amount of light by tracking the sun's position throughout the day. This will help guide you in flower placement. Place flat stones at various sunny locations in the garden for butterflies to bask on. During cool mornings or cold spells, butterflies will perch on these stones or on bare soil to sun themselves. This behavior is necessary to raise their body temperature sufficiently enough to allow them to fly. A few species of butterflies, such as the Wood nymph and satyrs, prefer shady conditions, and if your yard has a wooded area, you might consider laying out special potions to attract these species. Geyata Ajilvsgi, in her book, *Butterfly Gardening for the South*, has a number of effective and apparently irresistible recipes.

If there are any natural structures to block the wind, leave them standing. Butterflies avoid high winds and appreciate wind-breaks. They will often congregate behind breaks on blustery days to get out of the wind, allowing them to fly freely about your garden on an otherwise unsuitable day. You may want to add tall plants to buffer the wind if your garden does not possess natural barriers.

Whether you have a large house with extensive gardens and fields or a small garden apartment with a modest plot of yard space, anyone can attract and play host to butterflies.

Native wildflowers serve as butterfly lures. Growing native species not only restores habitat, but also provides special nectar sources for the butterflies. When selecting wildflowers, it is always best to select those native to your region, though a few non-natives such as West Indian bloodroot (*Ascelpias curassavica*) and Common Butterflybush (*Buddleia* spp.), or marigolds, do a magnificent job at attracting butterflies, and make great additions to the native butterfly garden.

A combination of wildflower species and grasses that bloom from early spring through early fall will keep butterflies well fed throughout the season. Most butterflies wander from place to place, stopping off temporarily at your garden to partake of food, water, and shelter on their way to somewhere else. When food sources disappear, butterflies go elsewhere. Gardeners from Central Texas can enjoy amazingly extended flowering seasons with many attendant butterfly species, both residents and migrants.

Try to use large splashes of color when designing the layout of your garden. Butterflies are first attracted to flowers by their color, and a large mass is easier for them to spot. According to some experts, their favorite color is purple, followed by blue, yellow, white, pink, and orange. Members of the composite family, such as asters, coreopsis, boneset, goldenrods, and sunflowers, are excellent nectar sources.

Leave old trees as well as some younger trees, as butterflies like to perch on them and their larvae may use them for food. For instance, the beautiful swallowtail caterpillar prefers wild cherry. Mourning cloak caterpillars feed on elms and willows, as well as hackberries. Spicebush caterpillars prefer, in addition to spicebush, red bay and sweet bay trees. Small trees, such as hawthorns, buckeyes, and sumacs offer nectar sources and shelter as well.

If you love butterflies, you will have to learn to love and provide for their larvae, too. Adult butterflies will definitely hang around, if you feed and house their caterpillars. Admittedly, caterpillars look rather like worms—a life form not held in high regard by many people. It is important, however, to provide a good quantity of larval host plants for them, as larval food plants lure females into the garden to lay their eggs. Don't get overly attached to the larval host plants, though, or you will be upset when you watch the hungry caterpillars eat them to shreds. That's how they grow. They will repay plants indirectly by performing pollination duties at the next stage. It all evens out in the long run.

Try to leave thick brush under some of the trees. This is where butterflies can find shelter and warmth on colder days or when it rains. These are also often the areas where larvae go to pupate. Dead and hollow stumps are also good places for insects to take refuge from inclement weather or predators.

If you love butterflies, you will have to learn to love and provide for their larvae, too.

Table 8.4: Larval Host Plants

Common Name	Botanical Name
Anacacho Orchid Tree	*Bauhinia congesta*
Black Dalea	*Dalea frutescens*
Cenizo	*Leucophyllum frutescens*
Cedar Elm	*Ulmus crassifolia*
Dill	*Anethum graveolens*
Flame Acanthus	*Anisacanthus wrightii*
Lantana	*Lantana horrida*
Milkweed	*Asclepias* spp.
Parsley	*Petroselinum crispum*
Passionflower	*Passiflora* spp.
Spanish Dagger	*Yucca treculiana*
Sunflower	*Helianthus annuus*
Texas Mountain Laurel	*Sophora secundiflora*
Yarrow	*Achillea millefolium*

Provide damp areas or shallow puddles. If at all possible install a seep irrigation system. Don't set up sprinklers, though, as this washes the nectar out of the flowers. A permanent wet patch or seep with various species of sedges and moisture-loving wildflowers will surely attract a multitude of butterflies. As a matter of fact, a damp patch of sand, baited with a touch of manure or fermented fruit, will attract butterflies in a "puddle assemblage." Soil "enriched" by urine or ashes from fires can also be especially attractive to them. Large congregations of "puddlers"—mostly males who derive important elements from this foul feast—will descend to partake of the goodies. Here, they will be less wary of observers—a good spot to take photos.

People who want to go all out might well choose to offer butterfly "delicacies" that are anything but delicate. Beautiful butterflies do not always behave the way we might expect. Shunning our most prized roses, many prefer to feed on rotten fruit, carrion, mud puddles, oozing sap, human sweat, and even animal scat. Of course, this step is not for everyone, but if you choose to take it, you can attract species you might not otherwise see. The dazzling Red-spotted purple, Hackberry, and Goatweed butterflies can be the prize. In fact, many attractive members of the *Nymphalidae* (Brush-footed butterfly family) are attracted to these putrid buffets.

Do not use insecticides anywhere near your butterfly garden, near the larval food plants, or near the adult nectar sources. These chemicals will kill butterflies in both the adult and larval stages. Treat any pest problem you have manually. If you have fire ants, use a juvenile growth hormone such as Logic, diatomaceous earth, or boiling water, but not poisons. Integrated pest management is the best technique in any situation.

Remember butterfly gardens develop gradually. They are not made overnight or even in one year. Each year, you can increase the number of nectar plant selections and lengthen the blooming period

You can be certain that butterflies will come to your gardens and flourish there if they find nectar plants, and, most important, the larval host plants on which the females lay their eggs.

Xeriscape for Central Texas

to span the seasons. Planning, patience, and persistence are the keys to success. The more home gardeners add to the interactive communities of butterflies and native plants, the more stable and colorful your habitat will become. Table 8.5 lists some of the food and nectar plants for butterflies and moths in Central Texas.

Table 8.5: Butterfly Nectar Plants

Common Name	Botanical Name
Agarita	*Berberis trifoliata*
Butterfly Bush	*Buddleia davidii*
Butterfly Weed	*Asclepias turberosa*
Buttonbush	*Cephalanthus occidentalis*
Canna Lily	*Canna x generalis*
Carolina Jessamine	*Gelsemium sempervirens*
Coral Vine	*Antigon leptopus*
Coreopsis	*Coreopsis lanceolata*
Desert Willow	*Chilopsis linearis*
Flowering Sedum	*Sedum spectabile*
Glossy Abelia	*Abelia x grandiflora*
Lantana	*Lantana horrida, L. camara*
Marigolds	*Tagetes* spp.
Mexican Oregano	*Poliomintha longiflora*
Passionflower	*Passiflora incarnata*
Pavonia	*Pavonia lasiopetala*
Pentas	*Pentas lanceolata*
Purple Coneflower	*Echinacea purpurea*
Spirea	*Spiraea* spp.
Summer Phlox	*Phlox paniculata*
Texas Star Hibiscus	*Hibiscus coccineus*
Verbena	*Verbena bipinnatifida*
White Mistflower	*Eupatorium wrightii*
Yarrow	*Achillea* spp.
Zinnias	*Zinnia acerosa, Z. grandiflora*

By planting local native wildflowers, shrubs, and trees in a rich, well-designed butterfly garden, you will not only provide much needed corridors between remaining patches of natural habitat, you will also be contributing in a significant measure to conserving our native butterfly population.

Many of our butterflies are now disappearing, not just those recognized as endangered species. By protecting, restoring, and managing natural habitats in our own backyards, we can be instrumental in protecting and restoring numbers of those species whose disappearance we are already witnessing. You can be certain that butterflies will come to your gardens and flourish there if they find nectar plants, and, most important, the larval host plants on which the females lay their eggs. Finally, by planting local native wildflowers, shrubs, and trees in a rich, well-designed butterfly garden, you will not only provide much needed corridors between remaining patches of natural habitat, you will also be contributing in a significant measure to conserving our native butterfly population.

The *Texas Wildscapes* Program

If you're interested in transforming your yard into a low-maintenance, wildlife-friendly habitat, the Texas Parks and Wildlife Department's *Texas Wildscapes* program can help you get started. You can begin creating your own habitat by ordering the *Texas Wildscapes Information Packet* from the Texas Parks and Wildlife Department. To order information, write:

TPWD Nongame and Urban Program
4200 Smith School Road
Austin, Texas 78744

Or you can call 389-4403 if you live in Austin; outside of Austin, call 1-800-792-1112. You can also find information on the TPWD web site at:

[http://www.tpwd.state.tx.us/nature/plant/wldscape.htm].

The $15 packet includes booklets on butterfly gardening, hummingbird gardening, and other backyard wildlife written by TPWD staff biologists. You will also receive a National Wildlife Federation book, *The Backyard Naturalist*, a color brochure produced by the Native Plant Society of Texas on ornamental trees, information on feeders, nest box dimensions, lists of native plants, and an application form.

After designing your habitat, submit the completed application form and a rough sketch of your yard to the TPWD *Wildscapes* program. The department will review your application, and upon approval, you will receive a certificate of achievement and a decorative green and white sign to designate the site. The *Wildscapes* application fee not only pays for the program, it helps support nongame education, management, and research throughout Texas. By following the department's suggestions, you can create a beautiful, easy-to-care-for landscape for your home and enjoy the company of many wildlife species year around.

Sometimes we get overwhelmed by the multitude of environmental challenges we hear about—acid rain; ozone depletion; polluted lakes, rivers, and coastlines; and global warming—to the point that we feel that there is nothing we can personally do. But if we start in our own backyard, each one of us can make a difference.

Sometimes we get overwhelmed by the multitude of environmental challenges we hear about—acid rain; ozone depletion; polluted lakes, rivers, and coastlines; and global warming—to the point that we feel that there is nothing we can personally do. But if we start in our own backyard, each one of us can make a difference.

Acknowledgments

The information on Texas Wildscapes was excerpted from the *Texas Wildscapes Information Packet* produced by the Texas Parks and Wildlife Department, Nongame and Urban Program. A special thanks goes to John Herron, Director of the Nongame and Urban Program, for granting permission to reprint the Wildscapes information in this publication.

Xeriscape for Central Texas

The section on *Co-Existing with Deer* is based on Xeriscape Garden Club Fact Sheet #13, which was originally authored by Will Walker and Susan DuBar (with credit to the Lady Bird Johnson Wildflower Research Center publication *Deer Resistant Plants* for the information and wording about deer characteristics.)

The extensive list on deer resistant plants was compiled by Austin landscape designer Brenda Barger. Brenda thanks author and landscape designer, Jill Nokes, for sharing her "desperate deer plant list" and her own extensive experience working in deer habitats. *Barton Springs Nursery* (Austin, TX) also shared their valuable customer survey on deer resistant plants, and Chip Schumacher of New Braunfel's *Hill Country Gardens* provided an extensive list of deer resistant plants.

When it comes to the voice of experience, Austin gardeners frequently turn to Patti Simons, a.k.a. the "Deer Lady," a former certified deer rehabilitator and expert gardener who proves you can co-exist with deer and have a beautiful garden. Patti presented her techniques of "camouflage gardening" with deer to the Xeriscape Garden Club of the Austin Area, Inc. in 1996.

Bibliography

Damude, Noreen. *Butterflies and How to Attract Them to Your Garden*. Austin, Texas: Texas Parks and Wildlife Department Nongame and Urban Program.

Damude, Noreen. *Hummingbirds and How to Attract Them to Your Garden*. Austin, Texas: Texas Parks and Wildlife Department Nongame and Urban Program.

Foss, Diana. *Designing a Wildscape*. Austin, Texas: Texas Parks and Wildlife Department Nongame and Urban Program.

Appendices...

A: Conversion of Existing Landscapes
B: Sustainability and Xeriscape
C: Color Throughout the Year
D: Shade Tolerant Plants
E: Perennials and Grasses
F: Hydrozone Coding
G: Water Harvesting
H: Central Texas Resources
I: Recommended Reading & References

These appendices contain additional information that the authors chose not to include in the individual chapters, yet wanted to include in the book. The basics for converting an existing landscape is here, as well as extensive lists for year-round color, shade tolerant plants, and perennials and grasses. Also included is a list of resources with addresses, phone numbers, and web addresses for those of you seeking more specific information and/ or examples of Xeriscape in action. Finally, the authors have compiled a list of their favorite gardening books. **Happy Gardening!**

211

A: Conversion of Existing Landscapes

The benefits that apply to a new landscape also apply to changing an existing high water use landscape to a Xeriscape having reduced water costs, maintenance time, pesticides, and fertilizer. Phasing in the new Xeriscape can reduce the costs of changing your landscape.

To kill perennial turf grasses such as Bermuda and St. Augustine effectively, use an herbicide with glyphosphate as an active ingredient. Examples are "Doomsday," "Kleenup," "Roundup," or a 10% vinegar and water solution. When you use this type of herbicide, the turf grass must be growing vigorously, so that you kill the maximum amount of grass. In the central Texas area, turf grass grows best when the nighttime temperatures are consistently above 68 to 70 degrees (usually from June to late September). Water turf areas daily for about 30 minutes during the week before you plan to spray. Do not mow during this period.

Select a calm morning for spraying. Spray the lawn with an even application of herbicide using a heavy spray to avoid drift onto desirable plants. Shield fragile plants with cardboard. If you apply the herbicide correctly, 90% of the grass will die in seven to 10 days. Spot kill any areas that survive the initial spray. Two weeks after you spray, scalp the lawn by setting your lawn mower on its lowest setting. You can also rent a verticutter or power rake. Remove all the dead grass (it is okay to compost, the herbicide is gone).

After preparing the soil, you can now safely plant trees, shrubs, ground covers, or succulents. Provide the new plants with generous watering basins even if you install a drip irrigation system.

Complete your conversion by spreading up to four inches of mulch. Spot kill any grass if it reappears.

B: Sustainability and Xeriscape

John Gleason

Sustainability means *meeting our needs in the present without compromising the needs of future generations*. The issue of sustainability requires that you take a long-term, "big-picture" view of things. It means balancing economical, environmental, and social concerns, whether you're creating (or managing) a city or landscape. It pragmatically recognizes that our environment is our "life-support" system, and acknowledges that "What we do for the earth, we do for ourselves." A sustainable approach toward landscaping is one of the many ways that homeowners can soften their impact on the local environment. Thus, "landscaping which meets our needs in the present without compromising the needs of future generations" can be part of the "cure" for restoring health to our urban environment. In this case, CURE stands for:

- **C**ommunity Gardening.
- **U**sing Resources Effectively.
- **R**educe, Reuse, and Recycle.
- **E**nvironmental Protection.

The following information explains sustainable landscaping through the principles of CURE.

Community gardening involves landscaping efforts that are beneficial to our whole community. It's gardening with people of all races and generations, especially children. Community gardening is a tool for environmental education and promotes awareness. It means volunteering for local environmental projects and garden clubs.

Use resources effectively. Like Xeriscape, sustainable landscaping involves efficient and effective use of our resources. While Xeriscape emphasizes water-use efficiency, sustainable landscaping seeks to conserve all resources, including water, energy, land, and our affluence.

Reduce, reuse, and recycle efforts help to convert potential waste into valuable resources. Compost and organic mulch are good examples of the sustainable approach that gardeners have been employing for many years. Beside recycling on-site, gardeners can purchase recycled materials or products, and use high-quality, durable products that can be repaired instead of discarded.

Environmental protection means using best management practices (BMPs) to minimize the amount and severity of non-point pollution entering our local waterways. BMPs include using Integrated Pest Management (IPM) and appropriate amounts of fertilizer. It also means using alternative fuels and limiting emissions.

With the right knowledge, skill, and attitude, Central Texas gardeners can avoid being part of the problem by becoming involved with the solution. The Xeriscape Garden Club membership believes that the way we design and manage our landscapes can help to ensure the long-term survival of our regional ecosystem. We promote a sustainable human culture that can involve itself intelligently and productively with our developed landscape.

Xeriscape for Central Texas

C: Color Throughout the Year

Common Name	Botanical Name	Color	Light	Ht. × Spacing	
Woody and Herbaceous Perennials (*including some self-sowing annuals*)					
Columbine	*Aquilegia canadensis*	Red/Yellow	Part-Shade, Shade	24"	24"
Hinckley's Columbine	*A. chrysantha v. hinkleyana*	Yellow	Part-Shade, Shade	24"	24"
Wood Sorrel	*Oxalis drummondii*	Pink	Part-Shade, Shade	12"	12"
Winecups	*Callirhoe involucrata*	Magenta	Sun, Part-Shade	12"	24"
Damianita	*Chrysactina mexicana*	Yellow	Sun	18"	24"
Dayflower	*Commelina spp.*	Light Blue	Part-Shade, Shade	12-18"	18"
Magenta Dianthus	*Dianthus sp.*	Magenta	Sun, Part-Shade	6-12"	24"
Four Nerve Daisy	*Hymenoxys scaposa*	Yellow	Sun	8"	12"
Blackfoot Daisy	*Melampodium leucanthemum*	White/Yellow	Sun	12"	24"
Narcissus	*Narcissus spp.*	Yellow, White	Sun, Part-Shade	12-18"	
Prairie Beardstongue	*Penstemon cobaea*	Pale Lavender, Pink	Sun, Part Shade	24"	24"
Brazos Penstemon	*Penstemon tenuis*	Purple	Sun, Part-Shade	24"	24"
Drummond Phlox	*Phlox drummondii*	Red-Pink	Sun, Part-Shade	6-12"	12"
Frog Fruit	*Phyla nodiflora var. incisa*	White	Sun, Part-Shade	3-4"	18-24"
Spring Obedient Plant	*Physostegia angustifolia*	Lavender	Sun, Part-Shade, Shade	36-60"	24"
Cherry Sage	*Salvia greggii*	Red, Pink, White, Coral	Sun, Part Shade	36"	36"
Lyre-Leaf Sage	*Salvia lyrata*	Blue	Part-Shade	12"	12"
Bog Sage	*Salvia uliginosa*	Blue	Sun, Part-Shade	60"	36"
Texas Betony	*Stachys coccinea*	Coral	Sun, Part-Shade	18"	30"
Blue-Eyed Grass	*Sisyrinchium ensigerum*	Blue	Part-Shade, Shade	8-10"	12"
Giant Spiderwort	*Tradescantia gigantea*	Purple	Sun, Part-Shade, Shade	18-36"	18"
Moss Verbena	*Verbena tenuisecta*	Purple	Sun	12-18"	36"
Wood Violets	*Viola missouriensis*	Purple	Part-Shade, Shade	12"	12"
Johnny Jump-Ups	*Viola cornuta*	Purple/Yellow	Sun, Part-Shade	7-10"	8"
Flowering Shrubs					
Agarita	*Berberis trifoliata*	Yellow	Sun, Part-Shade	4-6'	3-4'
Texas Barberry	*Berberis swayseyi*	Yellow	Sun, Part-Shade	4-6'	3-4'
Primrose Jasmine	*Jasminum mesneyi*	Yellow	Sun, Part-Shade	8'	8'
Flowering Quince	*Chaenomeles speciosa*	Scarlet, Pink, White, Orange, & Salmon	Sun	6'	6'
Flowering Vines					
Coral Honeysuckle	*Lonicera sempervirens*	Red, Yellow	Sun, Part-Shade		
Carolina Jessamine	*Gelsemium sempervirens*	Yellow	Sun, Part-Shade		
Lady Banks Rosa	*Rosa banksiae*	White, Yellow	Sun		

Early Spring (February & March)

Appendix C: Color Throughout the Year

Common Name	Botanical Name	Color	Light	Ht. ×	Spacing
Flowering Trees					
Oklahoma Plum	*Prunus gracilis*	White	Sun, Part-Shade	24-72"	18-36"
Mexican Plum	*Prunus mexicana*	White	Sun, Part-Shade	15-25'	15-20'
Texas Mountain Laurel	*Sophora secundiflora*	Purple	Sun, Part Shade	12-20'	6-12'
Mexican Buckeye	*Ugnadia speciosa*	Pink	Sun, Part-Shade	8-15'	8-15'
Woody and Herbaceous Perennials (*including some self-sowing annuals and biennials*)					
Yarrow	*Achillea millefolium*	White	Sun, Part-Shade, Shade	12"	24"
Calylophus	*Calylophus berlandieri*	Yellow	Sun	12"	24"
Oxeye Daisy	*Chrysanthemum leucanthemum*	White/Yellow	Sun, Part-Shade	12-24"	12"
Coreopsis	*Coreopsis spp.*	Yellow	Sun	18-24"	18-36"
Lavender Lace Dianthus	*Dianthus superbus*	Lavender	Part-Shade	12-18"	24"
Snakeherb	*Dyschoriste linearis*	Purple	Sun, Part-Shade	9"	18"
Purple Coneflower	*Echinacea purpurea*	Purple, White	Sun, Part-Shade	24"	18"
Indian Blanket	*Gaillardia pulchella*	Red, Red/Yellow	Sun	18-24"	18"
Whirling Butterflies	*Gaura lindheimeri*	White/Pink	Sun, Part-Shade	18-48"	24-48"
Daylilies	*Hemerocallis spp.*	Various	Sun	30-36"	18-24"
Heartleaf Hibiscus	*Hibiscus cardiophyllus*	Red	Sun	36"	24'
Iris	*Iris spp.*	Various	Sun, Part-Shade	12-36"	18"
Butter 'n Eggs	*Linaria vulgaris*	Yellow	Sun	18"	12"
Blue Flax	*Linum lewisii*	Blue	Sun	12-24"	12-18"
Bluebonnets	*Lupinus texensis*	Blue, Pink	Sun	18-24"	18"
Rose Campion	*Lychnis coronaria*	Magenta	Sun	30"	30'
Tahoka Daisy	*Machaeranthera tanacetifolia*	Purple	Sun	12-18"	24"
Beebalm	*Monarda spp.*	Red	Sun, Part-Shade	12-24"	24-30"
Fluttermills	*Oenethera missouriensis*	Yellow	Sun, Part-Shade	12"	18"
Mexican Primrose	*Oenothera speciosa*	Pink	Sun	8-16"	24"
Peruvian Rock Rose	*Pavonia hastata*	Pale Pink to White	Sun, Part-Shade	48-72"	24-36"
Rock Rose	*Pavonia lasiopetala*	Pink	Sun, Part-Shade	24-48"	36-48"
Hill Country Penstemon	*Penstemon triflorus*	Magenta	Sun, Part-Shade	18-24"	12-18"
Drummond Phlox	*Phlox drummondii*	Red, White, Pink	Sun	8-24"	
Prairie Phlox	*Phlox Pilosa*	Pink	Part-Shade, Shade	18-12"	12"
Mexican Oregano	*Poliomentha longiflora*	Pink	Sun, Part-Shade	24-36"	36"
Wild Petunia	*Ruellia spp.*	Purple, Pink, White	Sun, Part-Shade, Shade	12-48"	18"
Purple Leaf Sage	*Salvia blepharophylla*	Red	Part Shade, Shade	24"	30"
Englemann Sage	*Salvia englemannii*	Blue	Sun	18"	24"
Mealy Blue Sage	*Salvia farinacea*	Blue	Sun	12-24"	24"
Majestic Sage	*Salvia guaranitica*	Blue, Purple	Sun, Part-Shade	48"	24"
Indigo Spires Salvia	*Salvia longispicata x farinacea*	Blue	Sun, Part-Shade	48"	60"
Bicolor Sage	*Salvia sinaloensis*	Blue	Part-Shade	12"	18"
Bog Sage	*Salvia uliginosa*	Blue	Sun, Part-Shade	60"	36"
Lavender Scullcap	*Scuttellaria seleniana*	Lavender	Sun, Part-Shade	36"	36"

Spring (April & May)

Appendix C: Color Throughout the Year

	Common Name	Botanical Name	Color	Light	Ht. × Spacing	
Spring (April & May)	Pink Scullcap	*Scuttellaria suffrutescens*	Pink	Sun	12"	24"
	Buttercups	*Turnera ulmifolia*	Yellow	Sun, Part-Shade	36"	24"
	Zexmenia	*Zexmenia hispida*	Orange	Sun	24"	36"
	Flowering Shrubs					
	Texas Sage	*Leucophyllum frutescens*	Lavender, White	Sun	6'	6-8'
	Monterrey Cenizo	*Leucophyllum langmanae*	Lavender	Sun	4-6'	4--6'
	Grape-Scented Sage	*Salvia melissodora*	Lavender	Sun	6'	4'
	Yellow Bells	*Tecoma stans var. Angustata*	Yellow	Sun	3-6'	3-4'
	Skeleton Leaf Goldeneye	*Viguiera stenoloba*	Yellow	Sun	3'	3'
	Flowering Trees					
	Anacacho Orchid Tree	*Bauhinia lunaroides*	White	Sun, Part-Shade	8-15'	6-15'
	Texas Redbud	*Cercis canadensis var. Texensis*	Lavender	Sun, Part-Shade	15'	12-15'
	Mexican Redbud	*Cercis canadensis var. Mexicanus*	Lavender	Sun, Part-Shade	12'	12'
	Golden Ball Lead Tree	*Leucaena retusa*	Yellow	Sun	15-20'	12-15'
	Eve's Necklace	*Sophora affinis*	Pink	Sun, Part-Shade	10-20'	6-10'
	Flowering Vines					
	Crossvine	*Bignonia capreolata*	Yellow/Red	Sun, Part-Shade		
	Wisteria	*Wisteria sinensis*	Purple	Sun, Part-Shade		
	Annuals					
	Cosmos	*Cosmos spp.*	White, Yellow, Orange, Pink, & Red	Sun	3-6'	18-24"
	Larkspur	*Delphinium ajacis*	Pink, White, Blue	Sun, Part-Shade	36-48"	12"
	Shirley Poppy	*Papaver rhoeas*	White, Pink, Red	Sun	24-30"	
	White Lace Flower	*Ammi majus*	White	Sun	36"	12"
	Hollyhocks	*Alcea rosea*	Assorted	Sun, Part-Shade	2-8'	
Early to Mid-Summer (June & July)	**Woody and Herbaceous Perennials** (*including some biennials*)					
	Agapanthus	*Agapanthus africanus*	Purple	Part-Shade	36"	24"
	Tropical Milkweed	*Asclepias curassavica*	Yellow/Red	Sun	48"	24"
	Swan River Daisy	*Brachycomb multifida*	Lavender	Sun, Part-Shade	12"	18"
	Cannas	*Canna spp.*	Red, Orange, Yellow	Sun, Part-Shade	36-60"	48-60"
	Texas Star Hibiscus	*Hibiscus coccineus*	Red	Sun, Part-Shade	5-6'	3-6'
	Pink Lantana	*Lantana camara*	Pink/Yellow	Sun	36"	48'
	Texas Lantana	*Lantana horrida*	Orange/Yellow	Sun	48"	48'
	Lantana hybrids:					
	'Cream Spreader'	*Lantana hybrid*	Ivory	Sun	18"	36"
	'Flame Red'	*Lantana hybrid*	Red/Orange	Sun	30"	36"
	'Irene'	*Lantana hybrid*	Magenta	Sun	24"	24"
	'New Gold'	*Lantana hybrid*	Gold	Sun	18"	48"
	Trailing Lantana	*Lantana montevidensis*	Purple, White	Sun, Part-Shade	18"	48"
	Lion's Tail	*Leonotis leonurus*	Orange	Sun	36-72"	24-36"
	Texas Bluebells	*Lisianthus russelianus*	Blue, Purple, Pink	Sun, Part-Shade	18-24"	12"

Appendix C: Color Throughout the Year

Common Name	Botanical Name	Color	Light	Ht. × Spacing	
Cardinal Flower	*Lobelia cardinalis*	Red	Sun, Part-Shade, Shade	48"	12"
Turk's Cap	*Malvaviscus arboreus*	Red	Sun, Part-Shade, Shade	36"	30"
Catmint	*Nepeta faassenii*	Lavender	Sun	24"	24"
Rock Penstemon	*Penstemon baccharifolius*	Red	Sun, Part-Shade	18"	18"
Plumbago	*Plumbago auriculata*	Blue	Sun, Part-Shade	24-36"	18"
Pitcher Sage	*Salvia azurea var. Pitcherii*	Blue	Sun	36"	24"
Tropical Sage	*Salvia coccinea*	Red, Pink, White	Part-Shade	36"	24"
Cedar Sage	*Salvia roemeriana*	Red	Part-Shade	12"	24"
Flowering Shrubs					
Flame Acanthus	*Anisacanthus wrightii*	Red, Orange	Sun	48"	36"
Buddleia	*Buddliea davidii*	Purple, Pink, White	Sun	4-8'	6-10'
Bird of Paradise	*Caesalpinia gilliesii*	Yellow	Sun	5-10'	5-10'
Pride of Barbados	*Caesalpinia pulcherrima*	Red/Yellow	Sun	6-10'	6-10'
Oleander	*Nerium oleander*	White, Pink, Red	Sun	6-12'	6-12'
Flowering Trees					
Desert Willow	*Chilopsis linearis*	Pink/Lavender, White	Sun	12-15'	10-15'
Vitex, Chaste Tree	*Vitex agnus-castus*	Purple, Pink, White	Sun, Part-Shade	12-18'	20'
Flowering Vines (*Note: many are annuals or tropicals*)					
Bougainvillia	*Bougaainvilla spp.*	Fuschia, Coral, Red, Pink	Sun		
Trumpet Vine	*Campsis radicans*	Orange	Sun		
Clematis	*Clematis spp.*	Purple, Magenta, White	Sun, Part-Shade		
Pea Vine	*Clitoria ternata*	Purple	Sun, Part-Shade		
Morning Glories	*Ipomea spp.*	Varied	Sun		
Moonflower Vine	*Ipomea alba*	White	Sun		
Cypress Vine	*Ipomea quamoclit*	Red	Sun, Part-Shade		
Mandevilla	*Mandevilla spp.*	Pink	Sun, Part-Shade		
Passion Flower	*Passiflora spp.*	Purple	Sun, Part-Shade		
Mexican Flame Vine	*Senecio Confusus*	Orange	Sun		
Skyflower Vine	*Thunbergia grandiflora*	Light Blue	Sun		
Summer Annuals					
Periwinkles	*Catharanthus roseus*	Pink, Mauve, White	Sun	12"	8-12"
Spider Flower	*Cleome spinosa*	Pink, Purple, White	Sun, Part-Shade	48"	18"
Blue Daze	*Evolvulus glomeratus*	Blue	Sun	8-12"	18-24"
Globe Amaranth	*Gomphrena globosa*	Purple, Red	Sun	12-18"	10-12"
Sunflowers	*Helianthus annuus.*	Yellow, Red, White	Sun	2-8'	2-3'
Petunias	*Petunia hybrida*	Asstd.	Sun	10-16"	6-8"
Portulaca	*Portulaca grandiflora*	Asst.	Sun	6"	4"
Black-Eyed Susan	*Rudbeckia hirta*	Yellow	Sun	30-36"	12"
Zinnias	*Zinnia spp.*	Assorted	Sun		

Early to Mid-Summer (June & July)

Xeriscape for Central Texas

	Common Name	Botanical Name	Color	Light	Ht. × Spacing	
Late Summer (August & September)	**Woody and Herbaceous Perennials**					
	Lindheimer's Senna	Cassia lindheimerii	Yellow	Sun	24-48"	24"
	Dwarf Plumbago	Ceratostigma plumbaginoides	Blue	Part-Shade, Shade	6-12"	18"
	Joe Pye Weed	Eupatorium virginianum	Purple	Part-Shade	36-48"	24"
	Maximillian Sunflower	Helianthus maximilianai	Yellow	Sun	4-6'	36"
	Gayfeather	Liatris spp.	Pink, Lavender	Sun	24-36"	18-24"
	Russian Sage	Perovskia atriplicifolia	Lavender-Blue	Sun	36-48"	24-36"
	Fall Obedient Plant	Physostegia virginiana	Purple, White	Sun, Part-Shade	36-48"	24"
	'Goldsturm' Rudbeckia	Rudbeckia fulgida 'Goldsturm'	Gold	Sun, Part-Shade	24"	24"
	Yellow Sage	Salvia madrensis	Yellow	Sun, Part-Shade	6'	4'
	Surprise Lily	Lycoris radiata	Red	Sun, Part-Shade	12-18"	12"
	Flowering Shrubs					
	Firebush	Hamelia patens	Red-Orange	Sun-Part-Shade	48"	48"
	Blue Mist Shrub	Caryopteris clandonensis	Blue	Sun, Part-Shade	24"	24"
	Flowering Trees					
	Tree Senna	Cassia corymbosa	Yellow	Sun	5-8'	5-8'
	Annuals					
	Mexican Sunflower	Tithonia rotundifolia	Orange	Sun	4-6'	2-3'
	Flowering Vines					
	Coral Vine	Antigonon leptosus	Coral Pink	Sun, Part Shade		
Fall (October & November)	**Woody and Herbaceous Perennials**					
	Fall Aster	Aster oblongifolius	Purple	Sun, Part-Shade	24-36"	30-36"
	Black Dalea	Dalea frutescens	Purple	Sun	24-36"	24-36"
	Blue Mist Flower	Eupatorium coelistinum & E. greggii	Blue	Sun, Part-Shade	18"	36"
	Fragrant Mist Flower	Eupatorium havanense	White	Sun, Part-Shade	36"	48"
	Mexican Bush Sage	Salvia leucantha	Purple	Sun, Part-Shade	48"	48"
	Mountain Sage	Salvia regla	Orange	Part-Shade	36-48"	36"
	Goldenrod	Solidago spp.	Yellow	Sun	36-60"	18"
	Copper Canyon Daisy	Tagetes lemonnii	Yellow	Sun	48"	48"
	Mexican Mint Marigold	Tagetes lucida	Yellow	Sun	36	24"
	Plateau Goldeneye	Viguiera dentata	Yellow	Sun, Part-Shade	3-6'	3-4'
	Plants with Colorful Fall Berries					
	Beautyberry	Callicarpa americana	Purple	Part-Shade	3-6'	4-6'
	Yaupons	Ilex vomitoria	Red	Sun, Part-Shade	12-20'	12-15'
	Possumhaw	Ilex decidua	Red	Sun, Part-Shade	8-20'	12-15'
	Coralberry	Symphoricarpos orbiculatus	Magenta	Sun, Part-Shade	3-6'	3-6'
	Cold-Hardy Annuals for Winter Color					
	Pansies & Violas					
	Snapdragons					
	Dianthus					
	Ornamental Cabbage & Kale					
	Cyclamen					
	Sweet Alyssum					
	Iceland Poppies					

D: Shade Tolerant Plants

Common Name	Botanical Name	Height x Spread	Color	Bloom Period
Perennials				
Bicolor Sage	Salvia sinaloensis	12" x 18"	blue	April-Sept
Big Red Sage	Salvia penstemenoides	36" x 24"	magenta	June-Sept
Blue Mist Flower	Eupatorium coelestinum	18" x 36"	blue	July-Oct
Bog Sage	Salvia uliginosa	60" x 36"	blue	Mar-Nov
Brazos Penstemon	Penstemon tenuis	24" x 24"	purple	Mar-June
Buchanan Sage	Salvia buchanii	18" x 24"	magenta	April-Sept
Butterfly Weed	Asclepias tuberosa	18-24" x 24"	orange	April-Sept
Cedar Sage	Salvia roemeriana	12" x 12"	red	April-Sept
Chi-Chi Ruellia	Ruellia brittonia 'Chi-Chi"	36-48" x 24"	pink	April-Oct
Chile Pequin	Capsicum annuum	2-5' x 2'	white/red berries	April-Nov
Columbine	Aquilegia chrysantha var. Hinckleyana	24" x 24"	yellow	Feb-May
Coreopsis	Coreopsis lanceolata	18-24" x 12"	yellow	April-June
Fall Aster	Aster oblongifolius	36" x 48"	pink, purple	Sept-Dec
Fall Obedient Plant	Physostegia virginiana	36-48" x 24"	purple or white	July-Oct
Flowering Maple	Abutilon pictum	36" x 36"	yellow, pink	July-Nov
Forsythia Sage	Salvia madrensis	72" x 48"	yellow	Aug-Oct
Fragrant Mist Flower	Eupatorium havanense	36" x 48"	white	Aug-Sept
Gregg's Mist Flower	Eupatorium greggi	18" x 36"	blue or white	Mar-Nov
Hill Country Penstemon	Penstemon triflorus	18-24" x 12-18"	magenta	April-May
Lavender Lace Dianthus	Diathus superbus	12-18" x 24"	lavender	May-Nov
Lavender Scullcap	Scutellaria wrightii	6-8" x 6-12"	purple	Mar-Nov
Lyre-Leaf Sage	Salvi lyrata	12" x 12"	blue	Feb-April
Magenta Dianthus	Dianthus sp.	6-12" x 24"	magenta	Mar-May
Majestic Sage	Salvia guaranitica	48" x 24"	blue or purple	April-Oct
Mealy Blue Sage	Salvia farinacea	36" x 24"	blue	Mar-Nov
Mexican Marigold Mint	Tagetes lucida	24" x 36"	yellow	Oct-Nov
Mexican Oregano	Poliomentha longiflora	36" x 48"	pale lavender	May-Aug
Mexican Sage	Salvia mexicana 'Lollie Jackson'	60" x 60"	purple	Sept-Oct
Missouri Violet	Viola missouriensis	4-6" x 8-12"	purple	Feb-Mar
Oxalis	Oxalis spp.	10-12" x 12"	pink	Mar-April
Pacific Chrysanthemum	Chrysanthemum pacificum	24-36" x 36"	yellow	Fall
Pink Rock Rose	Pavonia lasiopetala	24-36" x 36-48"	pink	April-Sept
Pink Scullcap	Scutellaria suffrutescens	12" x 24"	pink	April-Nov
Pringle's Bee Balm	Monarda pringlei	12-24" x 24-30"	scarlet red	April-July
Purple Coneflower	Echinacea purpurea	24" x 18"	purple	May-July
Purple Leaf Sage	Salvia blepharophylla	24" x 30"	red	April-Oct
Rock Penstemon	Penstemon bacharifolius	18" x 18"	red	June-Sept
Skeleton Leaf Goldeneye	Viguiera stenoloba	3' x 3'	yellow	May-Sept
Spring Obedient Plant	Physostegia angustifolia	36-60" x 24"	lavender	Mar-June

Xeriscape for Central Texas

Common Name	Botanical Name	Height x Spread	Color	Bloom Period
Texas Betony	*Stachys coccinea*	18" x 30"	coral	Mar-Oct
Turk's Cap	*Malvaviscus arboreus var. drummondii*	36-48" x 36-48"	red	June-Nov
Yarrow	*Achillea millefolium*	12" x 24"	white	Feb-May
Zexmenia	*Wedelia hispida*	2-3' x 24"	yellow	May-Nov

Ground Covers

Common Name	Botanical Name	Height x Spread	Color	Bloom Period
Ajuga	*Ajuga reptans*	3" x 12"	blue	
Asian Jasmine	*Trachelospermum asiaticum*	10-18" ht.		
Blue Shade Ruellia	*Ruellia sp. 'Blue Shade'*	8-10" x 18"	blue	
Blue-Eyed Grass	*Sisyrinchium sp.*	6" x 9"	blue	April-May
Bouncing Bette	*Saponaria officianalis*	12-18" x 36"	white or pink	Spr-Sum
Drummond Phox	*Phlox drummondii*	6-18" x 12"	shades of pink	Mar-April
Dwarf Plumbago	*Ceratostigma plumbaginoides*	6-8" x 18"	blue	
Fragrant Phlox	*Phlox pilosa*	8-12" x 12"	pink	April-May
Katie's Dwarf Ruellia	*Ruellia brittonia 'Katie'*	8-12" x 18"	purple	April-Oct
Lamium, Dead Nettle	*Lamium maculatum*	6" x 24"	pink or white	
Monkey Grass	*Ophiopogon japonicus*	6-12" x 6"	lavender	
Mountain Pea	*Orbexilum pedunculatum*	8-12" x 12"		
Pigeonberry	*Rivina humilis*	18" x 24"	pink	May-Nov
Purpleheart	*Setcreasea pallida*	12" x 36"	pale pink	
Snake Herb	*Dyschoriste linearis*	9" x 18"	purple	April-Oct
Trailing Lantana	*Lantana montevidensis*	12-18" x 36"	lavender, white	
"Profusion" Fleabane	*Erigeron sp.*	12-18" x 18"	white	March

Shrubs

Common Name	Botanical Name	Height x Spread	Color	Bloom Period
Agarita	*Berberis trifoliata*	36-48"		
American Beautyberry	*Callicarpa americana*	4-8' x 6-8'	purple	October-Dec
Aromatic Sumac	*Rhus aromatica*	3-8' x 3-8'		
Beach Vitex	*Vitex rotundifolia*	18-36" x 36-60"	lavender	May-Sept
Boxwood	*Buxus spp.*	2-8' x 2-8'		
Bush White Honeysuckle	*Lonicera albiflora*	4-8' x 4-6'	white	
Cherry Sage	*Salvia greggii*	36-48" x 36"	red, pink, white	Mar-Nov
Coral Berry	*Symphoricarpos orbiculatus*	3-6' x 3-6'	magenta fruit	Fall
Dwarf Barbados Cherry	*Malphighia glabra*	24-30" x 36"	pink	April-Nov
Dwarf Palmetto	*Sabal minor*	4-6' x 6-12'		
Dwarf Pittosporum	*Pittosporum 'Wheeler's Dwarf'*	4' x 4'		
Dwarf Wax Myrtle	*Myrica pusilla*	4-6' x 4-6'		
Dwarf Yaupon	*Ilex vomitoria 'nana'*	3-5' x 5-10'		
Evergreen Sumac	*Rhus virens*	6-10' x 6-8'		

Appendix D: Shade Tolerant Plants

Common Name	Botanical Name	Height x Spread	Color	Bloom Period
Japanese Yew	Podocarpus macrophyllus	10' x 5'		
Mock Orange	Philadelphus x virginalis	8' x 6'	white	
Nandina	Nandina domestica	4-6' x 4-6'		
Pittosporum	Pittosporum tobira	10' x 10'		
Spiraea	Spiraea spp.	4-5' x 6'	white	April-May
Texas Barberry	Berberis swayseyo	36-48"		
Texas Indigo Bush	Amorpha roemerana	3-9' x 3-5'	purple	April-June
Texas Mountain Laurel	Sophora secundiflora	12-20' x 6-12'	purple	Mar-May
Yaupon	Ilex vomitoria	6-12' x 6-10'		

Vines

Common Name	Botanical Name	Height x Spread	Color	Bloom Period
Boston Ivy	Pathenocissus tricuspidata	to 50'	red fall color	Fall
Clematis	Clematis spp	10-20'	purple, white, etc	May-July
Coral Honeysuckle	Lonicera sempervirens	3-18'	coral	Mar-Nov
Crossvine	Bignonia capreolata	to 50'	yellow/red	March
Cypress Vine	Ipomea quamoclit	10-15'	red	June-Nov
Passion Flower	Passiflora spp.	15-20'	purple	May-Oct
Pea Vine	Clitoria ternata	10-15'	purple	June-Nov
Snapdragon Vine	Maurandya antirrhiniflora	3-8'	purple	April-Nov
Virginia Creeper	Parthenocissus quinquefolia	to 50'	red fall color	Fall

Yuccas, etc

Common Name	Botanical Name	Height x Spread	Color	Bloom Period
Coral Yucca	Hesperaloe parviflora	36" x 36"	coral	May-Nov
Manfreda	Manfreda spp.	4-12" x 18"	yellow	April-July
Sacahuista	Nolina texana	18-36" x 6'	white	May-June
Twisted Leaf Yucca	Yucca rupicola	4" x 24"	white	May-July

Ferns

Common Name	Botanical Name	Height x Spread	Color	Bloom Period
Autumn Fern, Wood Fern	Dryopteris spp.	12-24" x 24"		
Holly Fern	Cyrtomium falcatum	24" x 36"		
Maidenhair Fern	Adiantum capillus-veneris	18" x 10"		
River Fern	Thelypteris kunthii	30-40"x 36"		

Sedges & Grasses

Common Name	Botanical Name	Height x Spread	Color	Bloom Period
Bamboo Muhly	Muhlenbergia dumosa	48-60" x 36"		
Berkeley Sedge	Carex tumulicola	14" x 24"		
Cedar Sedge	Carex planostachys	12" x 18"		
Dwarf Maiden Grass	Miscanthus sinensis 'Yaku-Jima'	36-48"		
Giant Lirope	Liriope gigantea	24-36" x 36"		
Inland Sea Oats	Chasmanthium latifolium	2-3' x 3'		
Liriope	Liriope muscari	12-18" x 12"		

Xeriscape for Central Texas

Common Name	Botanical Name	Height x Spread	Color	Bloom Period
Maiden Grass	*Miscanthus sinensis* 'Gracillimus'	48" x 48"		
Mexican Feathergrass	*Stipa tenuissima*	18-24" x 18"		
Texas Sedge	*Carex texensis*	6" x 6"		
Umbrella Sedge	*Cyperus alternifolia*	36" x 36"		
Weeping Muhly	*Muhlenbergia dubiodes*	18-24"		

Bulbs

Common Name	Botanical Name	Height x Spread	Color	Bloom Period
Agapanthus	*Agapanthus africanus*	36" x 24"	purple	May-July
Amaryllis	*Hippeastrum spp.*	24" x 18"	red, pink, white	Feb-March
Grape Hyacinth	*Muscari armeniacum*	6-8" x 6"	purple, white	Feb-Mar
Snowflakes	*Leucojum aestivum*	18" x 18"	white	March
Spanish Bluebells	*Hyacinthoides hispanica*	18" x 12"	purple, pink	Feb-March
Spiderlily	*Hymenocallis spp.*	36" x 36"	white	Mar-April
Surprise Lily	*Lycoris radiata*	18-24" x 12"	red, pink, yellow	September

Annuals

Common Name	Botanical Name	Height x Spread	Color	Bloom Period
Begonias	*Begonia semperflorens*			
Caladiums	*Caladium bicolor*			
Coleus	*Coleus hybridus*			
Four O'clocks (self-sowing)	*Mirabilis jalapa*			
Impatiens	*Impatiens wallerana*			
Nicotiana	*Nicotiana alata*			

E: Perennials and Grasses

Common Name	Botanical Name	Light	Water	Height × Spread	Color	Bloom Period
Perennials						
Bicolor Sage	Salvia sinaloensis	S/PS	L	12" x 18"	blue	April-Sept
Big Red Sage	Salvia penstemenoides	PS	L	36" x 24"	magenta	June-Sept
Black Dalea	Dalea frutescens	S/PS	L	24-36" x 36-48"	purple	July-Oct
Blue Mist Flower	Eupatorium coelestinum	PS	L/M	18" x 36"	blue	July-Oct
Brazos Penstemon	Penstemon tenuis	S/PS	L	24" x 24"	purple	Mar-June
Buchanan Sage	Salvia buchanii	PS/SH	L	18" x 24"	magenta	April-Sept
Butterfly Weed	Asclepias tuberosa	S/PS	L	18-24" x 24"	orange	April-Sept
Calylophus	Calylophus drummondianus var. berlandieri	S	L	12" x 24"	yellow	April-June
Cedar Sage	Salvia roemeriana	PS/SH	L	12" x 12"	red	April-Sept
Chi-Chi Ruellia	Ruellia brittonia 'Chi-Chi'	PS/SH	L	36-48" x 24"	pink	April-Oct
Chile pequin	Capsicum annuum	PS/SH	L	24" x 24"	white/red berries	April-Nov
Columbine	Aquilegia chrysantha var. Hinckleyana	PS/SH	M	24" x 24"	yellow	Feb-May
Coreopsis	Coreopsis lanceolata	S/PS	L/M	18-24" x 12"	yellow	April-June
Damianita	Chrysactina mexicana	S	L	18" x 24"	yellow	Mar-Sept
Fall Aster	Aster oblongifolius	S/PS	L	36" x 48"	pink, purple	Sept-Dec
Fall Obedient Plant	Physostegia virginiana	S/PS	M	36-48" x 24"	purple or white	July-Oct
Flowering Maple	Abutilon pictum	S/PS	M	36" x 36"	yellow, pink	July-Nov
Four Nerve Daisy	Hymenoxys scaposa	S	L	8" x 12"	yellow	Feb-Nov
Fragrant Mist Flower	Eupatorium havanense	S/PS	L	36" x 48"	white	Aug-Sept
Gregg's Mist Flower	Eupatorium greggi	S/PS	L/M	18" x 36"	blue or white	Mar-Nov
Heartleaf Hibiscus	Hibiscus martianus	S	L/M	36" x 24"	red	May-Nov
Hill Country Penstemon	Penstemon triflorus	S/PS	L	18-24" x 12-18"	magenta	April-May
Indian Blanket	Gaillardia pulchella	S/PS	L	12-24" x 12"	yellow/red	May-July
Lantana hybrids	Lantana hybrid	S	L	18-30" x 24-48"	various	Mar-Oct
Lavender Lace Dianthus	Diathus superbus	PS	L/M	12-18" x 24"	lavender	May-Nov
Lavender Scullcap	Scutellaria wrightii	PS	L	6-8" x 6-12"	purple	Mar-Nov

Xeriscape for Central Texas

Common Name	Botanical Name	Light	Water	Height × Spread	Color	Bloom Period
Lindheimer's Cassia	Cassia lindheimeriana	S	L	18-36" x 24"	yellow	Aug-Sept
Lyre-Leaf Sage	Salvia lyrata	PS	L	12" x 12"	blue	Feb-April
Magenta Dianthus	Dianthus sp.	PS	L/M	6-12" x 24"	magenta	Mar-May
Majestic Sage	Salvia guaranitica	PS/SH	L	48" x 24"	blue or purple	April-Oct
Mealy Blue Sage	Salvia farinacea	S/PS	L	36" x 24"	blue	Mar-Nov
Mexican Marigold Mint	Tagetes lucida	S/PS	L	24" x 36"	yellow	Oct-Nov
Mexican Oregano	Poliomentha longiflora	S/PS	L	36" x 48"	pale lavender	May-Aug
Missouri Violet	Viola missouriensis	PS/SH	L/M	4-6" x 8-12"	purple	Feb-Mar
Oxalis	Oxalis spp.	PS/SH	L	10-12" x 12"	pink	Mar-April
Oxeye Daisy	Chrysanthemum leucanthemum	S/PS	L/M	6-24" x 12"	white/yellow	April-June
Pacific Chrysanthemum	Chrysanthemum pacificum	S/PS	L/M	24-36" x 36"	yellow	Fall
Pink Lantana	Lantana camara	S	L	36" x 48"	pink/yellow	Mar-Oct
Pink Rock Rose	Pavonia lasiopetala	S/PS	L	24-36" x 36-48"	pink	April-Sept
Pink Scullcap	Scutellaria suffrutescens	S/PS	L	12" x 24"	pink	April-Nov
Pringle's Bee Balm	Monarda pringlei	PS	L/M	12-24" x 24-30"	scarlet red	April-July
Purple Coneflower	Echinacea purpurea	S/PS	L/M	24" x 18"	purple	May-July
Purple Leaf Sage	Salvia blepharophylla	PS/SH	L/M	24" x 30"	red	April-Oct
Rock Penstemon	Penstemon bacharifolius	S/PS	L	18" x 18"	red	June-Sept
Skeleton Leaf Goldeneye	Viguiera stenoloba	S/PS	L	3' x 3'	yellow	May-Sept
Spring Obedient Plant	Physostegia angustifolia	S/PS	M	36-60" x 24"	lavender	Mar-June
Standing Cypress	Ipomopsis rubra	S/PS	L/M	48" x 8"	red	April-June
Texas Betony	Stachys coccinea	S/PS	L	18" x 30"	coral	Mar-Oct
Texas Lantana	Lantana horrida	S	L	48" x 48"	orange/yellow	Mar-Oct
Texas Star Hibiscus	Hibiscus coccineus	S/PS	L	5-6' x 3-6'	red	June-Sept
Trailing Lantana	Lantana montevidensis					
Turk's Cap	Malvaviscus arboreus var. drummondii	S/PS	L	36-48" x 36-48"	red	June-Nov
Whirling Butterflies	Gaura lindheimeri	S/PS	L	18-48" x 24-48"	white/pink	Apr-Nov
Winecups	Callirhoe involucrata	S/PS	L	6-12" 24-36"	magenta	Feb-June
Yarrow	Achillea millefolium	S/PS	L	12" x 24"	white	Feb-May
Zexmenia	Wedelia hispida	S/PS	L	2-3' x 24"	yellow	May-Nov

Appendix E: Perennials and Grasses

Common Name	Botanical Name	Light	Water	Height × Spread	Color	Bloom Period
Ground Covers						
Ajuga	*Ajuga reptans*	PS/SH	L/M	3" x 12"	blue	
Asian Jasmine	*Trachelospermum asiaticum*	S/PS/SH	M	10-18" h		
Blue Shade Ruellia	*Ruellia sp. 'Blue Shade'*	PS/SH	L	8-10" x 18"	blue	
Blue-Eyed Grass	*Sisyrinchium sp.*	S/PS/SH	L	6" x 9"	blue	April-May
Bouncing Bette	*Saponaria officianalis*	PS/SH	L	12-18" x 36"	white or pink	Spring to Summer
Drummond Phox	*Phlox drummondii*	S/PS	L	6-18" x 12"	shades of pink	Mar-April
Dwarf Plumbago	*Ceratostigma plumbaginoides*	PS	L/M	6-8" x 18"	blue	
Fragrant Phlox	*Phlox pilosa*	PS	L	8-12" x 12"	pink	April-May
Gregg's Dalea	*Dalea greggii*	S	L	12" x 48"	purple	April-Nov
Katie's Dwarf Ruellia	*Ruellia brittonia 'Katie'*	PS/SH	L/M	8-12" x 18"	purple	April-Oct
Lamium, Dead Nettle	*Lamium maculatum*	PS/SH	L/M	6" x 24"	pink or white	
Monkey Grass	*Ophiopogon japonicus*	PS/SH	L/M	6-12" x 6"	lavender	
Mountain Pea	*Orbexilum pedunculatum*	PS/SH	L	8-12" x 12"		
Pigeonberry	*Rivina humilis*	PS/SH	L	18" x 24"	pink	May-Nov
Purpleheart	*Setcreasea pallida*	PS/SH	L/M	12" x 36"	pale pink	
Snake Herb	*Dyschoriste linearis*	S/PS	L	9" x 18"	purple	April-Oct
Trailing Lantana	*Lantana montevidensis*	S/PS	L	12-18" x 36"	lavender, white	
'Profusion' Fleabane	*Erigeron sp.*	S/PS	L	12-18" x 18"	white	March
Shrubs						
Agarita	*Berberis trifoliata*	S/PS/SH	L	36-48"		
American Beautyberry	*Callicarpa americana*	PS/SH	L/M	4-8' x 6-8'	purple	Oct-Dec
Aromatic Sumac	*Rhus aromatica*	PS/SH	L	3-8' x 3-8'		
Beach Vitex	*Vitex rotundifolia*	PS	L/M	18-36" x 36-60"	lavender	May-Sept
Boxwood	*Buxus spp.*	PS/SH	L/M	2-8' x 2-8'		
Bush White Honeysuckle	*Lonicera albiflora*	PS/SH	L	4-8' x 4-6'	white	
Cherry Sage	*Salvia greggii*	S/PS	L	36-48" x 36"	red, pink, white	Mar-Nov
Coral Bean	*Erythrina herbacea*	S/PS	L/M	4-5' x 6'		
Coral Berry	*Symphoricarpos orbiculatus*	PS/SH	L/M	3-6' x 3-6'	magenta fruit	Fall

225

Xeriscape for Central Texas

Common Name	Botanical Name	Light	Water	Height × Spread	Color	Bloom Period
Dwarf Barbados Cherry	*Malphighia glabra*	PS/SH	L	24-30" x 36"	pink	April-Nov
Dwarf Palmetto	*Sabal minor*	PS/SH	M/H	4-6' x 6-12'		
Dwarf Pittosporum	*Pittosporum 'Wheeler's Dwf'*	PS/SH	M	4' x 4'		
Dwarf Wax Myrtle	*Myrica pusilla*	S/PS/SH	L/M	4-6' x 4-6'		
Dwarf Yaupon	*Ilex vomitoria 'nana'*	S/PS/SH	L	3-5' x 5-10'		
Evergreen Sumac	*Rhus virens*	S/PS/SH	L	6-10' x 6-8'		
Japanese Yew	*Podocarpus macrophyllus*	PS/SH	L/M	10' x 5'		
Mock Orange	*Philadelphus x virginalis*	PS	M	8' x 6'	white	May-June
Nandina	*Nandina domestica*	PS/SH	L/M	4-6' x 4-6'		
Pittosporum	*Pittosporum tobira*	PS/SH	M	10' x 10'		
Spiraea	*Spiraea spp.*	PS/SH	L/M	4-5'x 6'	white	April-May
Texas Barberry	*Berberis swayseyo*	S/PS/SH	L	36-48"		
Texas Indigo Bush	*Amorpha roemerana*	PS	M	3-9' x 3-5'	purple	April-June
Texas Mountain Laurel	*Sophora secundiflora*	S/PS/SH	L	12-20' x 6-12'	purple	Mar-May
Yaupon	*Ilex vomitoria*	S/PS/SH	L	6-12' x 6-10'		

Vines

Common Name	Botanical Name	Light	Water	Height × Spread	Color	Bloom Period
Boston Ivy	*Pathenocissus tricuspidata*	PS/SH	L/M	to 50'	red fall color	Fall
Clematis	*Clematis spp*	PS	M	10-20'	purple, white, etc	May-July
Coral Honeysuckle	*Lonicera sempervirens*	S/PS	L/M	3-18'	coral	Mar-Nov
Crossvine	*Bignonia capreolata*	S/PS	L	to 50'	yellow/red	March
Cypress Vine	*Ipomea quamoclit*	PS/SH	L/M	10-15'	red	Jun-Nov
Passion Flower	*Passiflora spp.*	PS/SH	M	5-20'	purple	May-Oct
Pea Vine	*Clitoria ternata*	PS/SH	L/M	10-15'	purple	Jun-Nov
Snapdragon Vine	*Maurandya antirrhiniflora*	PS	L	3-8'	purple	April-Nov
Virginia Creeper	*Parthenocissus quinquefolia*	PS/SH	L/M	to 50'	red fall color	Fall

Yuccas, etc

Common Name	Botanical Name	Light	Water	Height × Spread	Color	Bloom Period
Coral Yucca	*Hesperaloe parviflora*	S/PS	L	36" x 36"	coral	May-Nov
Manfreda	*Manfreda spp.*	S/PS	L	4-12" x 18"	yellow	April-July
Sacahuista	*Nolina texana*	S/PS	L	18-36" x 6'	white	May-June
Twisted Leaf Yucca	*Yucca rupicola*	PS/SH	L	4" x 24"	white	May-July

Appendix E: Perennials and Grasses

Common Name	Botanical Name	Light	Water	Height × Spread	Color	Bloom Period
Ferns						
Autumn Fern, Wood Fern	*Dryopteris spp.*	SH	L/M	12-24" x 24"		
Holly Fern	*Cyrtomium falcatum*	SH	L/M	24" x 36"		
Maidenhair Fern	*Adiantum capillus-veneris*	SH	M	18" x 10"		
River Fern	*Thelypteris kunthii*	SH	L/M	30-40"x 36"		
Sedges & Grasses						
Bamboo Muhly	*Muhlenbergia dumosa*	S/PS	L	48-60" x 36"		
Berkeley Sedge	*Carex tumuicola*	PS/SH	L/M	14" x 24"		
Big Bluestem	*Andropogon gerardii*	S	L	4-6' x 3'		
Big Muhly	*Muhlenbergia lindheimeri*	S/PS	L	36-48" x 48"		
Blue Gramma	*Bouteloua gracilis*	S	L	8-24" x 12"		
Blue Lyme Grass	*Elymus arenarius*	S/PS	M	12-36" x 36"		
Bushy Bluestem	*Andropogon glomeratus*	S/PS	M	2' x 2'		
Canadian Wild Rye	*Elymus canadensis*	S/PS	L/M	2-5' x 2'		
Cedar Sedge	*Carex planostachys*	PS/SH	L	12" x 18"		
Deer Muhly	*Muhlenbergia rigens*	S/PS	L/M	24-36" x 48"		
Dwarf Maiden Grass	*Miscanthus sinensis 'Yaku-Jima'*	S/PS	L/M	36-48"		
Evergreen Miscanthus	*Miscanthus transmorrisonensis*	S/PS	M	3-4' x 4'		
Feathertope	*Pennisetum villosum*	S	L/M	12-24" x 24"		
Fountain Grass	*Pennisetum alopecuroides*	S/PS	L/M	36-48" x 36"		
Giant Lirope	*Liriope gigantea*	PS/SH	L/M	24-36" x 36"		
Giant Reed	*Arundo donax*	S/PS	L/M	10-15' x 18'		
Indian Grass	*Sorghastrum nutans*	S	L/M	2-3' x 3'		
Inland Sea Oats	*Chasmanthium latifolium*	PS/SH	L	2-3' x 3'		
Liriope	*Liriope muscari*	PS/SH	L/M	12-18" x 12"		
Maiden Grass	*Miscanthus sinensis 'Gracillimus'*	S/PS	L/M	48" x 48"		
Mexican Feathergrass	*Stipa tenuissima*	PS	L	18-24" x 18"		
Oriental Fountain Grass	*Pennisetum orientale*	S/PS	L/M	24-36" x 36"		

Xeriscape for Central Texas

Common Name	Botanical Name	Light	Water	Height × Spread	Color	Bloom Period
Pampas Grass	Cortaderia selloana	S	L/M	8-12' x 12'		
Porcupine Grass	Miscanthus sinensis var. strictus	S/PS	M	4-6' x 6'		
Ravenna Grass	Erianthes ravennae	S	L/M	4-5' x 4-5'		
Ribbon Grass	Phalaris arundinacea	PS	M	18-30" x 36"		
Rushes	Juncus spp.	S/PS/SH	H	24-36" x 36"		
Sideoats Gramma	Bouteloua curtipendula	S	L	12-24" x 18"		
Silver Bluestem	Botriochloa saccharoides	S	L	12-18" x 18"		
Switchgrass	Panicum virgatum	S/PS	L/M	4-7' x 5'		
Tender Fountain Grass	Pennisetum setaceum	S/PS	L/M	36-48" x 48"		
Texas Sedge	Carex texensis	PS/SH	L	6" x 6"		
Umbrella Sedge	Cyperus alternifolius	PS/SH	M/H	36" x 36"		
Weeping Love Grass	Eragrostis curvula	S	L	12" x 24"		
Weeping Muhly	Muhlenbergia dubiodes	S/PS	L	18-24"		
Zebra Grass	Miscanthus sinensis 'Zebrinus'	S/PS	M	5-6' x 6'		

Bulbs

Common Name	Botanical Name	Light	Water	Height × Spread	Color	Bloom Period
Agapanthus	Agapanthus africanus	PS	M	36" x 24"	purple	May-July
Amaryllis	Hippeastrum spp.	PS	M	24" x 18"	red, pink, white	Feb-March
Grape Hyacinth	Muscari armeniacum	PS/SH	L/M	6-8" x 6"	purple, white	Feb-Mar
Snowflakes	Leucojum aestivum	PS	M	18" x 18"	white	March
Spanish Bluebells	Hyacinthoides hispanica	PS/SH	M	18" x 12"	purple, pink	Feb-March
Spiderlily	Hymenocallis spp.	PS/SH	M	36" x 36"	white	Mar-April
Surprise Lily	Lycoris radiata	PS	L/M	18-24" x 12"	red, pink, yellow	September

Annuals

Common Name	Botanical Name	Light	Water	Height × Spread	Color	Bloom Period
Begonias	Begonia semperflorens					
Caladiums	Caladium bicolor					
Coleus	Coleus hybridus					
Four o'clocks (self-sowing)	Mirabilis jalapa					
Impatiens	Impatiens wallerana					
Nicotiana	Nicotiana alata					

F. Hydrozone Coding

The Alpha-Numeric Hydrozone Coding System

JOHN GLEASON

This system uses a combination of letters and numbers to indicate the moisture level of a plant's native habitat and relative soil moisture preferences and tolerances. A plant is much less likely to survive if soil moisture levels are outside its range of adaptation. While many plants will use and transpire all the water they receive, others will "drown" when given too much water. Conversely, many species are intolerant of drought. Fortunately, lots of plants are tolerant of a wide range of soil moisture conditions. The alphanumeric system was designed to accommodate plant diversity. Combining the proper letter code with an appropriate number code will give the whole range of moisture levels for a particular species.

LETTER CODES

The alphabetic portion of the code is an adaptation of a system which is well established in botanical and ecological science. The system and a comprehensive plant list can be found in a publication entitled *National List of Plant Species That Occur in Wetlands: South Plains (Region 6)*. In this system, the letters indicate a range of estimated probabilities (expressed as a frequency of occurrence) of a species occurring in wetland versus non-wetland areas across the entire distribution of the species. These indicators are used on a national as well as regional level. In the plant list, the indicators established for the Texas region are used. The indicator categories should not be equated to degrees of wetness. Many obligate wetland species occur in permanently or semi-permanently flooded wetlands, but a number of obligates are restricted to wetlands which are only temporarily or seasonally flooded. Please refer to the chart and the diagram below.

LETTER CODES EXPLANATION

Letter Code	Zone Category	Frequency of Occurrence in Wetlands (under natural conditions)
U	Upland	Occurs almost always (probability > 99%) in uplands (non-wetlands)
FU	Facultative Upland	Usually occurs in uplands (probability 67% to 99%, but occasionally found in wetlands
F	Facultative	Equally likely to occur in wetlands or nonwetlands (probability 34% to 66%)
FW	Facultative Wetland	Usually occurs in wetlands (probability 67% to 99%), but occasionally found in uplands
O	Obligate Wetland	Occurs almost always (probability > 99%) in wetlands

NUMBER CODES

The numeric portion of the code generally indicates the potential drought tolerance of a particular species. The various levels of drought tolerance are explained in the following chart. Since this system and the drought tolerance codes assigned to each species are preliminary, they are simply "suggested" for your consideration. Unfortunately, except for certain crop plants and most turf grasses, little research has been done regarding the specific moisture needs of most plants. The information presented in the plant list has been derived from the following sources:

Xeriscape for Central Texas

- Observation of the plants in their native habitats (particularly during droughts).

- Scientific and horticultural references.

- Communications with landscape professionals.

Since some plants (e.g., wetland species) are not drought tolerant at all, a different meaning to the number code is assigned to them. If an inch or foot (" or ') symbol follows the number, then the number indicates the typical water depth (or range of depths) in which the plant customarily grows.

The Alpha-Numeric Hydrozone Coding System, and the codes given to individual species, may be revised as changes are suggested. The author welcomes suggestions for improvement of the system and encourages the submission of changes to the species codes that may be misclassified or unlisted. Improvement of the format and changes to any of the data is dependent on input from knowledgeable professionals. The author sincerely appreciates your help in this task.

Appendix F. Hydrozone Coding

Moisture Level	Nbr Code	Native Landscape Example	Water Use/ Hydrozone Category	Drought Tolerance	Soil Moisture Regime Moisture = Rain, Inundation, or Irrigation		
					Basis	Dry Period	Days
D r y	18		Very Low	Extremely Tolerant	Quarterly	Almost a year	360
	17	Desert				3/4 of a year	270
	16					1/2 a year	180
	15	Chaparral				1/4 of a year	90
M o i s t	14		Low	Highly Tolerant	Monthly	2 1/2 months	75
	13	Upland prairie				2 months	60
	12					1 1/2 months	45
	11	Lowland prairie				1 month	30
	10		Moderate	Moderately Tolerant	Weekly	3 weeks	21
	9	100-year floodplain				2 weeks	14
	8					1 1/2 weeks	10
	7	Riparian				1 week	7
	6		High	Intolerant	Daily	6 days	6
	5	Bankfull				5 days	5
	4					4 days	4
	3	Moist fringe				3 days	3
	2					2 days	2
	1					1 day	1
W e t	0	Water Level					
	1"						
	3"	Draw-down area					
	6"						
	9"	Marsh					
	1'						
	18"	Marsh/Aquatics					
	2'						
	3'	Aquatics					
	4'						

HYDROZONE CODE EXAMPLE

Lindheimer Muhly, FW 13, often grows in wet areas, but is highly tolerant of drought. In a Xeriscape, this species could be used with others in a "low" hydrozone group. Since it also tolerates moisture, however, it could grow near a pond or other moist area.

GENERALIZED HYDROZONE GRADIENT

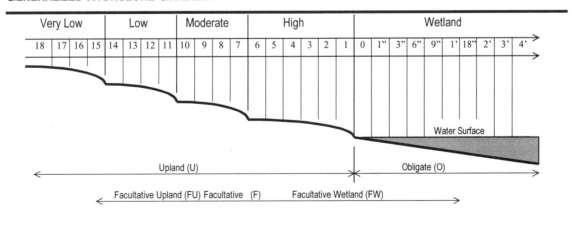

G. Water Harvesting

For centuries in Texas and throughout the world, people have relied on rainwater harvesting to supply water for household, landscape, livestock, and agricultural uses. Before large, centralized water supply systems were developed, rainwater was collected from a variety of surfaces—most commonly roofs—and stored on site in tanks known as *cisterns*. While there are many good reasons to harvest rainwater, it may not be cost effective if your house is already connected to a centralized water infrastructure or if the cost of the tank is prohibitive. A rainwater system compares quite favorably to the cost of drilling a well, though.

A compelling advantage of rainwater over other water sources is that it is one of the purest sources of water available. Rainwater quality almost always exceeds that of ground or surface waters: It does not come into contact with soil and rocks where it dissolves salts and minerals, and it is not subject to the pollutants that are often found in surface water. While falling rain is usually free of almost all contaminants, once rain comes in contact with a roof or collection surface, it can wash some contaminants into the storage tank. Therefore, if the rainwater is intended for use inside the household, appropriate filtration and disinfection practices should be employed. If the rainwater is to be used outside for landscape irrigation, the presence of contaminants may not be of major concern, and thus treatment requirements can be less stringent or not required at all.

If you would like to estimate the size of your roof catchment area, measure the ground surface below the eaves of your roof. Compute the square footage in the area covered by the building. As a rule-of-thumb, one inch of rain on 1,000 square feet of roof surface yields around 550 gallons of rainwater. Use the following worksheet to help you figure out if rainwater harvesting is appropriate for you.

1. Determine your roof catchment area _____ sq. ft.

2. Divide it by 1,000. This equals _____ .

3. Multiply it by 550 gallons to get gallons per one inch of rain _____ .

4. Multiply this by the annual rainfall (32" in much of central Texas) _____ inches

5. The amount of rainfall you can probably collect is _____ gallons

If you are truly interested in rainwater harvesting, consult the two books listed on the subject in *Appendix I: Rainwater Collection*. They are very helpful and can provide you with considerable hands-on information.

H: Central Texas Resources

Xeriscape Garden Club of the Austin Area, Inc.
P.O. Box 5502 • Austin, Texas 78763 • (512) 370-9505
Web Address: http://www.zilker-garden.org/xgc.html

MEETINGS

The Xeriscape Garden Club of the Austin Area, Inc. (XGC) is a non-profit organization formed in March 1987 to teach and promote water conservation and environmental protection through quality landscaping. Meetings are held the third Wednesday of each month, except December, at 7:30 P.M. in the Zilker Garden Center located at 2220 Barton Springs Road. Meetings are free and open to the public. Local experts, selected for their interesting presentations and unique knowledge of the Austin area, conduct the programs.

LEARN-BY-DOING PROGRAM

A monthly "Learn-By-Doing" session is held the Saturday following the regular monthly meeting from 8:30-11:00 A.M. at the Xeriscape Demonstration Garden. This program is in conjunction with regularly scheduled maintenance of the Demonstration Garden. Volunteers learn how to plan, prune, prepare soil, and weed, in addition to learning more about practical plant selections for the Austin area. Gatherings are small and informal, and landscape professionals join the group on a regular basis to give brief talks and answer questions on different landscape topics. Participation in maintenance is optional. Anyone is welcome to attend the presentations and ask questions.

Xeriscape Demonstration Garden
Zilker Botanical Gardens • 2220 Barton Springs Road • Austin, Texas
Web Address: http://www.zilker-garden.org

Open daily to the public, this garden is one of Austin's most important examples of "Xeriscape at Work" as a showcase of the seven principles of Xeriscape. In particular, it provides a display of over 50 native and low water use plants including trees, shrubs, ground covers, and wildflowers. The Xeriscape Garden Club of the Austin Area, Inc. is responsible for the maintenance and improvements to this garden. It is an excellent place to view Xeriscape plants that thrive in the Austin area. The beds are designed for specific micro-climates including full sun, partial sun, and full shade. The plants and irrigation system are matched to these micro-climates. Please direct your questions about the Demo Garden to the Xeriscape Garden Club at (512) 370-9505.

Xeriscape Advisory Board

A volunteer group of professionals and interested homeowners, this board was created to assist the City of Austin with the promotion of Xeriscape. The advisory board, along with the Xeriscape Garden Club and the City of Austin Water Conservation Division, sponsors yearly Xeriscape-related schools, tours, and contests.

Native Plant Society of Texas, Austin Chapter

P. O. Box 891 • Georgetown, Texas 78627 • (512) 238-0695
Web Address: http://lonestar.texas.net/~jleblanc/npsot-austin

The Native Plant Society of Texas is a non-profit organization with the goal to promote the conservation, research, and utilization of the native plants and plant habitats of Texas through education, outreach, and example. The Austin chapter of the Native Plant Society of Texas meets on the fourth Tuesday of each month (except December).

Lady Bird Johnson Wildflower Research Center

4801 La Crosse Avenue • Austin, Texas 78739 • (512) 292-4100
Web Address: http://www.wildflower.org

The purpose of the Lady Bird Johnson Wildflower Research Center is to educate people about the environmental necessity, economic value, and natural beauty of native plants. The Wildflower Center maintains one of the largest collections of information about native North American plants and makes this information available to more than 20,000 members across North America, as well as to landscape professionals and gardeners around the world.

Texas Parks and Wildlife Urban and Nongame Program

4200 Smith School Road • Austin, Texas 78744 • (800) 792-1112
Web Address: http://www.tpwd.state.tx.us/nature/nature.htm

Nongame and urban fish and wildlife resources contribute greatly to species richness in Texas and receive increasing appreciative and consumptive uses by the public. A recent national survey revealed that about four million Texans engage in appreciative uses of wildlife ranging from viewing and photography to nature study. Much of that use is directed toward nongame species. Further, many of these species provide Texans with special viewing opportunities and signify our natural heritage.

Travis County Agricultural Extension Service

1600-B Smith Road • Austin, Texas 78721 • (512) 473-9600
Web Address: http://www.co.travis.tx.us/index.htm

The county agricultural extension service conducts educational programs in the areas of family and consumer sciences, agriculture, horticulture, community development, 4-H, and youth. They usually hold a gardening school in the fall and the spring.

Texas A&M Horticulture Program

202 Horticulture Science Building • College Station, Texas 77843 • (409) 845-5269
Web Address: http://aggie-horticulture.tamu.edu

This is the entry to the information server of the Texas Horticulture Program. It provides access to the information resources of the teaching, research, and extension program at the Texas A&M University System.

Appendix H: Central Texas Resources

City of Austin Water Conservation Division

625 East 10th Street • Room 615 • Austin, Texas 787xx • (512) 499-2199
Web Address: http://www.ci.austin.tx.us/watercon
Drainage Utility Customers: (512) 499-1918
Water Utility Customers (Horticultural Info): (512) 499-3514

The Water Conservation Division of the City of Austin takes an active and progressive role regarding water conservation for the local community. Several programs are available which will assist you in your efforts to conserve water and lower your water bill. Currently available programs (as of this writing spring 1998) are described below.

FREE IRRIGATION SYSTEM AUDITS

If you have an underground sprinkler system and use more than 15,000 gallons per month in the summer, a city water auditor will check your system and determine an efficient watering schedule. In addition, the auditor can install low flow showerheads and faucet aerators. By following the recommendations, many customers have reduced their summer water bills by 20% to 50%. To schedule an audit, please call (512) 499-3514.

IRRIGATION AUDIT PROGRAM

If you are a City of Austin water customer, you are eligible to receive free, helpful advice regarding the proper management of your existing irrigation system. At your request, a City of Austin irrigation professional will visit your home and perform an irrigation audit on your system. The auditor will evaluate irrigation scheduling and system performance. Recommendations may be made regarding potential equipment upgrades. If so, you may want to participate in the Irrigation Rebate Program. Eligible upgrades will be identified at the time of the audit. Customers should call (512) 499-2199 to schedule an audit.

SINGLE FAMILY EFFICIENT IRRIGATION REBATE PROGRAM

If you are a City of Austin water customer, or live in a water district that receives water service from the City of Austin, take note of the following information. You can receive a water bill credit (CoA) or rebate (MUD) of up to $150.00 for upgrading your existing automatic sprinkler system with water conserving features. The incentives are designed to encourage water customers to upgrade existing irrigation systems to increase the efficiency of the system, reduce the quantity of water needed, and assist you with following the City of Austin recommended watering schedule of every five days. Funding is limited and is available on a first-come, first-served basis.

Program participants go through the following process:

- *Call for an irrigation audit.* To participate, sites must have an irrigation audit of the current system performed by City of Austin staff. The auditor will evaluate irrigation scheduling and system performance. Recommendations for eligible upgrades will also be identified at the time of the audit. Customers should call (512) 499-2199 to schedule an audit.

- After the irrigation audit is performed, customers are required to *submit an irrigation upgrade proposal prior to start of work*. Materials and labor costs must be shown separately. This proposal can be submitted by the company or their licensed irrigator and will consist of an itemized list of potential equipment

Xeriscape for Central Texas

improvements and their associated costs. All products should be selected from a list provided by the city. Rebates will not be paid for work that occurs before city approval.

- *Proposal reviewed by city.* The credit or rebate will be calculated at a certain percentage of the actual material cost of the products. The maximum rebate is $150.00 per water account. Labor costs must be for installation of water conserving devices. Labor charges on repairs will not be rebated.

- *Complete modifications.* Customers have 90 days to complete modifications to the irrigation system. After the work is completed, mail the original dated sales receipt(s) or final invoice from supplier and/or contractor to the City of Austin office.

- *Final inspection.* A city representative will call you to schedule a verification inspection after receiving proof of completion.

- *Credit or rebate issued.* For City of Austin retail customers, the credit will appear on the utility bill in the Adjustment/Fee section within 6 to 8 weeks after passing inspection. For MUD residents, a rebate check will be mailed to you, 6 to 8 weeks after final inspection. Each water customer may participate only once.

WATERWISE PROFESSIONAL CERTIFICATION PROGRAM

The City of Austin maintains a list of landscape professionals that are interested in water conservation. This list includes licensed irrigators, and it may be helpful if you are interested in finding a competent professional. The program does no testing of these individuals, however they are generally aware of water conservation techniques, equipment, and programs.

WATERWISE LANDSCAPE REBATE PROGRAM

This program encourages the use of plants that require little water and maintenance, as well as planting techniques that allow for mature height and spread of plants. Participation will reduce future demand on the water utility and create beautiful, low-maintenance landscapes. Call the Water Conservation Division at (512) 499-3542 for information and an application.

Lower Colorado River Authority
3701 Lake Austin Boulevard • Austin, Texas 78703 • (800) 776-5272
Web Address: http://www.lcra.org

The Lower Colorado River Authority (LCRA) is a conservation and reclamation district created by the Texas Legislature in 1934 to improve the quality of life in the Central Texas area. It provides many services to the area including electricity, managing floods, protecting the quality of the lower Colorado River and its tributaries, providing parks and recreational facilities, offering economic assistance, helping water and wastewater utilities, and providing soil, energy, and water conservation programs.

Appendix H: Central Texas Resources

Locally-Owned Nurseries

Support locally-owned nurseries. They are one of the best sources for information about the plants which thrive in your particular area. Employing a dedicated group of knowledgeable people, local nurseries sell plants which are best-suited for our harsh Central Texas climate.

Umlauf Sculpture Garden and Museum

605 Robert E. Lee Street • Austin, Texas • 78704 • (512) 445-5582

The City of Austin Parks & Recreation Department maintains a xeriscape garden featuring prairie buffalo grass and ground covers as a backdrop for the sculptures of Charles Umlauf.

Additional Central Texas Gardening Resources

ANTIQUE ROSE EMPORIUM
Route 5, Box 143 • Brenham, Texas • 77833 • (800) 441-0002

FREDRICKSBURG HERB FARM
402 Whitney Street • Fredricksburg, Texas 78624 • (800) 259-HERB
http://www.fredericksburgherbfarm.com

INTERNATIONAL FESTIVAL-INSTITUTE AT ROUND TOP
P.O. Drawer 89 • Round Top, Texas 78954 • (408) 249-3129
http://www.fais.net/~festinst/index.html

SAN ANTIONIO BOTANICAL GARDENS
555 Funston • San Antonio, Texas 78209 • (512) 821-5115
http://www.sabot.org

THE RIVERSIDE NATURE CENTER
150 Francisco Lemos Street • Kerrville, Texas 78029 • (830) 25RIVER
http://ns1.ktc.com/personal/jfwest/

WILDSEED FARMS
7 miles east on 290 • Fredricksburg, Texas • (800) 848-0078
http://www.wildseedfarms.com

Additional Gardening Web Addresses

AUSTIN BUTTERFLY FORUM
http://www.vrstore.com/ABF/index.html

GARDEN ESCAPE WEB SITE
http://www.garden.com/

GARDENING WEB SITE
http://www.gardening.com/

NEIL SPERRY'S WEB SITE
http://www.neilsperry.com

THE GARDENING LAUNCH PAD
http://www.tpoint.net/neighbor/

Remember...

Drought-tolerant landscaping conserves water, saves you money, and protects the environment. To learn more about these and other drought survival techniques, check with local landscape professionals and consider joining Austin's Xeriscape Garden Club. Xeriscape is *quality landscaping that conserves water and protects the environment*. When you conserve water, you support a cause with community-wide dividends. It may seem a big jump to be talking of regional benefits in the same breath as how we landscape our property. But the two are intimately linked through our consumption patterns. It is only by changing our own lives and habits that we can begin to protect our environment.

Note: There are many more resources in the Central Texas area than what we have listed in this section. We encourage you to check with your extension service or a local nursery professional for names and phone numbers of organizations, landscape professionals, and gardening experts in your area.

I: Recommended Reading & References

Xeriscape-Related

Duffield, Mary and Warren Jones. *Plants for Dry Climates.* Tucson: H.P. Books, 1981.

Ellefson, Connie Lockhart, Thomas L. Stephens, and Douglas Welsh. *Xeriscape Gardening: Water Conservation for the American Landscape.* New York: Macmillan Publishing Company, 1992.

Hogan, Elizabeth. *Waterwise Gardening: Beautiful Gardens with Less Water.* Menlo Park: Sunset Publishing Corporation, 1989.

Nehrling, Arno and Irene Nehrling. *Easy Gardening with Drought-Resistant Plants.* New York: Dover Publications, Inc., 1975.

Robinette, Gary. *Water Conservation in Landscape Design.* New York: Van Nostrand Reinhold Co., 1984.

General

Brenzel, Kathleen N., Editor. *Sunset Western Garden Book.* Menlo Park: Sunset Publishing Corporation, 1995.

Duffield, M.R. and W. Jones. *Plants for Dry Climates: How to Select, Grow and Enjoy.* Tuscon: HP Books, 1981.

Garrett, J. Howard. *J. Howard Garrett's Organic Manual.* Dallas: Lantana Publishing Company, 1989.

Hamilton, Geoff. *The Organic Garden Book.* London: Dorling Kindersley Limited, 1987.

Hazeltine, Cheryl and Joan Filvaroff. *The Central Texas Gardener.* College Station, Texas: Texas A&M University Press, 1980.

Odenwald, Neil G. and James R. Turner. *Southern Plants.* Baton Rouge: Claitor's Publishing Division, 1996.

Ogden, Scott. *Gardening Success with Difficult Soils: Limestone, Alkaline, Clay and Caliche.* Dallas: Taylor Publishing Company, 1992.

Sperry, Neil. *Neil Sperry's Complete Guide to Texas Gardening.* Second Edition. Dallas: Taylor Publishing Company, 1991.

Wasowski, Sally and Andy Wasowski. *Native Texas Plants: Landscaping Region by Region.* Houston: Gulf Publishing, 1991.

Landscaping and Design

Brenzel, Kathleen N., Editor. *Sunset Western Landscaping.* Menlo Park: Sunset Publishing Corporation, 1997.

Brookes, John. *The Book of Garden Design.* New York: Macmillan, Inc., 1991.

Diekelmann, John and Robert Schuster. *Natural Landscaping.* New York: McGraw-Hill, Inc., 1982.

Eck, Joe. *Elements of Garden Design.* New York: Henry Holt & Company, 1996.

Gent, Lucy. *Great Planting.* London: Ward Lock, 1995.

Harper, Pamela J. *Color Echoes.* New York: Macmillan Publishing Company, 1994.

Home Landscaping: Plants, Projects, and Ideas for Your Yard. Des Moines, Iowa: Better Homes and Gardens Books, 1996.

Keen, Mary. *Gardening With Color.* New York: Random House, Inc., 1991.

Leighton, Phebe and Calvin Simonds. *The New American Landscape Gardener.* Emmaus, Pennsylvania: Rodale Press, Inc., 1987.

Miller, G.O. *Landscaping with Native Plants of Texas and the Southwest.* Stillwater, Minnesota: Voyageur Press, 1991.

Murphy, Wendy, Joanne Pavia, and Jerry Pavia. *Beds and Borders. Traditional and Original Garden Designs.* Boston: Houghton Mifflin Company, 1990.

Overy, Angela. *The Foliage Garden.* New York: Harmony Books, 1993.

Paul, Anthony. *Creative Ideas for Small Gardens.* London: Harper Collins, 1994.

Phillips, Judith. *Southwestern Landscaping with Native Plants.* Santa Fe: Museum of New Mexico Press, 1987.

Soil

Peavy, Dr. William S. *Southern Gardener's Soil Handbook.* Houston: Gulf Publishing Company, 1979.

Trees & Shrubs

Cox, Paul W., and Patty Leslie. *Texas Trees.* San Antonio: Corona Publishing Company, 1988.

Hessayon, Dr. D. G. *The Tree & Shrub Expert.* Herts, England: pbi Publications, 1983.

Lynch, Brother Daniel, C.S.C. *Native & Naturalized Woody Plants of Austin & the Hill Country.* Austin, Texas: Acorn Press, 1981.

Vines, Robert A. *Trees, Shrubs, and Woody Vines of the Southwest.* Austin, Texas: University of Texas Press, 1960.

Ground Covers

Dimond, Don and Michael MacCaskey. *All About Ground Covers.* San Francisco: Ortho Books, 1982.

Antique Roses

Welch, William C., Margaret Sharpe and S. J. Derby. *Antique Roses for the South.* Dallas: Taylor Publishing Company, 1990.

Druitt, Liz. *The Organic Rose Garden.* Dallas: Taylor Publishing Company, 1996.

Phillips, Roger and Martyn Rix. *Roses.* New York: Random House, 1988.

Herbs

Hill, Madalene, Gwen Barclay, and Jean Hardy. *Southern Herb Growing.* Fredericksburg, Texas: Shearer Publishing, 1987.

Meltzer, Sol. *Herb Gardening in Texas*, 2nd Edition. Houston: Gulf Publishing Company, 1992.

Perennials & Wildflowers

Abbot, Carroll. *How to Know and Grow Wildflowers.* Kerrville, Texas: Green Horizons Press, 1982.

Ajilvsgi, Geyata. *Wildflowers of Texas.* Bryan, Texas: Shearer Publishing, 1984.

Appendix I: Recommended Reading & References

Andrews, J. *The Texas Bluebonnet.* Austin, Texas: University of Texas Press, 1986.

Cox, Jeff and Marilyn Cox. *The Perennial Garden.* Emmaus, Pennsylvania: Rodale Press, 1985.

Enquist, Marshall. *Wildflowers of the Texas Hill Country.* Austin, Texas: Lone Star Botanical, 1987.

Loughmiller, Campbell and Lynn Loughmiller. *Texas Wildflowers: A Field Guide.* Austin, Texas: University of Texas Press, 1994.

Welch, William C. *Perennial Garden Color.* Dallas: Taylor Publishing Company, 1989.

Wills, M. M. and H. S. Irwin. *Roadside Flowers of Texas.* Austin, Texas: University Press, 1961.

Annuals

Taylor's Guide to Annuals. Boston: Houghton Mifflin Company, 1986.

Bulbs

Ogden, Scott. *Garden Bulbs for the South.* Dallas: Taylor Publishing Company, 1994.

Turf, Ornamental Grasses, and Forbs

Gould, F. W. *Common Texas Grasses An Illustrated Guide.* College Station, Texas: Texas A&M University Press, 1978.

Gould, F. W. *The Grasses of Texas.* College Station, Texas: Texas A&M University Press, 1975.

Greenlee, John. *The Encyclopedia of Ornamental Grasses.* Emmaus, Pennsylvania: Rodale Press, 1992.

Hatch, S. L. and J. Pluhar. *Texas Range Plants.* College Station, Texas: Texas A&M University Press, 1993.

Knopp, William E. *The Complete Guide to Texas Lawn Care.* Waco, Texas: TG Press, 1986.

Rainwater Collection

Banks, Suzy and Richard Heinichen. *Rainwater Collection for the Mechanically-Challenged,* 1997.

Campbell, Stu. *The Home Water Supply: How to Find, Filter, Store, and Conserve It.* Pownal, Vermont: Garden Way Publishing, 1983.

Maintenance, Botany, Miscellany

Correll, Donavan S. and Marshall C. Johnston. *Manual of the Vascular Plants of Texas.* Dallas: The University of Texas at Dallas, 1979.

Michigan State University Cooperative Extension. *What Is IPM?* Common Sense Pest Control IV(3). 1988.

Nokes, Jill. *How to Grow Native Plants of Texas and the Southwest.* Austin, Texas: Texas Monthly Press, 1986.

Norwine, Jim, John R.Giardino, Gerald R. North, and Juan B. Valdes. *The Changing Climate of Texas: Predictability and Implications for the Future.* College Station, Texas: Texas A&M University.

Reiley, H. Edward and Carroll L. Shry, Jr. *Introductory Horticulture.* Albany, New York: Delmar Publishing, 1991.

Salisbury, Frank B. and Cleon W. Ross. *Plant Physiology.* Belmont, California: Wadsworth Publishing Company, 1992.

Spearing, Darwin. *Roadside Geology of Texas.* Missoula, Montana: Mountain Press Publishing Company, 1992.

Welsh, Douglas F. *TALC Certified Landscape Professional: Certification Manual.* College Station, Texas: The Texas A&M University System, 1990.

Zak, Bill. *A Field Guide to Texas Critters: Common Household & Garden Pests.* Dallas: Taylor Publishing Company, 1984.

Wildlife

Ajilvsgi, Geyata. *Butterfly Gardening for the South.* Dallas: Taylor Publishing, 1990.

Schneck, Marcus. *The Bird Feeder Guide.* New York: Barnes & Noble, 1989.

Additional Resources and Individual Contributions

Garden Pests and Lawn Management. The City of Austin (Brochure).

Integrated Pest Management. The City of Austin (Brochure).

Native Texas Nursery. Austin, Texas (Nursery Catalog.)

Shirey, Trisha. *Culinary Herbs for the Xeriscape*, 1997 (Herb Handout).

Texas Gardener. Waco, Texas: Suntex Communications, Inc. (The magazine for Texas gardeners by Texas gardeners, published bimonthly).

Texas Natives: Ornamental Trees. The Native Plant Society of Texas (Booklet).

The Antique Rose Emporium. Brenham, Texas. 1996 Reference Guide (Mail-order Catalog).

Tree Growing Guide For Austin And The Hill Country. Tree Folks (Brochure).

Welsh, Douglas F., Everett E. Janne, and Calvin Finch. *Fertilizing Woody Ornamentals.* Texas Agricultural Extension Service (A&M Handout).

Westin Gardens. Fort Worth, Texas (Rose Selection List).

Woody Plants (Chapter 14 out of *The Master Gardener's Reference Book.* Provided by Texas A&M University).